HAUNTED PROPERTY

HAUNTED PROPERTY

SLAVERY AND THE GOTHIC

Sarah Gilbreath Ford

University Press of Mississippi / Jackson

The University Press of Mississippi is the scholarly publishing agency of the Mississippi Institutions of Higher Learning: Alcorn State University, Delta State University, Jackson State University, Mississippi State University, Mississippi University for Women, Mississippi Valley State University, University of Mississippi, and University of Southern Mississippi.

www.upress.state.ms.us

The University Press of Mississippi is a member of the Association of University Presses.

Copyright © 2020 by University Press of Mississippi
All rights reserved

First printing 2020

∞

Library of Congress Cataloging-in-Publication Data

Names: Ford, Sarah Gilbreath, 1968– author.
Title: Haunted property : slavery and the gothic / Sarah Gilbreath Ford.
Description: Jackson : University Press of Mississippi, 2020. | Includes bibliographical references and index.
Identifiers: LCCN 2020014594 (print) | LCCN 2020014595 (ebook) | ISBN 9781496829696 (hardback) | ISBN 9781496829702 (trade paperback) | ISBN 9781496829719 | ISBN 9781496829726 | ISBN 9781496829733 | ISBN 9781496829740
Subjects: LCSH: Slavery in literature. | Gothic revival (Literature)—History and criticism. | African Americans in literature.
Classification: LCC PS374.S58 F67 2020 (print) | LCC PS374.S58 (ebook) | DDC 810.9/355—dc23
LC record available at https://lccn.loc.gov/2020014594
LC ebook record available at https://lccn.loc.gov/2020014595

British Library Cataloging-in-Publication Data available

To Connor

CONTENTS

ACKNOWLEDGMENTS
- IX -

INTRODUCTION
The Bill of Sale: Gothic, Property, Slavery, and the South
- 3 -

CHAPTER ONE
From Damsels to Specters in Harriet Jacobs's *Incidents in the Life of a Slave Girl* and Hannah Crafts's *The Bondwoman's Narrative*
- 29 -

CHAPTER TWO
Playing Con Games in Herman Melville's *Benito Cereno*, Mark Twain's *Pudd'nhead Wilson*, and Sherley Anne Williams's *Dessa Rose*
- 62 -

CHAPTER THREE
Specters on Staircases in William Faulkner's *Absalom, Absalom!*, Eudora Welty's *Delta Wedding*, and Toni Morrison's *Song of Solomon*
- 100 -

CHAPTER FOUR
Claiming, Killing, and Haunting in Toni Morrison's *Beloved*
- 128 -

CHAPTER FIVE
Claiming the Property of History in Octavia Butler's *Kindred* and Natasha Trethewey's *Native Guard*
- 154 -

EPILOGUE
What the Gothic Can Do
- 191 -

NOTES
- 196 -

WORKS CITED
- 208 -

INDEX
- 226 -

ACKNOWLEDGMENTS

The opportunity to write this book was afforded by the gracious support of my university, colleagues, friends, and family. Although I cannot pinpoint the exact moment when this project began because the various threads were sparked at different times, most of these wonderful sparks occurred in conversations with my students at Baylor University. I am thankful for their curiosity and enthusiasm.

This book benefitted from generous institutional support, including a Research Leave from the College of Arts and Sciences under the leadership of Dean Lee Nordt and travel funds for conferences from the English Department under the leadership of chair Kevin Gardner. I am fortunate to be in an incredibly supportive department, and several colleagues offered invaluable feedback on portions of the book: Jerrie Callan, Julia Daniel, Tara Foley, Hope Johnston, and Coretta Pittman. Many other colleagues offered encouragement throughout this process, including Mona Choucair, Richard Russell, Lisa Shaver, and Ron Thomas. Two graduate research assistants, Lajoie Lex and Loren Warf, also helped in innumerable ways. The English Department staff, Lois Avey and Julie Sherrod, were always helpful in making every task easier and every day more cheerful.

From the beginning of my career, the Eudora Welty Society has been an academic home for me, and I have learned so much about literature from its members, especially Mae Miller Claxton, Susan Donaldson, Julia Eichelberger, Michael Kreyling, Rebecca Mark, Suzanne Marrs, Pearl McHaney, David McWhirter, Harriet Pollack, Peggy Prenshaw, and Adrienne Akins Warfield. Audience members at the 2016 and 2018 meetings of the Society for the Study of Southern Literature offered helpful feedback on portions of the book. I am grateful to Editor Katie E. Keene and all of the wonderful people at the University Press of Mississippi who worked on the manuscript. The book benefitted immensely from the careful attention and incisive comments of the anonymous readers. An earlier version of chapter 5 was published in the *Mississippi Quarterly* (vol. 70/71, no. 3). An earlier version of chapter 3 was published in *New Essays on Eudora Welty, Class, and Race*, edited by Harriet Pollack (UP of Mississippi, 2019).

Every day that I worked on this project I was humbled by the courage and brilliance of the writers I study here.

On a personal level, I wish to acknowledge the encouragement of my wonderful village of dear friends. I am also ever grateful for my Arkansas family, including my brothers, David and Daniel, and my parents, E. C. and Barbara Gilbreath, whose support has been the very foundation of my life. And to my son, Connor, who grew tall during the writing of this book, all my love.

HAUNTED PROPERTY

- INTRODUCTION -

The Bill of Sale

Gothic, Property, Slavery, and the South

At the end of her slave narrative, Harriet Jacobs rejoices that she and her children are now free, but she also admits that "the dream of my life is not realized" (156). The lack of resolution in her narrative stems from her lack of property: "I do not sit with my children in a home of my own. I still long for a hearthstone of my own, however humble" (156). After a lifetime of abuse, captivity, and anxiety, this ending desire for a house may seem a little odd, as escaping from slavery and owning a hearthstone hardly seem equivalent desires. Jacobs's experience in slavery, however, taught her the correlation between property and identity. As someone's property, she was not considered a person but a thing to be owned. Jacobs then obtained her freedom through a purchase, and although she is grateful to her northern employer for engaging in the transaction, she is aghast that even in the North her freedom and indeed her very personhood must be bought with money. She calls on future readers to bear witness to this atrocity: "The bill of sale is on record, and future generations will learn from it that women were articles of traffic in New York, late in the nineteenth century of the Christian religion" (155). Now that the sale is complete and no one can claim ownership of her, she understands that to be a person in America is not only to be free of someone else's claims; it is to own property of your own.[1] Freedom, safety, and identity are indeed signaled and made manifest by that longed-for hearthstone.

What Jacobs's desire reflects is the entanglement of identity and property in the notion of the "American dream," the promise that unfettered by strict class boundaries a person can work hard to create whatever life he or she imagines.[2] Originally fed by eighteenth-century Enlightenment theories of the self as a powerful agent, the dream offers the promise of an identity that could be crafted from scratch on a blank slate by each person in each generation without the weight of inheritance, family, and bloodlines. Benjamin

Franklin promotes himself as the pattern of this dream in his autobiography, detailing his success as a business owner and famous statesman despite being the "youngest Son of the youngest Son for 5 Generations back" (5). His story is the realization of that grand American "pursuit of happiness." However, in penning those "certain and inalienable rights" as "life, liberty, and the pursuit of happiness," Thomas Jefferson was borrowing from John Locke's definition of rights as "life, liberty, and property." While the substitution of "pursuit of happiness" for "property" broadens the scope of a person's agency in the new republic, property continues to haunt that pursuit, leading to the problematic equations of happiness with tangible property and of identity with ownership: you are what you own.

Owning a house then becomes a kind of shorthand for identifying someone's success at crafting personhood and attaining that American dream. Marilyn Chandler ties the prominence of the house in American novels to the country's founding activity of settlement. She explains that "'the American dream' still expresses itself in the hope of owning a freestanding single-family dwelling, which to many remains the most significant measure of the cultural enfranchisement that comes with being an independent, self-sufficient (traditionally male) individual in full possession and control of home and family" (1–2). The key terms in her description, "possession" and "control," connect the physical topos of the house to the metaphysical grounds for autonomous and successful identity. A "freestanding" house is the measurement of freedom. That Jacobs sees liberty as essential to her life but identifies the "dream" of her life as owning a house is not surprising as much as shrewd. Jacobs, who has been treated as property, understands too well the importance of property to identity. She too wants that American dream.

The counter to this American dream of a "hearthstone of my own," however, is the American nightmare of slavery, where instead of the self being freely crafted, the self is reduced to property. Jacobs also understands too well this American nightmare, which she portrays through gothic tropes. Her master, Dr. Flint, plays the monster in the story by harassing her constantly, watching her every move, and threatening her with rape. Jacobs plays the damsel in distress, confined first in the Flint household and then later for seven years in the attic of her grandmother's house. As she waits for a way to escape to the North, she is figuratively entombed, becoming the ghost of her own story. When she finally achieves freedom, her lingering desire for a house signals the necessity of property to achieving full personhood. After being considered property herself and confined inside property, Jacobs can only be assured that a house is not a prison when she owns it. Although she hopes the American dream will counter the American nightmare, the ending note of her narrative is uncertainty.

From the very first American narratives, writers choose gothic conventions to question the American dream, revealing anxieties about property and property rights. Charles Brockden Brown's 1799 novel *Edgar Huntly*, for example, depicts the protagonist engaging in skirmishes in the Pennsylvania wilderness with ghostlike Indians who want to reclaim their territory. Ichabod Crane in Washington Irving's 1820 story "The Legend of Sleepy Hollow" is run out of town by the Headless Horseman because Crane wants to consume Katrina Van Tassel's property by selling her family's farm and heading west. And the haunting of Nathaniel Hawthorne's 1851 novel *The House of Seven Gables* begins with Colonel Pynchon accusing Matthew Maule of witchcraft so he can acquire his property and build the magnificent dream house with seven gables. Just as the American dream of working your way to success is evidenced by property, the American nightmare that your success was stolen from others is evidenced by haunted property. The dream house with the picket fence and the haunted house with broken windows are part of the same narrative. Hawthorne in fact describes a successful man by using the metaphor of a house with "spacious apartments," floors of "costly marbles," and "ceilings gorgeously painted," but with "some low and obscure nook" containing a "corpse, half-decayed, and still decaying" (229–30). The house becomes haunted because the success was bought with blood and rests on graves. Property haunted by its questionable acquisition then reoccurs throughout American literature from Sutpen's Hundred to Bigger's tenement building.

The anxieties expressed through gothic haunting about the provenance of the property needed for the American dream then become magnified by narratives like Jacobs's depicting slavery, where that property includes people. Critics have certainly argued that American gothic works are driven in large part by the sin of slavery.[3] In his 1960 book *Love and Death in the American Novel*, Leslie Fiedler argues that although a "dream of innocence" propelled Europeans to cross an ocean and build a new society, the "slaughter of the Indians, who would not yield their lands to the carriers of utopia, and the abominations of the slave trade, in which the black man, rum, and money were inextricably entwined in a knot of guilt, provided new evidence that evil did not remain with the world that had been left behind" (127). The guilt over the acquisition of property and the ownership of people appears in a gothic literature that Fiedler finds to be melodramatic and childish. Teresa Goddu's more recent examination in 1997 of how "slavery haunts the American gothic" agrees with Fiedler's assessment of the connection between the gothic and guilt over issues stemming from race but argues that gothic works are not escapist fantasies; they are rather "intensely engaged with historical concerns" (*Gothic* 4, 2). In essence, Goddu argues that critics should take the gothic more seriously in its exploration of slavery.

What is missing in the critical conversation on gothic works and slavery is the more direct target of the gothic energy in the narratives I explore here: the way that slavery turns people into property. Out of all of slavery's horrors, from violence and sexual assault to the separation of families, the status of enslaved people as property may seem academic and too far removed from the direct bodily harm of slavery to be the central catalyst for haunting. It is, however, the status of property that allows the perpetration of all of the other terrors by causing what happens to one person to be in the entire control of another person.[4] In examining the legal history of race in the United States, Cheryl I. Harris observes that "it was not the concept of race alone" that oppressed African Americans; "it was the *interaction* between conceptions of race and property that played a critical role in establishing and maintaining racial and economic subordination" (1716). The "hyper-exploitation of Black labor" was made possible "by establishing a form of property contingent on race—only Blacks were subjugated as slaves and treated as property" (Harris 1716). The Dred Scott case of 1857 established that since enslaved people were property, they could never be citizens. The formula is startling in its simplicity: white citizens owned property, while blacks were property and therefore not citizens. Property becomes the engine for the white accumulation of wealth and power fueled by the destruction of black personhood.

This link between race and property then continues in the postslavery era. Sandy Alexandre finds in her examination of lynching that the violence often "resulted from white aspirations to appropriate black property and resentment of black bids to own property" (4). Although the Supreme Court ruling in the 1917 *Buchanan v. Warley* case outlawed prohibitions to sell land to African Americans, the Fair Housing Act (Title VIII of the Civil Rights Act of 1968) had to tackle yet again the problem of racial discrimination in land ownership.[5] Thus, even after the end of slavery's definition of people as property, the ability of African Americans to own property continued to be curtailed, hampering access to that American right to pursue happiness through establishing personhood. The conflation of people and property in slavery produces an aftermath of dispossession and becomes the reason for the haunting in the eleven texts that I examine in this study. The idea of property hence occupies a key place in the American nightmare of slavery, which extends beyond emancipation, in addition to its role in the American dream of constructing identity. The conjunction of nightmare and dream is exemplified in Jacobs's tale of being owned, bought, and sold, followed by her longing to own property herself.

The dream and the nightmare appear simultaneously because Enlightenment ideas of freedom and agency not only arrived historically in tandem with the American institution of slavery; they were bound together. Edmund S. Morgan admits that "for a historian it poses a challenge to prove the connection" between liberty and slavery because of the "seemingly contradictory developments" (4). Yet he finds many links, such as America's dependence on French assistance for the shipping and trade that secured America's status as a free nation, assistance that was purchased by the tobacco produced by enslaved people. Morgan thus finds that "to a large degree it may be said that Americans bought their independence with slave labor" (5). The fusion that Morgan finds in the practical ground of commerce, Toni Morrison likewise finds in the realm of ideas. In her ground-breaking 1992 study, *Playing in the Dark: Whiteness and the Literary Imagination*, Morrison examines the "complex and contradictory situation in which American writers found themselves during the formative years of the nation's literature" (33). "Young America" was invested in the idea of the American dream, which she describes as the imagined "future of freedom" full of "'universal' longings," but in a country that also allowed slavery (33). Race-based slavery coexisted with Enlightenment ideals because "black slavery enriched the country's creative possibilities. For in that construction of blackness *and* enslavement could be found not only the not-free but also, with the dramatic polarity created by skin color, the projection of the not-me" (38). Morrison argues that the "concept of freedom did not emerge in a vacuum. Nothing highlighted freedom—if it did not in fact create it—like slavery" (38). While Jacobs's narrative demonstrates that the American dream and the American nightmare are connected by the fulcrum of property, Morrison reveals that slavery was not a departure from the republic's vision of freedom but was instead its evil twin.

If the dualities of freedom and slavery, the dream and the nightmare, the rags-to-riches story and the gothic haunted tale, are indeed conjoined, then gothic tales of slavery have to be read as something other than aberrations located only in the South. In examining the "empire of cotton," Sven Beckert explains that historians and economists have recently rejected the traditional view of slavery as a "Southern pathology" and "an unproductive system that retarded economic growth, an artifact of an earlier world" ("Slavery" 2). A "flurry" of recent books by a number of historians instead "all insist that slavery was a key part of American capitalism" ("Slavery" 1). As New England and the Mid-Atlantic states depended on the South's production of cotton, slavery was crucial to "the development of the United States as a whole" ("Slavery" 1). Edward Baptist, in his history of capitalism, adds that "enslaved African Americans built the modern United States, and indeed the entire modern world, in ways both obvious and hidden" (xxii). If slavery is not ancillary to the modern world but requisite to its existence, then gothic tales of slavery set in the South are not the literary equivalent of the weird uncle to be avoided at the American literary reunion, but are essential counternarratives to tales of freedom offered by the American dream. Benjamin Franklin may be able to write a narrative in which his hard work and cleverness result not only in a thriving printing business but in his meeting five kings during his lifetime (79). Harriet Jacobs, however, can only hope that she can participate in the attainment of property and thus identity now that her freedom has been purchased with money.

This book is an answer to Jacobs's call for future readers to witness that purchase and to contemplate the nightmare symbolized by that bill of sale. With other disciplines rethinking the role of slavery in the development of America and the larger modern world, literary scholars need to rethink the implications of the depictions of slavery in American literature. From early slave narratives to contemporary postmodern novels, authors have chosen to use the gothic as a tool to demonstrate how the conflation of people and property results in nightmares of haunting. This book will reimagine the southern gothic, which has too often been simply equated with the macabre or grotesque and then dismissed as regional. Instead, gothic tales of slavery are the very distillation of the anxieties about race and property located in the larger American tradition.

When these tales are moved from the margins to the center, we have the opportunity to put white and African American authors in conversation, not in order to flatten distinctions but to see how writers of various backgrounds and time periods explore this distillation. My study extends from nineteenth-century slave narratives to twenty-first-century poetry to demonstrate the myriad ways that slavery, property, and the gothic intersect throughout American literary history. Scholars have examined how individual authors such as William Faulkner or Eudora Welty use the gothic. No one, however, has written a broad analysis of the gothic in southern literature by examining and comparing multiple writers.[6] My study is the first extended examination of the southern gothic. When numerous writers are put in conversation, the shared focus of the gothic on the effects of slavery and property becomes magnified. While scholars such as Toni Morrison and Teresa Goddu have established the connection between the American gothic and race, no one has traced the key component of property in gothic depictions of slavery. Hence, I seek to put a variety of writers—male and female, white and African American, novelists and poets—in conversation to explore how the bill of sale haunts American literature.

Chapter 1 focuses on Harriet Jacobs's *Incidents in the Life of a Slave Girl* (1861) and Hannah Crafts's *The Bondwoman's Narrative* (written circa 1858 and published 2002). Although Jacobs and Crafts depict their personal experiences in slavery, they infuse their stories with gothic tropes to employ the power of fictionality. Gothic damsels in distress are beset by lascivious slaveholders and traders who are cast as monstrous villains. While enslaved, the damsels are haunted by the law's pronouncement of them as merely property, but they find refuge in haunted spaces, thereby claiming a different kind of ownership. This spectral possession is then doubled by the authors, Jacobs and Crafts, who shape their narratives as literary property they themselves can own.

Chapter 2 focuses on confidence games played in Herman Melville's *Benito Cereno* (1855), Mark Twain's *Pudd'nhead Wilson* (1894), and Sherley Anne Williams's *Dessa Rose* (1986). I argue that these con games expose the weakness in the legal construction of people as property. In each novel, white characters conflate enslaved people with animals, but this conflation allows black characters to hide their agency. Blinded by racism, white characters become the dupes of con games in which black characters outwardly perform the identity of property while covertly taking on the agency of people. By playing con games, the black characters diminish their fear of losing personhood but increase white observers' fear of losing racial boundaries, a shift revealed by gothic markers. Despite legal resolutions that seem to restore order in Melville's and Twain's texts, lingering haunting reveals that the racial categories in the end destroy everyone. Williams offers a twentieth-century answer to this destruction by rewriting history to imagine those who were formerly held in slavery escaping to the West, thereby crafting the only con game that works.

Chapter 3 examines parallel scenes in William Faulkner's *Absalom, Absalom!* (1936), Eudora Welty's *Delta Wedding* (1946), and Toni Morrison's *Song of Solomon* (1977), where a character rushes into a haunted house seeking to climb the stairs only to be thwarted by a seemingly supernatural African American woman. I read these scenes as signifying the women's contradictory roles as powerless property and powerful specters. Treated as property, the women do not just haunt the houses, they haunt *as* houses; they are conflated with the legal property of white families, even after the end of slavery. The women's status as housekeepers, however, allows them a "keeping," or possession of property, that provides them the power as specters to block the outsiders, who want to transgress the boundary of time to travel back into the past. Legal possession established by property rights confronts spectral possession signified by haunting. Although the chapter highlights significant differences in the three authors' treatment of this idea, the repetition of a specter standing on a staircase underscores both the human cost of the conflation of people with property and the destruction that ensues when the specters deny entry and claim possession.

Chapter 4 examines Toni Morrison's *Beloved* (1987). In reading Sethe's impossible choice between ending her children's lives or letting them be taken back into slavery, critics have largely blamed her daughter's death on the system of slavery. That critics do not want to blame Sethe for the murder is understandable, given how much she suffers under slavery. What critics miss, however, is Sethe's agency. In killing Beloved and attempting to kill the rest of her children, Sethe makes a property claim that speaks directly to the history of cases on American property law and slavery. In this chapter, I examine Sethe's choice in the context of *State v. Mann* and *Pierson v. Post*, arguing that her willingness to destroy makes her a valid property owner. Her legal possession, however, is answered by spectral possession when Beloved haunts to reclaim personhood.

Chapter 5 examines Octavia Butler's *Kindred* (1979) and Natasha Trethewey's *Native Guard* (2006). Butler's postmodern novel involving a woman from 1976 traveling back through time to the nineteenth-century world of slavery may seem to have little in common with Trethewey's poetry collection focusing on the death of her mother and the forgotten history of black Union soldiers stationed at Ship Island, Mississippi, during the Civil War. Both texts, however, show the haunting caused by the conflation of people with property, and they both reverse the direction of haunting to show the present haunting the past. Hence these narratives not only reveal that slavery haunts us; they expose how we haunt slavery. Through the haunting backwards, the authors claim the property of history, a claim that rewrites the paradigm of power and property in slavery. In claiming the past, the texts are able to reclaim ancestors as well. These two texts thus attempt to answer the stubborn problem of property evident throughout this study; instead of working within the system, conning the system, or destroying in order to claim, they intervene backwards into history to change what that history means for the present.

Together these five chapters reveal how the gothic acts as a magnifying glass to see more clearly how the American dream of obtaining property can become a nightmare of conflating people and property. As writers throughout American literary history return again and again to examine the depths of slavery, the repetition itself becomes gothic, doubling and redoubling. This uncanny echoing derives from the intertwining of four key components: the gothic, property, slavery, and the South.

THE GOTHIC

The gothic is the most persistent genre in American literature. In the late 1700s, the first novels written in America were either sentimental or gothic, and while the sentimental genre went out of fashion with the advent of realism in the late nineteenth century, today the gothic is as popular as ever.[7] From Charles Brockden Brown and Nathaniel Hawthorne to William Faulkner and Toni Morrison, the gothic has had incredible staying power in American literary history. Added to its persistence is its pervasiveness, appearing in high and low culture in every era. Found in canonical novels and Hollywood films, the gothic is America's fiction, as Leslie Fiedler argues, although he bemoans that even with the best writers "the machinery and décor of the gothic have continued to seem vulgar and contrived; symbolic gothicism threatens always to dissolve into its components, abstract morality and shoddy theater" (xxiv). Despite Fiedler's complaints, the sheer breadth of the gothic's range suggests that writers have found it useful, and that for better or worse the gothic lies at the heart of American identity. Even our simulacrums attest to the gothic's central place. In Disney World's "Liberty Square," an area that is designed to celebrate America, the "Liberty Tree Tavern" and the "Hall of Presidents" share the patriotic land with the "Haunted Mansion."[8] And in the cartoon *Peanuts*, when Snoopy repeatedly attempts to write the great American novel, even this cartoon dog knows he must begin with "It was a dark and stormy night."

America, however, does not own the gothic genre, nor can it claim to have invented it. Critics like to mark the gothic's birth with the publication of Horace Walpole's *The Castle of Otranto* in 1764, although common gothic elements, such as ghosts, hauntings, and scenes of confinement, appear in earlier literature. What Walpole did that was distinctive in 1764 was set a narrative designed to provoke fear in specifically "gothic" architecture. The setting itself became the key factor. Yet the term "gothic" applied to architecture is, as Jerrold E. Hogle explains, a kind of "misnomer" itself, as it was "invented as a pejorative descriptor by Italian art historians of the fifteenth century to associate the pointed-arch and castellated modes of architecture from the eleventh through the fourteenth centuries with the northern Germanic tribes of 'Goths' or 'Visigoths' who helped decimate imperial Rome" (2). The architecture was not the creation of the "Goths"; calling the buildings "gothic" was simply a way of saying they were crude. Crude or not, the architecture's heavy detailing and foreboding structures proved useful, as early practitioners of gothic literature, such as Ann Radcliffe and Matthew Lewis, took advantage of the castles and cathedrals with their garrets, dungeons, and crumbling ruins to create a genre emphasizing the haunting of the present by the past.

The plot twist in the story of the gothic is how the early United States without an ancient past and sans any notable architecture, much less gothic castles and cathedrals, could have been such a fertile place for a genre that had been so closely tied to particular settings. Enter Charles Brockden Brown, who fathers the American gothic with his 1798 novel *Wieland*, in which a man hears voices and in a religious mania kills his family. Peter Kafer asks, given the book's "oddness, its fierceness, its perversity, its patently uncertain morality," "Where had it come from?" (xvi).[9] In a country that succeeded in overthrowing the empirical power and was conducting a grand experiment in Enlightenment ideas of freedom, a literature of haunting and death seems odd. Toni Morrison remarks, "For a people who made much of their 'newness'—their potential, freedom, and innocence—it is striking how dour, how troubled, how frightened and haunted our early and founding literature truly is" (*Playing* 35). Brown's novel indeed seems to come out of nowhere, but he is not alone in writing gothic for long, as Washington Irving, Edgar Allan Poe, and Nathaniel Hawthorne soon join him. Brown and his successors are able to adapt the gothic to the different settings of the New World by substituting closets for garrets, caves for dungeons, and forests for castle ruins, but the question of why there was such a large appetite in the new republic for tales of haunting remains.

One explanation is offered by Charles Crow in his history of American gothic: "In the United States, a belief in progress is almost an article of faith. The Gothic, however, is deeply skeptical that either individuals or societies can be perfected. The Gothic insists that humans are flawed and capable of evil, and that the stories we tell ourselves in our history books may leave out what is most important for us to understand" (2). Just as in Morrison's argument where the presence of slavery is crucial to imagining freedom, the gothic plays an important oppositional role to Enlightenment thinking. Although America did not have an ancient past, the more recent past with the murder and oppression of Native Americans, the religious zeal of early colonists, and the revolutionary war provided plenty of fodder for early gothic writers. In their contemporary world also loomed the horror of slavery. Gothic texts in the late eighteenth and early nineteenth centuries show that the New World was not as "new" as pilgrims had hoped. It was not a sinless Eden. The gothic thus becomes popular because of its role as corrective. Certainly one of the most common conceptions of gothic literature is that it is "oppositional" (Crow 2). Given the unlikely beginnings of the gothic in American literature, the gothic's persistence could be due in part to the continuation of Enlightenment beliefs in progress that fuel the American dream and provide an enduring straw man as target for gothic writers.

Another explanation for its persistence is its slipperiness, as it morphs from one literary movement to the next. To say that the romantic work *The House of the Seven Gables*, the realist work *Native Son*, and the postmodern work *Beloved* are all gothic begs the question of whether there is a consistent definition of "gothic," or if we are indeed calling different aspects "gothic" in different time periods. Works of literary criticism on the gothic consistently begin with a disclaimer that the gothic cannot truly be defined (this sentence will serve as mine), before critics then proceed to offer a working theory (as I will do). Critics do tend to rally around particular ideas, however. Allan Lloyd Smith explains that the gothic focuses on "the *return* of the past, of the repressed and denied, the buried secret that subverts and corrodes the present" (1). This return of the past works against the "very American assumption," exemplified for Smith by Gatsby, that the "past can be superseded, transfigured, overcome by the valiant present" (1). Fred Botting and Peter K. Garrett both point out a second common description: the gothic as depicting transgression, but in contrast to the critics who see the gothic as oppositional to the status quo, these critics argue the transgression actually works to reinforce societal values. Garrett calls this a "safe experience of transgression" and comically imagines the gothic's slogan as "over two centuries of subverting the established order" (2). Eugenia DeLamotte and Eve Kosofsky Sedgwick typify critics who take their cues from the genre's dependence on architecture to discuss the structural aspects of gothic narratives. Sedgwick describes a "spatial model" in which the self is "massively blocked off from something to which it ought normally to have access" (12), while DeLamotte explains that "all major Gothic conventions involve either literal or metaphorical boundaries and sometimes both" (20). Other critics cite Freud's essay on the uncanny as related to the gothic. William Patrick Day in fact calls Freudianism and the gothic "cousins" (179). Maggie Kilgour in analyzing why the gothic genre is so "shadowy and nebulous" concludes that like "Frankenstein's monster" it feeds on and becomes entangled with other genres. And, finally, David Punter perhaps trumps this entire list of critics with his "bold" pronouncement: "in the context of the modern, Gothic is the paradigm of all fiction, all textuality," and then asks, "What might it mean to say that haunting is the form of all textuality?" (1).

It might mean confusion. Having taught five courses on American gothic literature to graduate and undergraduate students, I have seen firsthand the effect of the plethora of available definitions and approaches to the gothic. My students often begin to see the gothic in everything from Shakespeare and Milton to the biblical story of Christ's resurrection and Beyoncé's visual album *Lemonade*. We then have to ask if our reactions signal pervasiveness or paranoia.[10] My solution in this study is to pose the gothic not strictly as a genre with a set of particular and stable conventions but as a tool used by writers and a lens that can be used by readers.

Writers use the gothic as a tool to signal fear. Many writers, especially early practitioners of the gothic, are working in a recognizable gothic genre hoping to appeal to their readers' knowledge and tastes, but other writers I discuss in this study are not writing explicitly gothic works. The gothic instead appears in traces, along with other genres from realism to science fiction, producing the mix that Kilgore describes. Because early gothic novels repeatedly used a set of stock conventions, these conventions become like the elements of a mythic or biblical type scene, recognizable to a knowledgeable audience. Readers understand the gothic import of a dark night, a damsel in distress, a confining architectural space, a ghost, or a threat from a supernatural force. Authors can then draw from this arsenal of recognized elements to point to the thing in their narrative that is scary, uncanny, or wrong. Just as an ominous music score playing during a movie scene can cue the audience to anticipate trouble, a common trope such as a girl opening the attic door or a stranger riding into town alerts the reader to something amiss. Whatever the problem in the text—a transgression of social boundaries, a psychological breakdown, or an unsettled past event—writers employ the gothic as useful shorthand. I am thus suggesting that the gothic is an ideological tool for writers: the gothic teaches the reader what to fear.[11]

Just as the gothic is a tool for the writer, it can serve as a lens for the reader, a particular approach the reader takes towards a text. In using the word "lens," I want to acknowledge those many valid and helpful definitions that critics have employed to elucidate gothic works, approaches that I will be relying on in individual chapters to help identify and unpack gothic elements. I also recognize my own agency in selecting these particular eleven texts and studying them together under the umbrella of "gothic." Taking a gothic approach to a literary work is much like taking a feminist approach that pays close attention to gender or a deconstructionist approach that pays attention to the narrative gaps. Using the gothic as a lens entails looking for traces of those gothic conventions, even in works that might not otherwise be considered gothic, such as Eudora Welty's *Delta Wedding*, a modern novel focusing on the details of an impending wedding but also containing a scene where an old African American woman is practicing conjure in an abandoned and seemingly haunted house. This approach entails a kind of listening for the metaphorical creepy music in texts such as Herman Melville's *Benito Cereno*, when Captain Delano is uneasy about Don Benito's behavior as it alternates between extreme reserve and intense anxiety. Using a gothic lens means recognizing the conventions at play and reading for the moments of fear.

Fear is tricky, though. To say that the gothic can be a tool or lens to reveal fear is to enter into the amorphous nature of things that scare us. As pure emotion, fear is hard to identify, and its intangible essence actually heightens its power, as the goose bumps that precede the conscious naming of their catalyst reveal all that is outside the rational mind. By assigning agency to both authors and readers to declare fear, I want to acknowledge the negotiations that happen between the words on the page and the interpreters of those words. Does *Pudd'nhead Wilson*, for example, end up solidifying racial boundaries, thereby extending the haunting? Do Dana and Kevin in *Kindred* haunt the past they are in turn haunted by? Readers may end up with various answers to these questions. Throughout this study, I will, of course, be arguing for my own lens on the texts and my own readings by attending to the traces of gothic markers. These traces provide rich soil to explore what might be, or perhaps should be, fearful to a reader.

Positing the gothic as a tool and a lens can help us to explore how individual texts enact fear, but in constructing a broad view of how works use gothic tools to depict slavery in three different centuries, my study additionally takes a historical approach, specifically building off of the work of Morrison and Goddu. Morrison deconstructs an American literary history that pays scant attention to the "four-hundred-year-old presence of, first, Africans and then African-Americans in the United States. It assumes that this presence—which shaped the body politic, the Constitution, and the entire history of the culture—has had no significant place or consequence in the origin and development of that culture's literature" (*Playing* 5). She argues that even in texts by canonical white writers, such as Poe, "one can see that a real or fabricated Africanist presence was crucial to their sense of Americanness. And it shows" (*Playing* 6). My study will demonstrate how this presence shows in both white and African American writers' use of the gothic to reveal the loss of selfhood that African Americans experience in slavery. Goddu's approach to the gothic interrogates the assessments made by detractors of the genre and argues, "The gothic registers its culture's contradictions, presenting a distorted, not a disengaged, version of reality" (*Gothic* 3). In posing the gothic as a genre that engages with history, Goddu's work then examines "revolution, Indian massacre, the transformation of the market place" and especially "how slavery haunts the American gothic" (*Gothic* 3). By highlighting how the texts teach readers to fear losing selfhood and to identify with those held in slavery, my study reads the gothic as clearly engaged with history.

While haunting may provide a vocabulary for expressing the horrors of the past, the gothic, I will argue, also offers a language of spectral possession that can undermine the language of legal possession. David Punter, in arguing that the gothic battles the law, explains that "the law is the imposition of certainty, the rhetorical summation of the absence, or the loss, of doubt" (2–3). Yet laws determining the supposed "certainty" of racial lines are, as the authors repeatedly reveal in these texts, simply constructions and thus unstable. The gothic exploits this instability, thereby providing agency to those the law deems property. Punter explains the gothic's power "because of its freedom from the law, to play" (12). Although, as Botting and Garrett point out, transgression can ironically reify societal norms in that complex negotiation between author and reader, when the authors in this study play gothic, they use the gothic's oppositional power to combat the laws that sanction the loss of personhood in slavery. The writers are not just registering history or expressing horror; they are rather making a claim to the property of that history. Ghosts often linger to claim title, and haunting can be a powerful way to assert that the ownership of history is not settled. The target of gothic energy is thus the vexed but crucial notion of property.

PROPERTY

Issues of property began with the first European contact with the Americas. When Christopher Columbus "discovers" the New World and writes a report of his first voyage to King Ferdinand, he explains that in the Indies he "found very many islands filled with people innumerable, and of them all I have taken possession for their highnesses" (59). Columbus is anxious to have something to give Ferdinand and Isabella because he did not find the water route to the East he had promised; nor did he find anything as valuable as gold or silver. All he can offer the sovereigns is land, which he describes in exaggerated terms: "All [the lands] are most beautiful, of a thousand shapes, and all are accessible and filled with trees of a thousand kinds and tall, and they seem to touch the sky" (60). Even if Spain's new lands are, according to Columbus, a "marvel," the question is, by what means had Columbus "taken possession" of them. He did not purchase them, and he does not have title. Instead, the acquisition was "done by proclamation and with the royal standard unfurled, and no opposition was offered to me" (59). Columbus is surely not writing comedy here, but it is hard to miss the humor in this European proclaiming in a language that the native peoples do not understand his right to the land they live on while planting a flag in the ground and seeing if anyone protests. Since no dispute of Spain's property rights follows, Columbus assumes the right of an owner to give the various islands names that would appease his patrons. Columbus's method of "unfurling the royal standard" makes sense only in his own Old World paradigm, but that paradigm eventually wins in the New World as native peoples are forced to give up their rights to land. His act not only begets centuries of colonization; it also begs the question: In the New World, how does someone own a piece of land?

As complicated as this question is, land at least is tangible. Property in the more general sense includes not just concrete items, such as a plot of earth, a house, or a shirt, but also abstract things, such as a share of a business or even an idea. Key to understanding how people become property in American history is grasping that property is, as John Brigham puts it, a "legal construction" (3). Brigham explains that property is not a "material thing" but is "the relationship between people and the thing" that is created by law (3). In America, the Constitution creates this relationship in the "Fifth Amendment, with its protection against uncompensated 'takings' and guarantee of due process" (Brigham 3). C. B. Macpherson highlights the importance of law to defining property: "to have a property is to have a right in the sense of an enforceable claim to some use or benefit of something, whether it is a right to a share in some common resource or an individual right in some particular things. What distinguishes property from mere momentary possession is that property is a claim that will be enforced by society or the state, by custom or law" (3). Hence property is set up as a right governed and protected by the nation. One can own a piece of land or an idea because others agree to the legal construction of that ownership.

In the United States, property is not only a legal construction; it is also a way of establishing personhood. One significant influence on the conception of property rights in the United States was the Enlightenment philosopher John Locke, who argued in his *Second Treatise on Government* that "every man has a property in his own person. This nobody has any right to but himself. The labour of his body, and the work of his hands, we may say, are properly his. Whatsoever, then, he removes out of the state that nature hath provided and left it in, he hath mixed his labour with, and joined to it something that is his own, and thereby makes it his property" (274). Property can be claimed because a person's labor is combined with it. This idea is, of course, highly ironic considering the number of people who did not get to own their own bodies and thus did not get to claim the products of their labor. Philip Gould explains that Locke reconciled this "glaring yet apparently necessary aberration" by "carefully [placing] chattel slavery outside of that compact by distinguishing the 'state of nature' from the 'state of war,' in which slaves were presumably collected" (18). The result is that "only those persons who have placed themselves outside the social compact—such as criminals and war combatants—may choose enslavement over death" (Gould 18). Despite this strange logic designed to exclude enslaved people, Locke designates property as a natural right to those not enslaved along with the rights to life and liberty because he sees property as infused with the self.

Margaret Jane Radin calls this line of thinking the "personhood perspective" of property and explains that "to achieve proper self-development—to be a *person*—an individual needs some control over resources in the external environment. The necessary assurances of control take the form of property rights" (35). This connection of property and personhood results in the home becoming the tangible symbol of self-making: "It is not just that liberty needs some sanctuary and the home is a logical one to choose because of social consensus. There is also the feeling that it would be an insult for the state to invade one's home, because it is the scene of one's history and future, one's life and growth. In other words, one embodies or constitutes oneself there" (57). This connection makes the home a kind of extension of the person: "The home is affirmatively part of oneself—property for personhood—and not just the agree-on locale for protection from outside interference" (Radin 57).

As the house then becomes the locus of the ability to establish personhood, the gothic in its oppositional role employs the haunted house to express the fear that personhood was not achieved or that, as in Hawthorne's metaphor, there is a corpse hidden in the basement. The anxiety about property originates in English gothic novels, as Ruth Bienstock Anolik explains:

"The English Gothic is taken up by the issue of possession and is preoccupied with the legal and seemingly literal questions of ownership: the questions of who actually owns the *property* (the frequently contested castle), who owns the *self*, including the body and mind, who owns the *narrative* and the *text*" (*Property* 2). With plots often revealing the true heir, these novels typically focus on inheritance as the means of gaining property. Although American writers subsequently inherit the gothic's attention to issues of property, the particular anxieties shift. The source of uncertainty is not inheritance but the means of acquisition, questioning whether the property was perhaps stolen from Native Americans, seized during the revolution, or built with slave labor. Dale Bailey explains that the haunted house novel "while rooted in the European gothic tradition, has developed a distinctly American resonance" (6). In American literature, haunted house novels "present deeply subversive critiques of all that we hold to be true—about class, about race, about gender, about American history itself" (Bailey 6). The house becomes a crucial symbol so that, as Bailey points out, critics use it to show what is corrupt in American society, as when Henry David Thoreau in *Walden* critiques the many decades of life men spend acquiring houses. From Edgar Allan Poe's "The Fall of the House of Usher" to Shirley Jackson's *The Haunting of Hill House*, critiques of America find their place in haunted property.

Along with the anxiety about property, America inherited from England a connection between property and civic identity. The colonies largely copied British suffrage laws restricting voting to men who owned property. Alexander Keyssar explains that "on the eve of the American Revolution, in seven colonies men had to own land of specified acreage or monetary value in order to participate in elections; elsewhere, the ownership of personal property of a designated value ... could substitute for real estate" (5). The rationale for these restrictions was that citizens needed to be invested members of society to vote, and property ownership attested to commitment. Keyssar argues that an unspoken assumption was that "where economic opportunities were believed to abound," it followed that "anyone who failed to acquire property was of questionable competence and unworthy of full membership in the polity" (5). The connection of suffrage to property further underscores Jacobs's need to own that hearthstone as a way of asserting worth.

The right to property was moreover key to America's break with England. James L. Huston explains that "the heart of the American Revolution politically, economically, socially, and ideologically was a strident defense of the individual's right to property, in particular the right of an individual to earn, keep, and dispose of their property without the interference of any other power, especially the power of government" (7). America thus went further than its mother country in connecting property to personhood. Stuart Banner explains that "no one in England except the king owned land outright. Land could be held by a variety of tenures, but all of them implied some form of obligation to someone else higher up the ladder" (5). Ergo the sovereign granted the land and could ostensibly seize property at any time. By contrast, in America, "landowners still obtained their land from the sovereign—the federal or state government—but without any ongoing duties to render service or pay money" (Banner 5). Connecticut judge Jesse Roots declared, "The title of our lands is free, clear, and absolute. Every proprietor of land is a prince in his own domains" (Banner 5). Property therefore could not only make someone a person; it could make someone a prince. The appealing promise in Roots's declaration feeds that American dream of freedom equaling power, but when the object of that property is a person, the American nightmare is born.

SLAVERY

The answer, therefore, to the question of how one claims property in the New World is by constructing a legal fiction to which enough other people agree. The reward of accomplishing this construction is nothing less than personhood and power. Hence the stakes are high in defining what property is and who gets to own it. Harris declares that in the history of the United States, whiteness itself is a kind of property:

> Because whites could not be enslaved or held as slaves, the racial line between white and Black was extremely critical; it became a line of protection and demarcation from the potential threat of commodification, and it determined the allocation of the benefits and burdens of this form of property. White identity and whiteness were sources of privilege and protection: their absence meant being the object of property. (1720–21)

If whiteness is a "shield from slavery," blackness alternatively becomes the guarantee of slavery, as race and property are conflated (1720). When people become property in the slave system, a "hybrid" is created that Harris describes as "possessing inherent instabilities" because of the "dual and contradictory character of slaves as property and persons" (1718). She points to the Representation Clause of the Constitution whereby representation in the House of Representatives was figured by counting someone enslaved as three-fifths of a person. This odd accounting reflects the implications of property being first and foremost a legal fiction, which naturally benefits those doing the constructing.

This fictionality, though, underscores slavery's complexity. As Tim Armstrong argues, "slavery itself is *necessarily* metaphorical: no human being is in any direct or literal sense an instrument of another or a commodity" (2). Armstrong finds that the legal fiction becomes reality, though, at crucial moments: "the point of purchase or sale, and the point of an insurance claim" (40). These are moments when money changes hands, and the metaphorical becomes at least temporarily literal. In his influential study of slavery, Orlando Patterson calls slavery a "social death" but argues against the idea that slavery was about property because "to define slavery *only* as the treatment of human beings as property fails as a definition, since it does not really specify any distinct category of persons" (21). He argues instead that slavery is about "relations of power" and examines slavery as a practice across cultures and time periods (20).

In the chattel slavery practiced in America, however, that power relationship, even if artificially constructed, was legally defined as property and depended for its existence on that definition. Huston explains that "from the beginning of the Union, southerners demanded a basic contract that at all times had to be observed: slaves were property and property rights were inviolable. This was the foundation of all political defenses of slavery" (16). Enslaved people were thus "inert property," but this "legal transformation could never eliminate the volition of human beings" (Huston 44). Thus enslaved people had to be acknowledged at times as something other than "inert." A. Leon Higginbotham and Barbara K. Kopytoff provide more insight about which times people held in slavery were considered human and which times they were considered property. The decision depended upon what would benefit the owner, again highlighting the stakes involved in the act of defining. Higginbotham and Kopytoff analyze Virginia's slave laws to determine what happened in the cases where enslaved people were considered human. One situation involved the treatment of enslaved people in jail. They find that "the failure to provide humane treatment to the slave was a breach of a right of the owner, but not a breach of the human rights of the slave, for he was recognized as having no such rights. The humanity of the slave, requiring that he be treated with the care due other humans and not like other forms of property, became part of the owner's property rights" (520). Another situation involved the complications that arose when an enslaved person committed a crime or damaged someone else's property. In these cases, the enslaved people were classified as "servants," so "the master would not be held liable for the intentional wrongs of the slave unless the master had authorized them" (521). Higginbotham and Kopytoff find throughout their analysis of law that "property rights came first where slaves were concerned" (525). In his history of American law, Lawrence M. Friedman finds similar distinctions: "To be sure, the slave was a 'person,' for purposes of the criminal law, and indeed, more answerable for crimes than free whites. But in other regards, he was a commodity. He could not vote or hold office, he could not contract or own property; he was bought and sold like a bale of cotton" (197).

The stark contrast between the situation of people whose very whiteness acts as a form of property and people who are constructed as property when it benefits others demonstrates the crucial intersections of race and property. Gavin Wright explains that racial distinctions became more pronounced as the demand for slave labor grew: "the clarification and strengthening of property rights in slaves was intimately linked to intensified perceptions, ideologies, and rhetoric on racial inferiority" (13).[12] The desire for labor creates the need for a stronger concept of race, so that, as Ta-Nehisi Coates argues in examining the larger scope of American history, "Race is the child of racism, not the father" (7). Wright identifies the key factor in the "rise of African slavery in the Americas" as the introduction of property rights (14). The significance of this rise has been rediscovered recently by economic historians. Although Eric Williams argued in 1944 for the dependence of capitalism on slavery, until lately the general consensus was that slavery, which was seen as confined to the Caribbean and the South, was a holdover from the feudal system and disappeared as capitalism took hold.

This older idea was attractive because it enabled a particular narrative of the rise of industrial capitalism, a narrative that dovetails nicely with the American dream narrative of prosperity. Sven Beckert explains, "Too often, we prefer to erase the realities of slavery, expropriation, and colonialism from the history of capitalism, craving a nobler, cleaner capitalism.... Capitalism was in many ways a liberating force, the foundation of much of contemporary life; we are invested in it, not just economically but emotionally and ideologically. Uncomfortable truths are sometimes easier to ignore" (*Empire* xviii). Slavery's central role is one of the truths. Edward Baptist explains how vast indeed the slave system became when the plantations in the South started growing cotton: "in the span of a single lifetime after the

1780s, the South grew from a narrow coastal strip of worn-out plantations to a sub-continental empire" (xxi). Baptist details how "from 1783 at the end of the American Revolution to 1861, the number of slaves in the United States increased five times over, and all this expansion produced a powerful nation" (xxi).[13] This vast expansion built the cotton empire and, according to Baptist and Beckert, the modern capitalist world. The massive force of slavery depended on both strict racial boundaries and the legal constructions that caused people to become property.

Baptist calls the role of slavery in the making of American capitalism "the half that has never been told," the title of his book. Sven Beckert and Seth Rockman argue that "it is plainly obvious that the history of American capitalism is a history with slavery, yet it remains to be shown how exactly slavery is embedded within the larger story of capitalism" (3). This current view of slavery has gotten some push back from scholars still convinced by the traditional notion, typified by Eugene D. Genovese's 1974 *Roll, Jordan, Roll*, that slavery was "in the capitalist world but not of it" (Parry). My examination of these eleven literary works, however, supports the current view. Those in slavery, as the reading of Harriet Jacobs and Hannah Crafts in chapter 1 shows, connect their enslavement to the larger legal system of property that is part and parcel of that capitalist system. Later literary authors then explore how the connections between race and property extend beyond nineteenth-century slavery into twentieth-century discussions of the ownership of history.[14] From early slave narratives to contemporary American novels, the writers uncover the connections between the creation of personhood through property rights and the loss of personhood through slavery, between the dream and the nightmare.

THE SOUTH

One way American culture has avoided the ugliness of those dualities is by mapping them onto the North and the South. The North can appear to embody the Enlightenment ideals of freedom and progress because slavery supposedly existed only in the South.[15] The dream and the nightmare are compartmentalized by region, and the contradiction between freedom and slavery is maintained, letting America have its ideals *and* the massive commerce from the cotton empire constructed in the South. The South as a concept is therefore useful, as Jennifer Rae Greeson argues, which explains the staying power of regionalism in United States history. Greeson studies the rise of national literature and finds that the South plays the role of "*internal other* for the nation" (1). She explains that this geological separation, which she calls a "fantasy," also has a temporal dimension as "the South gives writers a backward glance, a conduit to the American colonial past against which they may gauge the rise of the independent, developing republic" (4). The temporal dimension to the otherness then carries into the modern era, as Leigh Anne Duck argues in her examination. She finds the same othering as Greeson: "a 'backward' South," connected to tradition and racism and a "modern or 'enlightened' nation," connected to democracy (3). Duck points out the incongruity in these categories: "These formulations disavowed both the contemporaneity of the South with the larger nation and the presence of apartheid in other areas of the country" (*Nation's* 3). For example, in a chapter focusing on William Faulkner's work, Duck finds that among modernist writers, Faulkner's use of the gothic was seen as "provincial"; "Faulkner's Gothicism was understood less as an aesthetic choice than as a reflection of the temporal alterity in which both author and subject matter were submerged" (*Nation's* 146, 149).

What Duck finds for the reception of Faulkner's work is true for the southern gothic in general. Not only do the American dream and the American nightmare become assigned to particular places, but the nightmare then positioned in this conceptual South becomes intertwined with the gothic. Goddu outlines this process:

> The South's oppositional image—its gothic excesses and social transgressions—has served as the nation's safely valve: as the repository for everything the nation is not, the South purges contrary impulses. More perceived ideas than social reality, the imaginary South functions as the nation's 'dark' other. By so closely associating the gothic with the South, the American literary tradition neutralizes the gothic's threat to national identity. As merely regional strategy, the gothic's horrifying hauntings, especially those dealing with race, can be contained. (Gothic 76)

The South becomes the gothic closet or attic, a place to put the monster and control the terror, allowing it to exist in the national house, but keeping the living room and kitchen free of specters. The South thus carries the burden of racism and slavery for the whole nation and presents this burden in gothic form.

Goddu's formulation of the region as the "imaginary South" is crucial. Scholars of southern literature have deconstructed the idea of a coherent and identifiable South. The South, especially in its role as "safety valve," is a construction, albeit a powerful one. To explain how a geographic location can also be imaginary, Thadious M. Davis uses the term "southscape." She examines the interactions between "natural environment and social collective" to find "the persistent conceptual power of the South as a spatial object and ideological landscape where matters of race are simultaneously opaque and transparent" (*Southscapes* 2). As the "'dark' other," the South becomes a kind of id for the superego North, a place to locate the nightmare, making race its central characteristic, thus making it transparent, as Davis puts it, but also sublimating the role of race in the making of the nation as a whole, making it opaque.

One problem with the South functioning as the nation's other is that because of the connections between freedom and slavery, the haunting is not contained in a region either geographical or imaginary. Gothic tales of slavery speak directly to the foundational principles of the nation. To keep the concept of the South useful, southern gothic has to be dismissed also. And it has, as critics have historically seen gothic tales set in the South as a kind of peculiar carnival show, entertaining in their perversity but not to be taken seriously. Ellen Glasgow, in fact, in coining the phrase "southern gothic" in 1935 was complaining about its ugliness: "All I ask [the writer of southern gothic] to do is to deal as honestly with living tissues as he now deals with decay, to remind himself that the colors of putrescence have no greater validity for our age, or for any age, than have—let us say, to be very daring—the cardinal virtues" (359). Glasgow does not perceive that the critique offered by the gothic can be crucial to undergirding those virtues. Any potential message instead gets overwhelmed by its ugly gothic clothing. Fred Botting typifies later critics who equate southern gothic with the bizarre when he describes Faulkner's fiction as "[presenting] a decaying, grotesque and absurd world through the disturbed consciousness of misfits and malcontents often on the verge of insanity" (160).

The conflation of southern gothic with the grotesque has cast a long shadow on southern literature. Susan Donaldson reflects on the choice of "Haunted Bodies" as the title of the collection she edited with Anne Goodwyn Jones in 1997 and explains their desire to bypass "literary and regional clichés" to focus specifically on the haunting involved in the "southern rape complex" ("Making Darkness" 262). In discussing why Eudora Welty in particular did not want to be called a gothic writer, Donaldson describes how "Southern Gothicism was generally considered a term of opprobrium and dismissal, shorthand for monolithic categorizations for the region's backwardness, violence, and injustice" ("Making Darkness" 261). For many in the twentieth century, "gothic" as a modifier of southern literature appeared to reflect a culture stuck in a past that while decaying was still exerting power.

"Gothic" as a description of American literature, however, has historically allowed for that potential "oppositional" stance to "monolithic categorizations" that Crow asserts (2). That the gothic can likewise be expansive instead of reductive for southern literature is the driving force of two recent essay collections. The 2014 collection *Critical Insights: Southern Gothic Literature* seeks to ignite the study of southern gothic, which has, according to the editor, Jay Ellis, been buried "under each of its respective terms" (vii). Ellis expands the concept of southern gothic by pointing to multiple influences from Europe to Africa. He then questions southern gothic's inferior status "below" New England and Northern gothic (xxiv). In the 2016 *The Palgrave Handbook of the Southern Gothic*, editors Susan Castillo Street and Charles L. Crow expand the concept of southern gothic by positing the South as obsessed with "crossroads and boundaries, whether territorial (the Mason-Dixon line) or those related to gender, social class, sexuality and particularly race" (2).[16] The readings in the volume then examine "crossings characterized by movement across many different disciplinary axes, with occasional collisions, conflicts and contradictions, and flashes of valuable and unsettling insight" (6). By choosing to focus on crossings and movement, Street and Crow open up the southern gothic to the possibility of change instead of nostalgia and stasis.

A third essay collection moves in a different direction by choosing to focus more closely on one concept. Eric Gary Anderson, Taylor Hagood, and Daniel Cross Turner, as the editors of *Undead Souths: The Gothic and Beyond in Southern Literature and Culture* (2015), reflect a marked distaste for the word "gothic," finding it tied too closely to old tropes, "long-standing images and ideas mummified and cracking into dust" (4). They opt instead for "undeadness" and offer a collection specifically focused on "representations of death and deathways as well as figures returned from the grave" (1). Their approach is grounded in "dynamic physicality" and borrows from Monique Allewart's description of the "parahuman" as well as Jane Bennett's concept of "vibrant matter" to focus on moments where seemingly "dead" people and seemingly "inanimate" material become forces with agency (6). While I appreciate the editors' desire to rid literary works of the baggage that the term "southern gothic" has carried, I am not ready to throw the whole gothic baby out because of the bathwater of older conceptions of the southern gothic. Undeadness is an interesting and powerful concept, but the vibrancy of seemingly dead or inert beings is only one thread in the larger fabric of the gothic. By imagining the gothic as a set of tools that writers can use, I find rich material in how spatial separations and confinements, homes fraught with the oppression of racial boundaries, temporal disruptions and reversals, and depictions of an unknown that questions rationality can all haunt in terrifying and potentially productive ways. If we dismiss the larger gothic framework because we read it only as a monolith, we miss out on the potentially oppositional gothic that exists in many forms, even in those "decayed" tropes, such as ghosts and haunted houses.

With an expansive set of tools, we can see this oppositional gothic at work not just in canonically gothic texts but also in smaller traces in texts whose larger framework does not elicit the classic terror of a haunted tale. In her 2005 essay "Ghosts and Shattered Bodies, or What Does It Mean to Still Be Haunted by Southern Literature?," Patricia Yaeger explains that ghosts are "notoriously hard to see" but that their "traces are everywhere" (87). She argues that "writers who refuse a monstrous hauntology" want the reader to feel that "within the humdrum world," "a haunting is taking place," a haunting she locates in "scraps" (99–100). In concert with Yaeger, and along with Ellis, Street, and Crow, I seek to expand the aperture to locate those undead as well as haunted spaces, time shifts, the unknown, and all of the other possibilities offered by the gothic. In the negotiations between page and person, the gothic in southern literature does not have to be only the conservative container of the past. It can also be the way out of the stultifying constraints of regional separateness. By continuing to use the term "gothic," we can furthermore assert southern literature's place at the center of American literature and at the heart of the nation's intertwining of race and property.

With the addition of these recent collections on the gothic, we now have significant readings of individual authors and texts. What we do not have yet is what I offer here: a study examining multiple authors and taking an expansive view to see what threads might be traced through the literature. Authors writing about slavery in different time periods from a myriad of perspectives choose over and over again to employ the gothic as a tool. Certainly, as Goddu points out, the sheer horrors of slavery need the terrifying conventions and magnified language of the gothic to give them adequate gravity in narrative form. But what my book will show is that both the gothic's link to issues of property and its ability to supply a nightmare powerful enough to disturb the American dream make it the perfect tool to examine slavery. That slavery is an issue of nation and not region is revealed when Hannah Crafts narrates her experience of being an enslaved person in Washington DC or when the original masthead of the slave ship in *Benito*

Cereno is a figure of Christopher Columbus or when Dana in *Kindred* finds eerie correspondences between slavery and her 1976 California world. Instead of its "below" status of a carnival show exhibiting the grotesque, I pose the gothic as a tool to explore the system of slavery as it fits into the nation and undergirds the larger modern world.

§ § §

Although Harriet Jacobs imagined that the bill of sale reflecting her status as property would be the concrete evidence future generations would use to witness the atrocity of slavery, that actual piece of paper has not been recovered by historians. What has been found is something perhaps even more disturbing: the newspaper advertisement published by her master announcing a $100 reward for her return. The ad states: "This girl absconded from the plantation of my son without any known cause or provocation" ("Runaway"). The simple desire for freedom was somehow an unknown cause. The ad also includes a warning that anyone "harboring or entertaining" her will be prosecuted "under the most rigorous penalties of the law." After the passage of the Fugitive Slave Act in 1850, which required that formerly enslaved people be returned to their slaveholders in the South, those who escaped slavery were not safe in the North. There was no free place, as Jacobs bemoans in her narrative. The advertisement exists as a vivid reminder of the implications of property laws and the actions of the entire nation in enforcing them.[17] Though the bill of sale ends her owner's property rights, it also carries a cost: "I well know the value of that piece of paper; but much as I love freedom, I do not like to look upon it" (155). Ellen Glasgow is right in saying that the gothic is not beautiful. The texts I examine in the following pages are hard to "look upon" because they make us confront brutality, abuse, human frailty, and sin, but they do this for critical reasons: to reveal the horrors of slavery, to uncover the dark potential of the pursuit of happiness, to acknowledge the existence of the American nightmare alongside the American dream, and to teach us what to fear.

- CHAPTER ONE -

From Damsels to Specters in Harriet Jacobs's *Incidents in the Life of a Slave Girl* and Hannah Crafts's *The Bondwoman's Narrative*

The title Harriet Beecher Stowe chose for her 1852 novel, *Uncle Tom's Cabin*, is nothing less than odd.[1] Early in the novel, Stowe depicts the slave cabin as charming, with a "neat garden patch" abounding in flowers, a kitchen smelling of "batter-cake," and a portrait of George Washington overseeing the general contentment (27, 28). A few chapters later, however, Tom is sold to a slave trader, and the novel never returns to the "cabin" referred to in the title. Even when the narrator proposes in chapter 21 to "glance back, for a brief interval, at Uncle Tom's Cabin, on the Kentucky farm, and see what has been transpiring among those whom he had left behind," the chapter is set instead in the Shelbys' parlor and the adjoining veranda (240). Although Tom fervently hopes to be reunited with his family, the plot moves him farther away from his Kentucky home, first to New Orleans and then to a rural Louisiana plantation. His wife, Chloe, also leaves the cabin behind when she moves to Louisville to try to earn enough money from her cooking skills to buy Tom. Mrs. Shelby vows to bring Tom back, and St. Clare promises Tom his freedom, but when Tom dies, his body is buried in Louisiana soil. As a setting, the cabin only occupies a sliver of the novel, one chapter of its forty-five.[2]

The title furthermore proves odd in the possession indicated by "*Tom's*." The charm radiating from the cabin certainly derives from Tom and Chloe's homemaking, but the cabin is not his.[3] Tom cannot own the property of the cabin because he himself is property, as Stowe underscores by opening the novel with Mr. Shelby and the slave trader negotiating his sale and by later titling the chapter of Tom's departure "The Property Is Carried Off" (94). These deficiencies in the novel's title reveal the harm in slavery's reduction of people to property: as property, enslaved people not only lose all rights to their own bodies, including where they reside, but they also cannot own property and therefore lose the protection that a home provides its occupants along with the identity conferred by that "'s." The identity the title gives Tom instead is "Uncle," which also proves inaccurate, in that Tom does not appear to be anyone's uncle in the text. Tom is an "Uncle" because this is the designation whites gave to those held in slavery to depict them as familial and nonthreatening.[4] Tom, however, desperately wants to claim the identity of husband and father in the Kentucky cabin, but that cabin becomes the sliver of a setting further receding from him because as property, Tom cannot claim his home.

The disparity between the possession of property by Tom in Stowe's title and the possession of Tom as property in Stowe's narrative is what both Harriet Jacobs and Hannah Crafts target in their slave narratives. In *Incidents in the Life of a Slave Girl* (1861), Harriet Jacobs tells the story of being sexually harassed by her master, hiding for seven years in an attic, and finally fleeing to the North. The narrative tracks how her condition as property thwarts her ability to have a safe home. Even at the end of her narrative, when she is free in New York, she still longs to own the home that would signify her identity as a person. Hannah Crafts escaped from slavery in 1857, likely finishing her manuscript in 1858.[5] *The Bondwoman's Narrative*, which remained unpublished until 2002, chronicles how the condition of being property negates the agency of enslaved people, particularly women whose black blood, even if undetectable to the eye, makes them vulnerable prey. Like Jacobs, Crafts spends the entire narrative seeking a safe home. Unlike Jacobs, she finds it, but only after escaping slavery and settling in New Jersey. In detailing the "incidents" from their experiences in slavery, both women explore the problems of property implicit in Stowe's problematic title.

That they choose to speak the truth about property through fictional gothic devices, though, may seem puzzling. Both writers were possibly influenced by Stowe's use of the gothic to heighten her novel's sentimental appeal, and Crafts borrows heavily from Charles Dickens's gothic novel *Bleak House*.[6] Yet, in contrast to these fiction writers, Jacobs and Crafts had to shape their narratives for audiences who expected a more rigid attachment to bare facts from formerly enslaved people advocating for abolition. Ann Fabian explains that these readers were looking for fugitives "who possessed the moral capacity to tell the truth, give their word, keep their promises, and ultimately become free laborers" (*Unvarnished* 85). Jacobs and Crafts register their awareness of these expectations in the very first sentences of their prefaces: Crafts offers a "record of plain unvarnished facts," while Jacobs announces, "Reader, be assured this narrative is no fiction" (3, 5).[7] Assuring the reader of the truth of a subsequently fictional narrative was typical in prefaces of early American novels, as authors tried to evade the general suspicion of fiction as dangerous.[8] Formerly enslaved people then borrow this rhetorical move as part of their strategy to, in William L. Andrews's words, "endow their stories with the appearance of authenticity" (*To Tell* 2). Andrews explains that the "reception of [a formerly enslaved person's] narrative as truth depended on the degree to which his artfulness could hide his art" (*To Tell* 2). Truth therefore is crucial as both declaration and construction.

Jacobs and Crafts, however, do not hide their highly fictionalized gothic trappings. Instead, they depict the personas of "Linda" and "Hannah" as gothic damsels in distress, who encounter ghosts, haunted spaces, and monstrous villains. Jacobs and Crafts thereby seemingly flaunt their authorial shaping of their life stories, even though it is the truth of those lived lives that give their depictions of slavery the significant force of candid revelation.[9] Teresa Goddu explores this tension, acknowledging that "the slave narrative's generic conventions seem to be in direct opposition to the gothic's: [the slave narrative's] documentary form and adherence to veracity announce a refusal of any imaginative rendering" (*Gothic* 136).[10] Her answer to this tension is that "the Gothic becomes the mode through which to speak what often remains unspeakable within the American national narrative—the crime of slavery" ("American" 63). In Goddu's analysis of Jacobs, she finds that "Jacobs at once narratively constructs the gothic event as actual and insists that it exceeds such representation" (*Gothic* 146).[11] Thus slavery as an "unspeakable fact" uses the power of the gothic to express reality and to assert that needed authenticity (*Gothic* 144).[12]

However, what I find in paying attention to the central problem of property in these texts is the power in the gothic's fictionality. Jacobs and Crafts employ the gothic as a malleable medium that allows them to shape their stories. They recast Linda and Hannah as haunted damsels instead of hunted property, leading readers to identify them as heroines threatened by slaveholders and traders, who are cast as monstrous villains. By employing these gothic constructions, the writers teach readers to fear a legal system that defines people as property. Legal possession in these narratives, however, must confront spectral possession. Linda and Hannah find refuge in spaces deemed haunted, such as a hidden attic, an abandoned cabin, or a prison, because they too are haunted property. Hence they become powerful specters haunting to seek title, and their gothic artfulness amplifies their power.

Moreover, in using fictional devices to recast their stories, Jacobs and Crafts claim a spectral possession of their lives, subverting the legal claim on their persons. Jacobs gives her narrative the subtitle "Written by Herself," clearly asserting her ownership, while Crafts's title identifies the narrative as the "Bondwoman's," a claim that becomes sharper considering that Hannah Crafts's real name was Hannah Bond.[13] Though they may be enslaved in the narratives they write, they now own these narratives. The logic of law must face the force of fiction. While scholars have certainly explored the gothic in both Jacobs's and Crafts's narratives, considering them together will reveal how their explorations of property confront the problem encapsulated in Tom's dispossession of his cabin and his person.[14] Jacobs and Crafts shape their stories to repossess and claim the property of their own lives, thereby creating their own "cabins."

DAMSELS AND MONSTERS

In writing the narratives of Linda and Hannah, Harriet Jacobs and Hannah Crafts portray their textual stand-ins as characters their audiences can readily identify and champion: damsels in distress. (Throughout I will be referring to Jacobs and Crafts as the authors and to Linda and Hannah as the characters in the text to highlight the shaping the writers do in telling their stories.) As a young girl, Linda realizes the difficulty of remaining unmolested among predatory owners; she exclaims, "The war of my life had begun; and though one of God's most powerless creatures, I resolved never to be conquered. Alas, for me!" (19). Alas, indeed, as she attempts to retain her selfhood without the protection of parents. After detailing the "fortunate circumstances" of her early childhood, Linda reveals that her mother died when she was six years old. Without a mother to guide her, her life story tracks the typical gothic damsel, whose orphan status leaves her subject to being harassed and haunted.[15] Linda is at least left with a brother, an aunt, and a forceful grandmother. Hannah is totally bereft of family. At the beginning of her narrative, she announces, "Of my relations, I knew nothing" (5). This lack of knowledge is nonetheless coupled with the unwanted knowledge of the effects of her parentage: "the African blood in my veins would forever exclude me from the higher walks of life. That toil unremitted unpaid toil must be my lot and portion, without even the hope or expectation of any thing better" (6).[16] As circumstances force Hannah to escape, and she finds herself first in an abandoned cabin complete with suspicious blood stains and later in a prison cell with rats, she voices her "alas" through prayers. In invoking biblical passages, Hannah echoes Mary Rowlandson, the Puritan captured by Native Americans whose narrative was an early American best-seller. Also a captive, Hannah likewise seeks divine protection yet repeatedly finds herself in harm's way.

As distressed damsels, Hannah and Linda sound a familiar note in the gothic.[17] Jerrold E. Hogle explains that even in the first gothic novel, Horace Walpole's *Castle of Otranto* (1764), "it is Otranto's Isabella who first finds herself in what has since become the classic Gothic circumstance: caught in 'a labyrinth of darkness' full of 'cloisters' underground and anxiously hesitant about what course to take there, fearing the pursuit of a domineering and lascivious patriarch" (9). The damsel character then crossed the Atlantic to appear in the first American gothic novel, Charles Brockden Brown's *Wieland* (1798). With the requisite orphan status, Clara Wieland confronts a villain hiding in her closet and a crazed murderous brother. Damsels act as the fuel for the gothic, and that it is almost always women that act as the conduit for the terror may be more than simply convention. Ruth Bienstock Anolik explains how in English novels the female characters are threatened by the central issue of dispossession: gothic plots of "imprisoned and endangered" women parallel the "civil death" that accompanied marriage, as the laws of coverture meant that women lost all rights to possess property ("Horrors" 678).[18] Though coverture is not a factor in these American works, the situation Linda and Hannah are in is likewise fraught with the legal issue of property. Jacobs and Crafts are in fact able to recast so easily and so powerfully their textual selves as gothic damsels, even without the trappings of castles or dragons, because Linda's and Hannah's distress derives from a lack of control over property, in their cases the property of their persons. Their tales of imprisonment and flight to counter this lack of control then fit the typical gothic narrative arc.

By employing the familiar character type, Jacobs and Crafts can thus appeal even to audiences far removed from slavery. Both writers amplify their depictions of suffering females for their readers by using second-person direct address.[19] Hannah Crafts uses the second person early in the narrative to make the reader feel that he or she is enduring the gothic space of a "dreary and solemn" house along with Hannah (15). Although this "you" aligns the reader with Hannah, an instance of second person late in the narrative pushes the reader even further to consider the dire consequences of race and property. Hannah is describing the horrible condition of the slave huts on the Wheeler plantation when she stops to ask, "What do you think of it?" (206). She then proceeds to align the reader with those enslaved, "to be made to feel that you have no business here, there, or anywhere except just to work—work—work" until "you really are assimilated to the brutes, that the horses, dogs and cattle have quite as many priveledges" (206). A reader invested in Crafts's narrative must understand what it is like to be property. Harriet Jacobs proves more persistent in her appeals to the reader, as Linda addresses "you" at least a dozen times. Many of these occurrences, as Robin R. Warhol points out, highlight the differences between the reader and the enslaved person, such as when Linda exclaims, "O, you happy free women, contrast your New Year's day with that of the poor bond-woman!" (17). The enslaved people who fear the January 1st sale of family members may be distant from the reader's world, but Jacobs and Crafts can borrow the damsel character with her pleas of "alas" from gothic fiction to teach the reader what to fear.

Specifically, they point to the monster. If damsels are the fuel of the gothic, the monstrous villains are its engine. Jacobs and Crafts can call evil by its name by clearly depicting slaveholders and slave traders as predators. Jacobs launches into an expose of Dr. Flint early in the narrative. After living in his house only a few weeks, Linda witnesses the brutal beating of an enslaved person who had "accused his master of being the father of [his wife's] child" (15). Linda then watches the sale of this man's wife because "she had forgotten that it was a crime for a slave to tell who was the father of her child" (16). Only twelve years old at the time, Linda already perceives Dr. Flint's evil nature. When at fifteen she is harassed by Dr. Flint, Jacobs uses gothic language to portray him as a villain: he is a "crafty man," who "[whispers] foul words," has "stormy terrific ways," and is in every way a "vile monster" (26). His "dark shadow" follows Linda everywhere (26). Crafts borrows the same gothic language for the central monster of her narrative, the lawyer and slave trader Trappe.[20] Trappe consistently appears to Hannah as a dark "shadow," and his black clothes seem less a marker of his position as a gentleman than a sign of his vile character. Trappe blackmails Hannah's mistress, Mrs. Vincent, over her supposed black blood, but the mistress explains that even before he revealed this secret, she felt "an indefinable presentiment of evil in his presence" (46). In separate analyses of *Incidents in the Life of a Slave Girl* and *The Bondwoman's Narrative*, Goddu argues that both Jacobs and Crafts locate "blackness" in the characters of Dr. Flint and Trappe, so that Jacobs "reverses the gothic's usual demonization: the master, not the black slave, is the source of horror and dread" and Crafts likewise "[demonizes] a wealthy white man rather than a black slave" (*Gothic* 147, "American" 67). Even though the gothic coding is reversed, the gothic tropes prove crucial in allowing Jacobs and Crafts to shape their readers' perceptions of these men as monsters.

Jacobs and Crafts also employ the characteristic gothic rendering of the villains' threat to the damsels as essentially sexual. Kari J. Winter identifies this threat as the key commonality of slave narratives and gothic fiction: "both genres focus on the sexual politics at the heart of patriarchal culture, and both represent the terrifying aspects of life for women in a patriarchal culture" (13). For women held in slavery, however, the threat of being at the mercy of a sexual predator arises because of the women's status as property. Unlike a typical gothic damsel, enslaved women are not in a precarious position that can be altered if they are saved; their very identity puts them at unending risk. Sex becomes a means for monsters to assert utter ownership. That Dr. Flint is asserting power is evident in his methods. He does not resort to raping Linda. Instead, he wants her to acknowledge her complete lack of agency by submitting to him: "My master met me at every turn, reminding me that I belonged to him, and swearing by heaven and earth that he would compel me to submit to him" (27). Trappe likewise does not force himself on Hannah or Mrs. Vincent, so he may appear to be something less than a villain. Hollis Robbins in fact argues, "Trappe is certainly not a good character—he is an extortionist and a slave speculator, but he is not a monster to Hannah. He feeds and clothes her ... and he sells her to a man who is rather kind to her, under the circumstances" (79). While Trappe may not threaten Hannah's life, when he sells her to a slave trader headed to the New Orleans market, where women are notoriously marketed as sex slaves, he indeed acts as a gothic monster because he reduces her to mere property. Hannah understands that Trappe wanted "to make me realize that in both soul and body I was indeed a slave" (112). If she is property, her body is not her own.

For gothic damsels, the possibility of rape proves even worse than death. In *Wieland*, Clara contemplates how she could end her life with a penknife to preempt being raped by the villain (111). Jacobs seems to share Clara's hierarchy. She portrays Dr. Flint several times threatening to kill Linda. When he asks her, "Do you know that I have a right to do as I like with you,—that I can kill you, if I please?" she responds, "You have tried to kill me, and I wish you had, but you have no right to do as you like with me" (35). Death is preferable. Unlike Clara, though, who seems to be projecting the idea that rape would cause her to be ruined or impure, Linda and Hannah see the monsters' threat as a question over the ownership of their very bodies, ergo a question of legal possession.

RACE AND LEGAL POSSESSION

While Jacobs and Crafts use the gothic construction of damsel and monster to help their readers to understand who the victims and villains are, to identify the key issue of sexual threat, and to perceive the underlying problem of property, unlike their gothic sisters, Linda and Hannah, do not lose control over property through marriage, inheritance, or foul play. They are property because of their race and are haunted by their owners' legal possession. Though the law haunts and traps the damsels, Jacobs and Crafts reveal the weakness of a system of property based on constructed racial categories that can easily dissolve.

Dr. Flint's legal possession of Linda is complicated, because she is actually owned by his minor daughter, a fact he raises only as deflection when asked if he is willing to sell Linda. Dr. Flint still pretends legal possession in pursuing her. For Linda, as for all the enslaved people in this study, the key catalyst for haunting is this conflation with property. When Jacobs uses those gothic tropes to construct Dr. Flint as monster, the devastating conclusion to Linda is "I was his property" (26). Linda bemoans that for the enslaved girl, "there is no shadow of law to protect her" (26). The master is both gothic shadow and the very law that denies personhood. In his 1853 book, *The American Slave Code*, William Goodell identifies the central "theory of slavery" as property. He quotes Judge Shroud as arguing "the cardinal principle of slavery—that the slave is not to be ranked among *sentient beings*, but among *things*, as an article of property, a chattel personal—obtains as undoubted law, in all these (the slave-holding) States" (27). For enslaved women, this status as an "article of property" equals sexual assault. In his 1858 defense of slavery, Thomas Cobb explains that the master has all rights to a enslaved person's body up to the denial of existence; therefore, "the penalties for rape would not and should not, by such implication, be made to extend to carnal forcible knowledge of a slave, the offense not affecting the existence of the slave, and the existence being the extent of the right which the implication of the law grants" (86). He later adds that "the occurrence of [a master raping a slave] is almost unheard of" (99). Linda, however, knows the possibility to be very likely from the moment she witnesses the sale of the woman who bore Dr. Flint's child. In positing absolute possession of women, the law sanctions rape.

Crafts's Trappe is the very embodiment of this law. When Trappe negotiates the sale of Hannah and Mrs. Vincent, he claims that "my conscience never troubles me" because if women "are to be sold it is rather the fault of the law that permits it than of me who profits by it" (102). He is seemingly devoid of any emotion, whether of pity for women sold into sexual slavery or of guilt for trading in human flesh. Selling young, good-looking women is his forte, and this sale is just another business transaction. His neutral affect, as a man simply following the law, belies the haunting hidden in his cold logic. In response to his explication, Mrs. Vincent swoons on a couch and then dies in the most melodramatic scene imaginable. Legal possession haunts, and cold logic kills. Ellen Weinauer explains that in antislavery texts, "the law itself becomes a kind of gothic villain, exerting a seemingly absolute and inescapable control over the lives of the enslaved" (272). For Jacobs and Crafts, that control leaves the damsels vulnerable to rape.

Yet slave law, however much it might have tried to make a person into a thing, had one major weakness. Unlike an animal, a house, or a piece of furniture, the enslaved person could contest this ownership. As James L. Huston explains, "Legal transformation could never eliminate the volition of human beings. Thus the property itself, the slaves, could contest the rule of the property holder (the slave master), a condition unlike any other property-holding arrangement" (44). Both Jacobs and Crafts speak back to the laws that enslave them. Jacobs continually points out to the reader how the law has failed to protect her: "O virtuous reader! You never knew what it is to be a slave; to be entirely unprotected by law or custom; to have the laws reduce you to the condition of chattel" (47).[21] Crafts likewise speaks back to the legal system. When Hannah is in prison, she remarks that "without having committed any crime, [I was] thus introduced into one of the legal fortresses of a country celebrated throughout the world for the freedom, equality, and magnanimity of its laws" (78). While both writers depict the volition of enslaved people against the legal system, this is not a game they can win because white men make (and can remake) the rules. When Dr. Flint discovers that Linda is pregnant with another man's child and claims, "You have been criminal towards me," the irony of his outrage is astounding, but he is not wrong (50). Linda understands that "[her] master had power and law on his side" (70). Yet the law is more than just on his side; it is in his very being, just as shadowy Trappe is the law in the flesh.

Linda and Hannah may not be able to overcome their legal status, but when Jacobs and Crafts change the script that these heroines inhabit to make them not just hunted property but also haunted damsels, the heroines' duality undermines the paradigm of legal possession. As the readers of Jacobs's *Incidents* identify Linda as the gothic damsel worthy of saving, the tension between this identity and the designation of her as the property of Dr. Flint generates the emotion of her story. Jacobs then intensifies the stakes of Linda's dire position by highlighting her virtue. Linda wants to maintain her purity, but "it is deemed a crime in [a slave girl] to wish to be virtuous" (28). Although she sees her eventual relationship with Mr. Sands as a sacrifice of her virtue, her explanation relies on gothic language: "I tried hard to preserve my self-respect; but I was struggling alone in the powerful grasp of the demon Slavery; and the monster proved too strong for me" (46). As property, Linda does not have the adequate agency to avoid a sexual relationship; as a damsel, though, she compels her readers' sympathy with her situation. As both at the same time, she presents a conundrum, as does Hannah, who also desires to maintain her virtue despite being property.

In writing Hannah, Crafts depicts an enslaved person who wishes to remain unmarried because "it was my unalterable resolution never to entail slavery on any human being" (213). Hannah (surprisingly to some critics) remains largely out of immediate danger from any thwarting of this plan, owing in part to a series of fortuitous events, such as the wagon accident that kills the slave trader who plans to sell her in the New Orleans market.[22] However, other stories that Crafts includes provide evidence of the peril of rape to an enslaved female. Mrs. Wright, for example, is in prison for helping an enslaved girl who was about to be sold to the New Orleans market. Even Hannah herself decides to escape when her owner, Mrs. Wheeler, gives her to an enslaved male to marry. She explains that "nothing but this would have impelled me to flight" (213). When she is threatened with rape, she "ran for [her] life" (216). Enslaved, the damsels have no legal standing, but they appear all too human in their desired morality.

They also appear all too white. Aspects of Linda's and Hannah's depictions as mixed race prove quite tricky to parse. If the emphasis on their light coloring is designed to make them more appealing to white readers, then the texts could be reifying the legal construction of racial hierarchies.[23] Crafts's text is more problematic than Jacobs's in this regard, as Crafts displays a clear disdain for darker people in her depiction of Hannah's revulsion towards the workers in the fields, those "promiscuous crowds of dirty, obscene and degraded objects" (213). Goddu admits that this "racial fear and loathing" is "deeply disturbing" given the text's seeming "commitment to rewriting those conventions" ("American" 70). The damsels' mixed race, however, might alternatively provide a critique of the legal construction of property. Just as the conflation of damsel and property disturbs the legal contention that humans can ever truly be things to be owned, the duality of black and white questions the strict racial categories that divide human from property in the first place. In positing whiteness itself as a kind of property, Cheryl I. Harris explains that "white identity and whiteness were sources of privilege and protection; their absence meant being the object of property" (1720–21). In the face of a bifurcated society, Jacobs and Crafts shape their damsels as both.

Jacobs and Crafts do not flinch from portraying mixed blood; instead, they lead with it. Linda announces in the first paragraph of the narrative that her parents were mulattos, while Hannah in her second paragraph explains that "my complexion was almost white" (6). Though they are haunted by monsters who are whiter, the difference is only a matter of degree. Daneen Wardrop contends that Jacobs employs gothic tropes to point to her "intertwined family" created by generations of "miscegenation, most often as the result of rape," resulting in "one 'branch' of the family [using] the other 'branch' as commodity" (23–24).[24] In the first chapter, Linda explains that her first mistress was the "foster sister" of her mother as her grandmother nursed them at the same time and they grew up together; by Wardrop's logic, they were also likely related. This sisterly bond is why Linda is so shocked that the mistress did not free her in her will but left her to Dr. Flint's daughter. Property rights allow this bizarre branching based on fractions of blood, as characters deemed white have all the power. Linda points out the irony that Dr. Flint "was too scrupulous to *sell* me; but he had no scruples whatever about committing a much greater wrong against the helpless young girl placed under his guardianship" (31–32). He does not scruple to make these demands because his very whiteness makes him in the spirit of the law if not the letter, the owner of Linda. Yet that Linda also has white blood questions his logic. White and black are not opposites but related, as Jacobs reiterates by including a vignette of two girls playing together: "one was a fair white child; the other was her slave, and also her sister" (27).

Crafts also portrays family relations across racial lines. Hannah is claimed as the "dear sister" of her "white" mistress, Mrs. Vincent, who then discovers that her own mother was black. Martha J. Cutter argues, "That this mistress can and does pass for white perhaps indicates that the difference between 'almost white' and 'white' may be no difference at all" (121). Trappe, in discovering her hidden racial lineage, may act as the law incarnate, but the consequence is a chaotic world: a mistress one day, enslaved the next.[25] Hannah, too, can pass as white. She has to tell Mrs. Henry that she has been an enslaved person because her appearance does not betray her mixed race, and Mrs. Wheeler references Hannah's "white face" when she sends her to live with the field workers (210). The implication that even "white" people can become enslaved echoes the assertion William Craft makes in his slave narrative that white children were kidnapped and sold into slavery (682). In

The Bondwoman's Narrative, even the pompous Mrs. Wheeler turns black, albeit only temporarily when she tries a new face powder.[26] In the inset story told by Lizzy, the family branches of various shades of color actually reside in the same house. Mrs. Cosgrove discovers secret rooms inhabited by enslaved children sired by her husband along with their mothers. Bridget M. Marshall argues that "Mrs. Cosgrove is troubled by images of the slaves' whiteness" and "haunted by the full implications of slavery (its sexual exploitation)," as that exploitation results in "still more—and still whiter—slaves" (124).[27] Even as Jacobs and Crafts use gothic tropes to portray Linda and Hannah as both enslaved people and damsels in distress, the writers portray the women as black property and white family at the same time. By openly revealing the mixed race of their textual selves, Jacobs and Crafts question the very underpinning of property law.

SPACE AND SPECTRAL POSSESSION

In revealing problems with the law's contradiction of racial boundaries, Jacobs and Crafts in effect argue that its own internal logic does not hold. Questioning legal possession may persuade readers that slavery is illogical, but the damsels remained trapped inside its legal system and haunted by the monsters' pursuit. Even though Linda and Hannah eventually escape from slavery, they point to sister-damsels still imprisoned. Jacobs and Crafts combat this seemingly intractable legal possession with spectral possession. By employing haunting, Jacobs and Crafts confront the cold logic of law with the force of the supernatural. Avery Gordon explains that "haunting is a very particular way of knowing what has happened or is happening. Being haunted draws us affectively, sometimes against our will and always a bit magically, into the structure of feeling of a reality we come to experience, not as cold knowledge, but as a transformative recognition" (8). As a supernatural phenomenon, haunting thwarts what society deems as natural, such as the "reality" of race, to transform the reader's recognition.

This transformation requires, as Gordon points out, a bit of magic, which Jacobs and Crafts find in the gothic's fictionality, specifically in the language of haunted spaces. Throughout the narratives, Linda and Hannah are searching for a safe space, a room without a lurking sexual predator, a cabin that will not disappear. Safe spaces, however, are hard to come by because the property the damsels inhabit is owned by the same white people who own them. There is no refuge from the threat of being property while they are inside property they do not themselves own. The gothic, however, provides a language of claiming that does not invoke property deeds or money. Ruth Bienstock Anolik explains that the gothic "posits a ludic, supernatural world in which the principles of legal ownership grounded in rationality and an existing social order, must give way to the irrational, to ghostly possession," so that "often, the true owner of the castle is the possessing ghost" ("Horrors" 667). Thus, to possess a safe space, the damsels need to become ghostlike.

Seeking refuge in haunted places may seem a strange strategy for these women. According to Sue Chaplin, gothic spaces traditionally "symbolise the dangerous, confined, and marginalised position occupied by women within patriarchal structures of power—the place of woman is hidden within, or secreted beneath the 'Gothic castle' of paternal law" (140). While Linda's and Hannah's need to hide and the very grim places they find as refuge certainly point to a reading that equates gothic space with a lack of power, Ellen Malenas Ledoux proposes an alternative reading. In the eighteenth-century British works she examines, she finds "hearty heroines" who know "Gothic spaces well and [are] not afraid to exploit that knowledge to circumvent often craven and feminized persecutors" (333). I contend that Linda and Hannah become "hearty" damsels whose status as haunted property allows them to possess haunted property.

In *Incidents*, Jacobs clearly distinguishes between safe and dangerous spaces: property owned by whites is perilous, while space claimed by blacks provides refuge. In gothic terms, Linda is haunted by slavery in white-owned space, and in turn she haunts slavery in black-owned space. Linda's childhood home is her original safe space and inspires the kind of space she will seek the rest of the narrative. The Brent home is "comfortable" and radiates warmth, family, and safety (9). The idyllic opening picture of this home echoes Stowe's early scene of Uncle Tom in his cabin with his wife and children. Because Linda is "fondly shielded," she does not know that she is a "piece of merchandise" (9). When her mother dies, the reality that someone else owns her ruptures this ideal. In her reading of Jacobs, Sally Gomaa identifies the "homelessness" tied to slavery that "communicates a universal feeling of vulnerability" (372). Although Linda will remain homeless, she searches for a home where she can again find comfort.

What she encounters instead when she enters Dr. Flint's house is "cold looks, cold words, and cold treatment" (12). Dr. Flint's house is, Linda admits, a "fine residence" and has the potential to be a haven for a "helpless young girl" who has been orphaned and placed under the "guardianship" of Dr. Flint (16, 32). At times, Dr. Flint even suggests that he sees himself as a paternal caretaker: "Did I not take you into the house, and make you the companion of my own children?" (32). But the house's "fine" appearance, which Dr. Flint "as a married man and a professional man" seems to care about greatly, belies its gothic character (29). As a predator trying to catch his prey, Dr. Flint knows he needs to control space. Linda is in part shielded from his advances because she sleeps in the room of her aunt, so Dr. Flint "resolved to remove the obstacle in the way of his scheme" by arranging to have his four-year-old daughter sleep in his room, with Linda as the necessary accompanying servant (29). That Dr. Flint would use his daughter in his scheme to rape a young enslaved girl is hard to believe, as Jacobs acknowledges when she attests, "Reader, I draw no imaginary pictures of southern homes. I am telling you the plain truth" (32). Dr. Flint is not, however, the only white person in this white-owned space. Mrs. Flint intervenes, which surely saves Linda, but Mrs. Flint in her distrust and jealousy then demands that Linda sleep in a room adjoining hers. She watches Linda while she sleeps, stalking her, so that she cannot rest. When Linda talks about the "circumstances in which I was placed," her phrasing reveals both her lack of power in that passive voice construction and the crucial role of place in that power dynamic (46). Her "place" in the Flint household is one of confinement and resembles a gothic prison.

In contrast to the "cold," gothic, white space of Dr. Flint's house is the house of Linda's grandmother. Her grandmother actually owns this house, a bona fide "'s": "by perseverance and unwearied industry, she was now mistress of a snug little home" (18). Even as a child, Linda understands the equation of the house to freedom, as she exclaims that she "longed for a home like hers" (18). She illustrates the warmth radiating from the house in literal terms by noting the "grand big oven there, too, that baked bread and nice things for the town" (18). This black-owned space becomes an important refuge for Linda; when she defies Dr. Flint by revealing that she is pregnant with another man's child, she escapes to her grandmother's house. At one point, she even hides when Dr. Flint comes by after the birth of her child to humiliate her. He is furious to find out she was indeed "at home" and evading his presence (52). Being "at home" in black-owned space gives Linda a small measure of protection and a greater measure of insight into how she can resist Dr. Flint's legal possession: she can change places, both literally in moving from his house to black-owned space, and later figuratively from being property that is haunted to being property that haunts.

First, though, she has to dodge Dr. Flint's ultimate power play: moving her into an isolated cottage "in a secluded place" (45). A cottage away from her aunt, Mrs. Flynn, her grandmother, and the rest of society, would leave her powerless.[28] In gothic works, a place generally becomes haunted by past events. Dr. Flint's house in town, for example, is haunted from the moment young Linda witnesses that brutal beating, but the isolated cottage is haunted by its future. Dr. Flint speaks of the cottage as something that would give Linda agency: "a home of my own" that would "make a lady of me" (45). She "shuddered" in reply, though, knowing that the space would not be hers to command as if she were a "lady" who owned it. Dr. Flint would not only own the space; he would fully own her and would "succeed at last in trampling his victim under his feet" (46). To thwart this move, Linda "made the plunge into the abyss" and begins her affair with Mr. Sands. Significantly, Linda connects the affair with her homelessness: "If slavery had been abolished, I, also, could have married the man of my choice; I could have had a home shielded by laws; and I should have been spared the painful task of confessing what I am now about to relate" (46). When the cottage is finished, Linda announces that she will not move into it because she is pregnant. In entering a relationship with another man, Linda is declaring that her body is hers to command. She subsequently wants to declare control of where that body resides. Later, Dr. Flint tries once more to convince Linda to move into his cottage, claiming that he offers "a home and freedom" where "the past [will] be forgotten" (69). Yet in white-owned space, there is no freedom, and the past continues to haunt.

For Linda, the first step to freedom is to inhabit black-controlled space: to hide in her grandmother's house. The startlingly aspect of this move is that Linda indeed finds refuge in a small attic, the very emblem of a haunted space. Jacobs underscores the garret's gothic qualities. Rats and mice run over Linda's bed, and the "darkness was oppressive" (92). When she creates a little hole in the wall, the first person she sees outside is Dr. Flint, which gives her a "shuddering, superstitious feeling" (93). As time goes on, the summer heat is oppressive, and the winter brings frostbite. During the second winter, she almost dies. Georgia Kreiger describes Linda's experience as a "live entombment" that parallels Linda's story of an enslaved man pressed in a cotton gin and left to die (613). Even as years go by, though, Linda continues to assert that she had "chosen this, rather than my lot as a slave" (92).

The garret is preferable and "safe" because it is not white-owned space. Samira Kawash examines the liminal position of the fugitive and argues that "in her garret Jacobs has effected an escape without going anywhere, as if the surface of slavery looped back on itself and created a little pocket where Jacobs can be *in*, but not a part of, the goings on of her community. It is, in fact, precisely because she is not anywhere within slavery, but in a pocket outside or alongside slavery, that her safety is guaranteed" ("Fugitive" 286). Although Linda is indeed not "within slavery," she inhabits black-owned space where, as many critics argue, she finds some measure of power. Jean Fagan Yellin explains that from this space Linda "manipulates the sale of her children to their father, arranges for her daughter to be taken north, tricks her master into believing that she has left the South, and quite literally directs a performance in which Dr. Flint plays the fool while she watches, unseen" (xxviii). The garret may be physically oppressive and reminiscent of the gothic spaces Chaplin describes that confine and marginalize women, but Linda, as a "hearty heroine," finds a way to exploit that space.

She can do so not only because the garret is within a black-owned house but also because she inhabits the position of a specter in haunted space. She can see without being seen. She watches, for example, her son, Benny, confront Dr. Flint. When Dr. Flint yells at Benny to "get out of the way, you little damned rascal! If you don't, I'll cut off your head!" Benny responds, "You can't put me in jail again. I don't belong to you now" (93). She sees townspeople speculating about where she might be hiding and debating whether they would turn her in if they found her. She witnesses an enslaved woman running from punishment, who jumps in the river and dies instead of remaining in slavery. She plays Santa Claus by sewing her children clothes and toys. Even though the children are not aware, at least early on, of her physical presence, she is witnessing their lives as well as the activities of the community in an invisible, spectral manner.

Linda additionally simulates a specter's ability to elide distance when she sends Dr. Flint a letter from New York. She encloses a letter to her grandmother indicating that she lives in Boston but is visiting New York and wants her children sent to her. Linda is able to pull off this feat by analyzing a New York newspaper for street names to mention and by soliciting a friend to post the letter from New York. Linda finds the whole trick "as good as comedy," but that she can imagine a life in Boston and pretend to be living there shows the power of fiction against the confinement of law (103). Dr. Flint is so distraught by losing control of her that he ends up making three trips to New York in pursuit. From her garret, the damsel now haunts the monster.

Linda finally escapes to the North, but because she exists in white-owned space in the house of Mr. and Mrs. Bruce, she is not safe. When Mr. Sands's brother-in-law writes to Dr. Flint divulging Linda's location, Linda must again flee from danger. Years later, when Linda is working for the second Mrs. Bruce, she is again in peril, as the Fugitive Slave Act makes her virtually "a slave in New York," and she has to escape once more (150). Mrs. Bruce fixes one part of Linda's problem by paying off Dr. Flint's daughter, in essence buying her to set her free. Linda can no longer be claimed as property, but the issue of whose space she inhabits continues. Debra Humphreys explains that Jacobs wrote *Incidents* "in private, at night" (153). She hides the activity that she uses to claim personhood because she is still in white-owned space. Linda admits that freedom is "a vast improvement in *my* condition" but this freedom appears qualified: "The dream of my life is not yet realized. I do not sit with my children in a home of my own. I still long for a hearthstone of my own, however humble" (156). Her lament echoes that of Sojourner Truth, who bemoans in her slave narrative that she lacks the ability to have a home "around whose sacred hearth-stone she could collect her family" (620). Just as Truth identifies the importance of a home in protecting her family, Linda wants that family connection in a home free from fear. Because of her experience in negotiating spaces from Dr. Flint's house and the proposed cottage to her grandmother's house and the garret, she knows that to be free from the haunting of legal possession completely, she needs to exist in property she owns. In the end, though, Linda is still homeless.

Crafts parallels Jacobs in her depiction of Hannah traversing safe and dangerous spaces. Like Linda, Hannah searches for a home and finds temporary refuge in haunted property. Without relatives, though, Hannah begins without the ideal image of a family home that Linda has. Hannah was instead "employed about the house," a rather detached description of her relationship with her abode. She does, however, find the model of the home she will seek when Hetty and Siah, an elderly white couple, befriend her. She spends time in their cottage as Hetty teaches her to read. Though the cottage is small, Hannah notes its "perfect neatness" and "quiet and orderly repose" (8). Here she is a person. When her master barges in one night and tells her to "begone home," she knows her friends will pay for their crime of teaching her to read (12). In examining the architectural spaces in *The Bondwoman's Narrative*, William Gleason explains that when the master orders her to go home, he is actually ordering her away from the place that has become her home (149). For my gothic reading here, it is as if the master is casting a spell or a curse, commanding the home to "be gone." She is now homeless, without the ownership of property that would help solidify her personhood.

As she searches for both home and personhood, she continually has difficulty discerning her level of safety in various places because of what Gleason terms their "architectural betrayal" (152). Reading through a gothic lens, what we see is the repeated trope of the deceit of the surface. In gothic texts, the monster can at first appear beautiful, or the haunted house can seem inviting. The damsel can thus be unaware of the danger even with foreshadowing. Eve Kosofsky Sedgwick explores the spatial dynamics of gothic works and finds that "it is the position of the self to be massively blocked off from something to which it ought normally to have access. This something can be its own past, the details of its family history; it can be the free air, when the self has been literally buried alive; it can be a lover; it can be just all the circumambient life, when the self is pinned in a death-like sleep" (12). Hannah is certainly blocked off from her self, in that she is not person but property, and this problem is reflected in her encounters with structures, as she does not have access to the things a home entails, namely, family and identity. The result is that she does not read spaces well, spaces which in her slave world are dangerously deceptive. Seemingly beautiful homes end up increasing her confinement. The places that appear to be haunted end up allowing her spectral possession.

The first beautiful space Hannah negotiates is her original master's house, "the ancient mansion of Lindendale" (13). Hannah has the opportunity to see the house in its full splendor when she helps prepare it for the arrival of the master's new wife. She is astounded by the "appearance of wealth and splendor, and the appliances to every luxury. What a variety of beautiful rooms, all splendid rooms, all splendid yet so different, and seemingly inhabited by marble images of art, or human forms pictured on the walls" (14). Those very "human forms" pose the first trial for Hannah, as she acknowledges that "memories of the dead give at any time a haunting air to a silent room" (16). Gazing at the master's family portraits, Hannah senses both "foreboding of some great calamity" and "superstitious awe" (17). The scene, however, takes an unexpected turn as Hannah decides that because "I was not a slave with these pictured memorials of the past," there was a "freedom" in their presence.[29] Priscilla Wald argues that *The Bondwoman's Narrative* is "not a haunted text" and points to Hannah's reaction in this scene of feeling "not haunted, but inspired" (213, 218). While it is true that Hannah is not haunted here by the characteristic monsters of the gothic—dead people returned to haunt as ghosts—she will be haunted throughout by live monsters in a system that deems her property.

Though Crafts makes dead people innocuous, the seemingly beautiful house conceals dangers, as the new mistress soon learns. On the night Mrs. Vincent arrives, a storm moves in, causing the wind to blow the branches of a linden tree that symbolizes the house's dark secrets. Hannah explains that an ancestor of the current master had used an iron loop to suspend an enslaved woman named Rose from the tree because she would not obey the master's command to kill her dog. The dog was given to her by her daughter, who had been sold away, and Rose, though she is property, dares to claim the property of the dog. The memory of her agonizing death haunts everyone who hears the tree branches move in the wind. The very house is haunted by slavery, and although Hannah feels safe among the portraits, she is, as subsequent encounters will evidence, a poor reader of space. She ends up needing to flee this house to protect Mrs. Vincent, that "dear sister," when Trappe threatens to reveal the mistress's mixed parentage.

Hannah, however, does not learn her lesson about the danger of beautiful spaces that are, as in Jacobs's rendering, white-owned and thus part of the system that makes her property as well. In her search for a home where she can claim personhood, she keeps finding property that keeps her enslaved. When she and Mrs. Vincent escape, they get lost, wander a while, and then decide to approach a farmhouse. Hannah spends several paragraphs detailing its charm, as it seems an "abode of competence and peace" with "a quiet air of domestic happiness" (60). Hannah concludes: "Slavery dwelt not there. A thing so utterly dark and gloomy could not have remained in such a place for a day" (62). The lady of the house mentions her lawyer brother, but Hannah's alarm is not aroused until they are alone in their room and see the face of Trappe appearing ominously in their window. Hannah is distraught that Trappe is "watching us, dogging our footsteps, and would be haunting us everywhere" (65). But he is not in fact "everywhere"; he is in the house whose charm seemed to suggest refuge but was white-owned space.

Hannah is tricked yet again by the beautiful appearance of the Henrys' house. Although she arrives here through the happenstance of the wagon accident, the Henrys' care for her leads her to hope she can stay. She takes pages to describe the various rooms of the Henrys' house because "every room seemed a wonder in itself" until she simply claims, "I could never sufficiently admire the order and harmony of the arrangements, which blent [blended] so many parts into a perfect whole" (127). The Henrys perfectly fit their charming house, as Mrs. Henry is "wise, pious, and gentle," and Mr. Henry is "a clergyman, and his naturally mild and genial disposition [has] been softened and tempered by the benignacy of religion" (128). This Christian couple housed in such beauty appears to double Hannah's friends Hetty and Siah with their quaint cottage, so Hannah begs Mrs. Henry to buy her because she wants this to be her "home" (130). Gleason points out the "deep irony" of Hannah labeling the house the name of the flower, "forget me not," because this is the "mandate from Mrs. Henry's dead father that prevents her" from helping Hannah (161). Mrs. Henry had promised her father that she would never buy or sell another enslaved person, so she refuses Hannah's pleas. Like the other beautiful white-owned spaces, the Henrys' house cannot be Hannah's home.

Even so, Hannah does not escape when she has the opportunity to do so with Charlotte and William. Stephanie Li, in comparing Hannah and Linda, argues that "Hannah is willing to forgo individual liberty for the opportunity to dwell in the utopian Henry household. Hannah's uncritical commitment to domestic values leads her to accept her bondage, unlike Jacobs who aspires to have her own home" (51). Yet Hannah also aspires to have a home and later her own home. For a while she just does not see, as a poor reader of space, how the Henrys' house cannot be a home, but as in earlier places, the beautiful turns gothic. The enslaved people start talking about a "ghostly visitant" (145).[30] Hannah figures out that this is just William arranging the escape, but when Charlotte and William flee, William's owner brings bloodhounds inside that beautiful home to track the runaways. The label "forget me not" takes a dark turn because now the fugitives would like to be forgotten. Later, Mrs. Henry arranges for Hannah to be sold to Mrs. Wheeler. Hannah detects "something in [Mrs. Wheeler's] manner that I did not like," but she has no say in the matter, and she is sold as property. Although she manages to get along with Mrs. Wheeler for a while, she eventually finds her situation dire enough to risk escaping. Mrs. Henry claimed earlier she could not buy Hannah, but she in effect sells her, and the beautiful house ends up putting Hannah in peril.

Contrasting with these seemingly beautiful places is an abandoned cabin that has every marker of being haunted but surprisingly allows Hannah some measure of agency. Just as Linda is able to find refuge in haunted property that allows her spectral possession, Hannah finds refuge in haunted property because she too is haunted property and for a time eludes legal possession. Hannah and her mistress stumble upon the cabin after they flee the house of Trappe's sister, having gotten lost in the "deep, dark wood," as if they are children in a fairy tale. The old cabin appears "forlorn and desolate" with paths "chocked with weeds" (67). Inside, everything is broken, from the leg of the bench to the iron pot and the crockery. More suspicious to Hannah is a "bundle of old clothes," which she intuits were "connected with some deed of crime" (67). These suspicions are later confirmed by the women finding a "hatchet, with hair yet sticking to the heft" and a "human skeleton, which the dogs and vultures had disentombed" (68). All of these details point to a horrific past event that could very well render the physical place of the cabin haunted. These clues link the violence to a specific narrative in early American tradition: the Indian captivity narrative. Hannah notes the residence had probably been of a "forester" and signals a frontier context by adding that the cabin "was formed much as Indians formed their wigwams" (67). The hatchet with hair on it evokes stories of scalping. That no one is left suggests that all the cabin's occupants were either killed or captured. Hannah and Mrs. Vincent, fleeing one kind of captivity in the guise of slavery, find themselves in the topos of a different captivity narrative, which only serves to increase their fear.

Hannah's mistress indeed responds to all of this stimulus in the expected way. She is haunted: "a superstitious horror took possession of my dear companion['s] mind. The scream of a nightbird, or the howl of a wolf, even the voice of the wind filled her mind with terror" (68). As time goes on, the mistress becomes "decidedly insane" and "fancied herself pursued by an invisible being, who sought to devour her flesh and crush her bones" (69). The gothic space of this abandoned cabin leaves her without agency or even mental clarity. Hannah, however, has a quite different reaction. As they first wander lost, she clearly identifies what is and is not frightening: "gloomy, indeed, was our walk, but gloomier were our thoughts. Serpents, wild beasts, and owls were our companions, yet our horror was of man" (67). Hannah is haunted by the men pursuing them and not by the standard markers of the gothic. When she first guesses that the cabin had been the scene of a violent episode, she does not flee from fear. Instead, she embraces the cabin's gothic status: "true, a more lonely and desolate place could not well be imagined, but loneliness was what we sought; in that was our security" (67). Here, she realizes, "at least we should be free" (67). As property haunted by legal possession, Hannah understands that she can hide in haunted property. Hannah tries to convince her mistress that the cabin's past could not harm them as they "were innocent of crime" (68). They are rather victims of the crime of slavery, and for a brief time in the cabin, they are not owned.

Eventually, however, hunters discover the cabin. When one hunter asks Hannah if she had not found the place "haunted," she replies, "no spirit had troubled me" (71). Trouble instead comes from the men who turn them in to the authorities. In prison, however, Hannah is once again able to claim spectral possession of a seemingly gothic space. The prison cell has all the trappings of an Edgar Allan Poe story. The women are led by a jailor with a "ghastly grin" to a "hot stifling" cell of almost "Egyptian darkness," an allusion to one of the plagues enacted on Egypt in the book of Exodus (80). Hannah wakes to find a "huge rat" eating her cheek, which leads her to "conjure strange fancies" where she recalls ghastly stories of people in prison being eaten alive by rats who "gnawed the quivering and palpitating flesh from their bones" (81). In this scene, Crafts lays the gothic on thick, and Marshall claims that "for the reader, it is difficult to disentangle the real horror of these situations—whether they are in an abandoned hovel that was the site of a murder or in a prison cell filled with rats—from the women's fanciful imaginings of terrors unseen" (120). Although Marshall's reading is certainly true for Mrs. Vincent at the cabin, it is not true for Hannah. And although both women are terrorized by the prison initially, Hannah is eventually able to convert the gothic space of the prison cell by her spectral possession. In this instance, the specter is imagined as spirit, derived from Hannah's Christian beliefs. When the one candle she begged the jailor for burns out leaving her in "inexpressible horror," she whispers, "God," and then feels "a heavenly assurance of his protection and presence" (82). She remembers that even in her captivity, "the God of Israel was my refuge" (82). Calling on the name of God in jail aligns Hannah with heroes of scripture, such as Joseph and Paul, yet another way Crafts signals to her reader that Hannah is a hearty heroine. The nightmare of being devoured alive transforms into a "blessed dream of my mother, whom I had never seen. My angel mother" (82). Hannah's mother, however, is not just a vision in a dream: "I still love to fancy that she was near me at the time; that a spirit herself she influenced me spiritually, and that her blessed and holy presence was made the medium of my consolation" (82). That Hannah's "consolation" had the "medium" of spirit shows how Hannah combats the legal possession of her very body with weapons spiritual and spectral. This imaginative vision of her mother shows not only the power of fiction but also the force of a different kind of possession.

Having grasped the "refuge" she can have even confined in a jail cell, Hannah meets Mrs. Wright. In one sense, Mrs. Wright is powerless and insane because she imagines the prison is her palace. Yet, in another sense, she has the agency to claim a spectral possession of a gothic space. Although she is unjustly imprisoned for helping a young enslaved girl escape, she explains that she has "learned to appreciate all the comforts of the place. I have the honor of living here now, and I live well and easy too. The state cares for me, provides for me, furnished me a home" (83). Not only have her hallucinations turned the jail into a home and the jailor into her servant, but her seeming sanity in deeming a society that sells humans insane makes her a perfect model of Emily Dickinson's declaration that "Much Madness is divinest Sense—/ To a discerning Eye—" (278). She even fits Henry David Thoreau's pronouncement: "Under a government which imprisons any unjustly, the true place for a just man is also a prison" (960). Hannah likewise is able to reflect on the "strange ideas of right and justice" that would put her in jail (78). Though they are physically in prison, the women critique the legal system and achieve a measure of spectral possession. Mrs. Wheeler's comment that "misery dwells in palaces" certainly proves true in *The Bondwoman's Narrative* as beautiful places are perilous while gothic spaces provide refuge.

Unlike Linda, Hannah eventually finds the home she seeks. After her escape, which is miraculously assisted by the residents of her earlier ideal home, Hetty and Siah, Hannah finally finds refuge in a house that is in no way haunted: her own. She and her husband have a "neat little Cottage" in New Jersey where she is finally free of all of the terrors of the past. Gleason asserts that "Crafts suggests that a true escape from slavery requires more than freedom from incarceration; it demands a habitation, a free home, or at least a safe one. Complete self-ownership, in other words, requires home-ownership" (154). Possession of self and home align for Hannah in contrast to Linda whose freedom is not complete without that "hearthstone" of her own. In Hannah's wonderful world of property ownership, the previous specters of her narrative come to life. William, who played a ghost in slavery, lives in a "tiny white cottage" along with Charlotte (246). In case the reader does not at first see the importance of the space, Crafts reiterates, "It is theirs" (246). Even more astonishing is the appearance of her mother. Crafts is cagey about the mechanics of the fairy-tale ending: "We met accidentally, where or how it matters not" (245). When Hannah was in the jail cell, her mother was only a spirit, and Hannah says that "my spirit [had] gone out in intense longing many, many times" for her (245). Now she can clasp her arms around her. Until the end, Hannah's possession of her self is spectral and hidden in haunted spaces. With this ideal resolution, her personhood is literalized in the physical presence of her mother, the possession of a cottage, and the claiming of that self in a home of her own.

WRITING AS SPECTRAL POSSESSION

While Linda and Hannah claim refuge and even spectral possession within the narratives, the writing of these narratives allows Jacobs and Crafts to claim the texts of their lives. The primary American model for crafting a life in words is Benjamin Franklin's autobiography. In his text, Franklin jokes about his life being a kind of book. He claims that "I should have no Objection to a Repetition of the same Life from its Beginning, only asking the

Advantage Authors have in a second Edition to correct some Faults of the first" (3). As he narrates events, Franklin labels the mistakes he made earlier in life "errata," which is a printer's term for a transposition of letters when setting out letter blocks. In modern parlance, it is a typo, something easily fixed. In editing the errors, Franklin assumes full ownership of the story of his life, using that "Advantage" to suit his purposes. He decides, for example, to tell the reader that he had little formal schooling and taught himself to read and write because he wishes to portray himself as a self-made man and the very product of Enlightenment thinking (8–20). Benjamin Franklin's self is thus created in and through language.

When both Jacobs and Crafts decide to put pen to paper to tell the stories of their experiences in slavery, they, too, grasp the right as authors to shape those narratives. To do so, they borrow some of the accoutrements of fiction. In her review of *The Bondwoman's Narrative*, Hilary Mantel ponders Crafts's choice. She acknowledges that, despite the preface's declaration of "plain unvarnished facts," "a glance at any page shows it to be something far more artful." Mantel's explanation for Crafts's use of fiction is that "autobiographies display the triumph of experience, but novels are acts of hope." Crafts and Jacobs need to borrow from fiction that "hope," the imaginative reshaping of their lives, so that instead of existing as someone else's property, they are central characters of their stories. In writing the story of Jane Franklin, Ben's sister, Jill Lepore reflects on what fiction offered women: "In the eighteenth century, history and fiction split. Benjamin Franklin's life entered the annals of history; lives like his sister's became the subject of fiction. Histories of great men, novels of little women" (241). As Louisa May Alcott's writing illustrates, the power of fiction is that it can elevate a seemingly common life.

The gothic heightens this power as it, in Charles Crow's words, makes "the invisible visible" (10). While fiction supplies latitude in crafting a story, the gothic additionally provides its spectral power. David Punter discusses how the gothic combats the law and explains that "the law is the imposition of certainty, the rhetorical summation of the absence, or the loss, of doubt" (2–3). It would therefore seem impossible to counter this force, just as Linda and Hannah cannot win when they critique the law because they do not create the rules of the game. Punter, however, asserts that ghost have "armies" as well (3). The power of the gothic is its ability "because of its freedom from the law, to play" (12). To play means to use the imagination, to posit the spectral realm beyond the material, to employ the ghosts' lack of temporal limitations, and to seize the possibility of fiction. Both play and hope exist outside of the law and, crucially for Jacobs and Crafts, outside of legal possession. To claim ownership of their lives, they must claim the "Advantage" of authors to write themselves into personhood.

Since that play gives them power, they do not hide it. Beth Maclay Doriani argues that Jacobs's use of the word "incidents" in her title indicates "her control" and shows that the scenes included were "carefully selected and shaped" (208). Christina Accomando likewise asserts that Jacobs "calls attention to craft in various ways." Specifically, Jacobs presents "two different versions of something to reveal the differences between versions depending on the framer and his or her agenda" (232). Accomando focuses on Jacobs's critique of the law's objectivity, but the presence of different versions also supports Jacobs's craft, as she claims the right as an author to choose which version of an incident to validate. A poignant example is when Linda's aunt dies, and Mrs. Flint requests that she be buried in their family gravesite because Mrs. Flint wants her servant buried at her feet. Linda can guess that Mrs. Flint thinks that she is being magnanimous to suggest that an enslaved person be buried in the white cemetery, but Linda counters with a different version. She declares that her aunt had been "slowly murdered" by "incessant, unrequited toil, and broken rest" (115). Linda imagines that "Northern travelers" (people much like her audience) would see Mrs. Flint's attendance at the funeral as a "tribute of respect," but Linda claims, "*We* could have told them a different story" (116). Linda describes this different story, which would have "a chapter of wrongs and sufferings" (116). She ends by honing in on her personal experience: "We could also have told them of a poor, blighted young creature, shut up in a living grave for years, to avoid the tortures that would be inflicted on her, if she ventured to come out and look on the face of her departed friend" (116). Although Linda only imagines concocting this story with that past modal verb tense "we could have told," Jacobs in writing Linda's story dares to tell it. In her narrative play, she even witnesses the funeral she was prevented from attending.

Jacobs's artfulness also extends to selecting which "incidents" to include to best craft a self that would appeal to her particular audience of Northern white women. Jacobs could have easily only included episodes that showed white people in the worst light, as they all benefitted from the institution that made her property, but she instead goes out of her way to include many depictions of kind white people, usually women, who help Linda and her family. Though the inclusion may soften the harsh depictions of other white characters, such as the Flints, it more importantly provides models for her readers. Early in the narrative, Linda highlights a woman who buys her grandmother when Dr. Flint puts her up at auction; the woman then gives

Linda's grandmother her freedom. Linda later mentions two southern wives who forced their husbands to free children they had with enslaved women. Another highlight is Miss Fanny, an old family friend who checks on Linda when she is sent to a plantation. A second old friend conceals Linda in her house for a short time at great risk to herself and her family. The first Mrs. Bruce hires Linda, and the second Mrs. Bruce sends her out of town when she is threatened, eventually making sure she is safe by paying for her freedom. The narrative thread of these many instances of assistance becomes an implied argument that in the face of predatory men, women across racial lines need to help each other.

In selecting and shaping events, Jacobs is doing the work any writer of an autobiography has to do, but she also amplifies the artfulness by employing gothic tropes. In chapter 9, Jacobs pauses the narrative arc of Linda's life to include "Sketches of Neighboring Slaveholders" (40). This inclusion is clever in enlarging the force of the text's critique of slavery beyond the story of her one life. In shaping these stories, however, Jacobs is sure to include the most macabre aspects. Here she tells the story of the enslaved man pressed in the cotton gin, "which was screwed down, only allowing him room to turn on his side when he could not lie on his back" (42). Jacobs adds gruesome details: "When the press was unscrewed, the dead body was found partly eaten by rats and vermin" (42). She tells of a neighboring planter who was known for letting bloodhounds "loose on a runaway, and if they tracked him, they literally tore the flesh from his bones" (40). This planter's death is imagined as painful: "his shrieks and groans were so frightful that they appalled his own friends" (40). When his body is buried, people keep digging it up, believing the rumor that his money was buried with him, until finally, "his body was found on the ground, and a flock of buzzards were pecking at it" (41). The passive voice construction of "was found" carefully excludes the source for the information, which might be rumor or perhaps a product of Jacobs's own version of play. The artfulness is even more overt in the sketch of this man's brother, who was horribly creative in punishing the people he held in slavery, such as suspending people over an open fire. In Jacobs's rendering, his deeds haunt him: "Murder was so common on his plantation that he feared to be alone after nightfall. He might have believed in ghosts" (40). The use of the conditional "might" indicates this gothic twist is a product of Jacobs's imagination.

Perhaps the most significant use of the gothic filter is what Jacobs does to Dr. Flint. Having cast him as the monster opposite her damsel, Jacobs as the writer of the narrative seizes control of him, and Dr. Flint becomes her property. One sign of her ownership is how she imagines him as an animal. As I explore in chapter 2, a common way slaveholders tried to justify treating enslaved people as property was to portray them as animals.[31] Jacobs, however, turns the tables and often describes Dr. Flint as animallike. For example, when Dr. Flint demands that Linda name the father of her baby, he then "sprang upon [her] like a wolf" (50). He and his fellow slaveholders become a "cage of obscene birds" (45). Because Dr. Norcom, the real slaveholder Dr. Flint is based on, died before Jacobs wrote her narrative, he exists only in her words and only in the guise she has given him. The characters Jacobs designs, the choices she makes, and the fictional and gothic tropes she employs together form the text of her life. While Linda does not have the home she wants at the end of the story, Jacobs creates her own space for personhood through her narrative.

Like Jacobs, Crafts borrows from fictional tropes to tell the narrative of her life the way she wants to tell it. Even more than Jacobs, though, Crafts mixes different genres. Adebayo Williams contends that Crafts's text is a "mélange of fictionalized autobiography, the gothic, the romance, the sentimental novel, and bristling social commentary held together in a precarious synthesis by a plot relying on impossible and improbable coincidences. The entire work indeed raises the question: When is a novel?" (139).[32] One answer to this question of genre is indeed a temporal matter. Crafts uses past tense throughout most of the text to give it the appearance of a personal story told from memory, but at key moments she switches to present tense to capture the sense of a narrative enfolding or of a fiction that can have any number of outcomes. For example, when Hannah talks about how her new mistress, Mrs. Vincent, seems strangely troubled, she says that Mrs. Vincent avoids the housekeeper because "perhaps she fears that Mr Trappe has taken her into his confidence, or perhaps it is something else. Who can tell?" (35). The present tense along with the "perhaps" adds suspense to the scene and highlights Crafts's shaping of the narrative.[33] A second example is when Hannah portrays Mr. Wheeler trying to convince Mrs. Wheeler to petition for him to get a government post: "The lady looks at him and wonders what he is driving at" (168). The present tense allows the reader to witness along with Hannah the clever way Mr. Wheeler plays on Mrs. Wheeler's vanity and jealousy: "I was thinking, however, that as [Mrs. Perkins's] good looks accomplished much, perhaps your beauty might do more" (168). The reader is in on the joke, getting to guess Mr. Wheeler's motives. Crafts plays with narrative further in chapter 13, when she uses present tense to imagine what the president might think: "The great President of the Great Republic looks perhaps from the windows of his drawing room, and wonders at the mud and slush precisely as an ordinary mortal would" (161). Though only an "ordinary mortal," Crafts can construct even the president as a character in the narrative she authors.

Certainly one source of the fictional thread running through *The Bondwoman's Narrative* is in fact fiction. As critics have noted, Crafts borrows from novels, such as *Uncle Tom's Cabin*, *Jane Eyre*, and *Bleak House*.[34] Robert S. Levine also traces several connections to Nathaniel Hawthorne's *The House of Seven Gables*, focusing on the similarities between Trappe and Judge Pyncheon ("Trappe(d)"). Crafts additionally appropriates an entire gothic scene from Hawthorne's novel. When Hannah and Mrs. Vincent are discovered in the cabin, one of the hunters reveals that Mrs. Vincent's husband had died. Hannah then proceeds to relate the scene of his death "from what [she] could gather," although she does not give the sources for this gathering (74). Although she begins in past tense, as if relaying information told to her, she switches into present tense to imagine the master killing himself, a scene that no one witnessed. The scene parallels chapter 18 of *The House of Seven Gables* when Hawthorne's narrator mocks Judge Pyncheon as he is dead in his ancestor's chair: "Pray, pray, Judge Pyncheon, look at your watch, now! What, not a glance? It is within ten minutes of the dinner-hour!" (273). Hannah steps into the role of this omniscient narrator, imagining Mr. Vincent's "dinner is waiting" as "the wine leaps and sparkles" (75). Mr. Vincent is obviously late because "his carriage is waiting" and "it is a long time for him to linger in his room" (75). Hannah builds suspense as the housekeeper "becomes seriously alarmed" (75). The servants then find a "red stream that still oozed slowly from a ghastly wound in his throat" (76). In Hawthorne's text, Judge Pyncheon died in his chair with blood gushing down his chest, fulfilling the curse he inherited that "God will give him blood to drink!" (8). Mr. Vincent is similarly cursed, sitting in the room overlooking the linden tree that is haunted by the death of an enslaved woman, and he kills himself because his wife has black blood. Crafts borrows from Hawthorne to play gothic.

In addition to borrowing fictional elements to tell her story, Crafts creates her own whole cloth, primarily to heighten the gothic flavor of the narrative. The signal that she has let her imagination loose is the word "fancy," which Crafts uses more than twenty times. Hannah explains that her "fancy painted [Hetty and Siah] as immured in a dungeon for the crime of teaching a slave to read" (13). When she is passing through the gloomy rooms of Lindendale, she comments that "we have heard or fancied of spiritual existences" around us (15). She "fancied" that Mrs. Vincent "was haunted by a shadow or phantom"

(27). She "half fancied" that all the doors slam shut in Trappe's house when she and Mrs. Vincent enter. When Mrs. Vincent dies on the couch, Hannah "half fancied that a deeper shadow passed over [Trappe's] countenance" (96, 103). While Hannah uses "fancy" to show off her creative abilities, this talent for fictionalization is tied to her very personhood. At the beginning of the narrative, when Hannah explains that her "almost white complexion" is mixed with "African blood," what she designates as the marks of that blood are "a rotundity to my person," "a wave and curl to my hair," and a preference for "fancy pictorial illustrations" (6). Hannah connects the creative element of her life story, her "fancy," with her very identity.

Moreover, the fairy-tale ending that gives Hannah all the elements of personhood—freedom, a profession, a family, a house of her own—is a product of this fancy: "I found a life of freedom all my fancy had pictured it to be" (244). Critics certainly comment that the ending seems wildly unbelievable. Andrews argues, though, that the ending might be Crafts's attempt to "reward her fugitive slave heroine" by imagining "what *ought* to happen to a woman of color who virtuously endures spiritual trials and moral tests" ("Hannah" 39). When Hannah says, "I found a life of freedom," the verb "found" signals that important place of home that she searches for throughout the story. Crafts, however, as the author speaking through Hannah, also "found" a life in the sense of originating or creating it. Perhaps the real-life Hannah Bond used the pseudonym "Hannah Crafts" to indicate her agency as she "crafts" this narrative.[35] In her text, Crafts not only takes Franklin's "Advantage" as an author to write her life; she constructs the picture her fancy prefers, a picture full of hope.

As in Jacobs's narrative, the monster is dead before the end, so he is entirely contained within the bindings of the book. Crafts kills off Trappe in a chapter aptly entitled "Retribution." Hannah is on the last leg of her escape from slavery on a riverboat when she overhears two gentlemen talking about his death. She "learns" (Crafts surely fancies) that he was murdered in his house, which, in contrast to Hannah's dream cottage, is "lonesome and retired" (239). He is killed by brothers of women he had captured (239). On the riverboat, Crafts puts Hannah's feelings into the two men's words when they conclude "love of gold had blunted all the finer sensibilities of his heart, and he would not have hesitated a moment to sell his own mother into slavery could the case have been made clear that she had African blood in her veins" (239). Crafts thus gets her ultimate revenge on the slave trader by pitting her gothic energies of fancy against his legal possession. Her spectral possession of his fictional character means that she ends his life just as she writes her personhood into being. The damsels turn into hearty heroines when they claim possession of haunted property. The heroines then turn into authors who write the story of that transformation, claiming it as their own.

AFTERLIFE

Writing their narratives gives Jacobs and Crafts a chance to assert their personhood. Jacobs, however, also wanted to change her audience's stance toward slavery. Throughout her story, Jacobs references the 1850 Fugitive Slave Act, which completely changed the legal landscape by requiring citizens of the North to return runaways, in essence making the North slave territory too. In her preface, Jacobs declares her "desire to arouse the women of the North to a realizing sense of the condition of two millions of women at the South, still in bondage, suffering what I suffered, and most of them far worse" (5). Active in the abolitionist movement, Jacobs doubtless saw her narrative as alerting those Northern women to the harm caused by the FSA: "Surely, if you credited one half of the truths that are told you concerning the helpless millions suffering in this cruel bondage, you at the north would not help to tighten the yoke" (26).

Moreover, her tone towards her audience expressed through that second-person "you" gets more strident as the narrative progresses. When Linda is reunited with her son in the North, she says, "O reader, can you imagine my joy? No, you cannot, unless you have been a slave mother" (135). The desire to put the reader in the shoes of an enslaved person transforms late in the text into seeing the reader as part of the system. This complaint becomes more pointed when Mrs. Bruce buys Linda to save her from recapture. Linda notes the irony: "A human being *sold* in the free city of New York! The bill of sale is on record, and future generations will learn that women were articles of traffic in New York, late in the nineteenth century of the Christian religion" (155). The problem of conflating people with property is not confined to the South. Jacobs tells readers that the problem is in their home and on their watch. Jacobs writes the narrative hoping for the future to witness history and for the present to intervene to change it.

Jacobs was therefore highly motivated by her mission, but the task was challenging. Although Jacobs had told her story orally at abolitionist events, she initially professed doubts about her ability to write it well. Yellin explains how Jacobs approached Stowe to help her write it, much like Olive Gilbert had helped Sojourner Truth (xviii). Stowe, however, countered that she could use Jacobs's material in her own book, *Key to Uncle Tom's Cabin*, a planned sequel to her best-selling novel that would provide primary source material. Rebuffed, Jacobs began sending pieces to newspapers, beginning with the revealing announcement "poor as I may be, I had rather give [my story] from my own hand, than have it said that I employed others to do it for me" (qtd in Yellin xix). Jacobs evidently learned from her interaction with Stowe that she wanted to tell her own story, and she realized that could tell it better than a professional writer. In a letter to a newspaper, Jacobs claims that "in *Uncle Tom's Cabin* [Stowe] has not told the half" ("Letter" 170). She even includes a sly dig at Stowe in her own preface by claiming, "Only by experience can any one realize how deep and dark, and foul is that pit of abominations" (5). Putting her experience in words gives Jacobs the agency as an author to call her Northern readers to action.

Crafts's motivation, on the other hand, is harder to decipher since she did not publish her manuscript. Gregg Hecimovich, who in 2013 determined that Crafts was the author of the text, explains that originally Crafts seemed to be hiding any features or names that would identify her, as fugitives often did. Crafts, for example, wrote "Wh—r" instead of "Wheeler" (xix). At some point in the writing process, however, she wrote, "Their names are Wheeler" and then went back and wrote "Wheeler" in every previous blank (xx). Did she at this point decide not to write for a larger public? Or did she cease caring about detection? Henry Louis Gates Jr., who published her manuscript in 2002, explains, "What she did with her manuscript after its completion or whether she ever tried to find a publisher for it, is still unknown. Nor is there evidence that anyone ever read *The Bondwoman's Narrative* or even knew of its existence during its author's lifetime. How it survived, who treasured and transmitted it over the generations, and for what reasons—all this, too, remains in the darker corners of history" (xiv-xv). Augusta Rohrback, however, suggests that Crafts "demonstrates a canny understanding of the literary marketplace" and that the narrative uses "cliff-hangers" and "breaks up nicely into installments," as if it were going to be published serially (4, 6). The preface at the very least suggests that she considered a larger audience; she asserts "a generous public" (3). She also ends with a bow to this audience: "I will let the reader picture it all to his imagination and say farewell" (246). The narrative seems aware of a possible reader, but all we know for sure is that she wrote it.

Whatever the manuscripts meant to these writers, both texts returned from the dead in the twentieth century to have yet another life. *Incidents* appeared in 1973, although as Nellie Y. McKay and Frances Smith Foster explain, "it generated a controversial debate among scholars who disputed the validity of its authorship and its authenticity as a slave narrative" (xiii). In 1981, Yellin published research validating the narrative and became, in McKay and Foster's words, "the founding mother of modern criticism on Jacobs' text" (xv). "Founding" is an interesting description, as it suggests an origination and perhaps yet another claim to ownership. For twentieth-century critics, in fact, Jacobs's text became a female answer to Frederick Douglass's slave narrative, a building block in African American literary tradition, and a prime source for historians and feminists. Thus *Incidents* is yet another kind of property in its twentieth-century form.

As is *The Bondwoman's Narrative*. Gates purchased the manuscript at an auction, and when he realized that parts of it could be identified as true, such as the existence of John Hill Wheeler, he set out on a quest to find the author, eventually involving Hecimovich. The published text became a New York Times best-seller, causing some critics to raise questions about ownership. Gill Ballinger, Tim Lustig, and Dale Townshend point out the "troubling analogies" that "Gates bought Crafts at an auction, spent some months in eager 'pursuit' of her ... and finally sold her at what seems to have been a sizable personal profit" (210). Karen Sanchez-Eppler also critiques the artifact of the current text, especially the addition of the words "a novel" to the manuscript's title: "These words are as clear a marketing ploy as the swirls that surround them; they announce a book that might be the first novel produced by a black woman anywhere, a book that could be the only novel written by an African-American woman who had been a slave" (254). Whether the text is a slave narrative or a novel, whether it is autobiographical or wholly fiction, whether it is "true" or not, Crafts's manuscript remains important to readers and critics as a kind of property whose ownership is complicated.

That these slave narratives are reborn as property in their modern form raises questions that the rest of the texts in this study have to negotiate. The remaining eight writers were not enslaved, and eight of the nine texts were written after slavery was abolished. Thus these writers have to think about who is allowed to tell the story of slavery, how later generations should remember those who suffered, and who finally owns the past. These are all obviously difficult questions, but Jacobs's and Crafts's texts provide a key path in their use of the gothic to explore the dynamics of slavery. Peter Garrett explains that "writing always stems from reading, fiction from earlier fiction, but Gothic makes that process particularly clear in its persistent repetition and reworking of a small set of devices ... One effect of these iterations is to invite us to read the narratives they link as versions of a common story, their figures and situations echoing or reflecting one another" (4–5). What Jacobs and Crafts both reveal is a common story of haunting that results from the conflation of people with property. Combatting this problem requires personhood, and personhood requires ownership of property. In depicting spectral possession, Jacobs and Crafts address this need for property in a form that is then echoed in the later works. If the key to an enslaved person's powerlessness is the inability legally to claim property—the inability to have "'s" after a name—Jacobs and Crafts find in the gothic a way to steal the keys and declare ownership.

CHAPTER TWO

Playing Con Games in Herman Melville's *Benito Cereno*, Mark Twain's *Pudd'nhead Wilson*, and Sherley Anne Williams's *Dessa Rose*

In his 2017 book *Bunk: The Rise of Hoaxes, Humbug, Plagiarists, Phonies, Post-Facts, and Fake News*, Kevin Young traces all manner of con games in American history and finds that many rely on racial categories. Young points to the example of P. T. Barnum's "notorious" exhibit called "What Is It?" in which Barnum "would dress a black man in animal hides" (37). Appearing just months after Darwin's *On the Origin of Species* (1859), Barnum's display allowed visitors "to find the answer to the exhibit's question: a black man they were invited to see as a, or as *the* missing link in evolution" (37). Barnum's hoax relied on his audience's gullibility in accepting a man as part animal and succeeded because of nineteenth-century constructions of race. Young explains: "I've come to realize the hoax regularly steps in when race rears its head—exactly because it too is a fake thing pretending to be real" (40).

What Young finds in Barnum's freak show world also operates in the works of Herman Melville's *Benito Cereno* (1855), Mark Twain's *Pudd'nhead Wilson* (1894), and Sherley Anne Williams' *Dessa Rose* (1986). This chapter argues that these works use con games to expose the weakness in slavery's definition of people as property, a definition relying on the same constructions of race that Barnum exploited. The insider to any con game knows that two levels of reality coexist: the illusion created by the con artist and the hidden second world where the con artist is profiting in some way from the observer's confidence in the illusion. In Barnum's show, throwing an animal hide on a man provided the illusion of a being who was half-man, half-animal. Likewise, in these three novels, white characters think of enslaved people as animals to justify the legal system that deems enslaved people as property, but what is hidden is ironically the agency of those held in slavery, allowing them to conduct con games. The enslaved people thus act as insiders, who understand not just the terror of being labeled as property on the level of an animal but also the fallacy of this designation. The white beneficiaries of the slave system act as outsiders to slavery's constructed nature. Being duped by a con leads a white person to fear the loss of boundaries between self and other, owner and property, white and black.

By playing con games, the enslaved people attempt to shift the locus of fear from their own loss of personhood to their white observers' loss of these stable boundaries, a shift revealed by gothic markers. In all three novels, the gothic appears in its typical guises of ghosts, haunted houses, nefarious strangers, and dark dungeons. What the gothic teaches the reader to fear, though, depends upon the point of view, which proves tricky in Melville's and Twain's works. For most of *Benito Cereno*, the point of view is limited to the white dupe of the con, and only towards the end does the narrative explore the fear felt by those in slavery of losing personhood.[1] In *Pudd'nhead Wilson*, Twain reverses Melville's order by beginning with an enslaved person's view but abandoning this point of view as the focus shifts to how the con disrupts the white community's boundaries. In both novels, the disruption of boundaries may even seem to be averted at the end when the con games fail and order is restored by legal trials.

What critics largely miss when discussing the novels' problematic endings, however, is the lingering effect of the con games.[2] The ghosts do not vanish. Traces of haunting remain in the very existence of a con game that can, even for a limited time, overturn racial constructions and expose the vulnerability of observers. More disturbing is the continued fear of people losing personhood, a haunting that the trials do not exorcise with their legal spells. This second form of haunting feeds the first: as long as the law haunts those enslaved, the fear that the law is simply a fictional construct continues to haunt slaveholders. Tracing the moments of fear reveals the vulnerability of a system predicated on tenuous racial categories, a weakness the con games both exploit and expose.

The intertwining of the con and the gothic in these nineteenth-century texts has a twentieth-century answer in Williams's *Dessa Rose*. In crafting the novel, Williams drew from two historical events: an enslaved woman who was executed in 1829 because of her role in a rebellion and a white woman who used her North Carolina farm in 1830 as a haven for runaways. In her fictional rewriting, Williams imagines the two women meeting and eventually working together in a charade of selling enslaved people. Echoing the nineteenth-century texts, the con game in *Dessa Rose* depicts both the fear felt by those held in slavery of losing personhood and the whites' fear of crossed boundaries. *Dessa Rose*, though, has one glaring difference: the con works. In her twentieth-century version, Williams allows the fugitive and the white woman to confront each other's fears. After a successful con, the formerly enslaved people escape to the West with the money they gain. While in Melville's novel the enslaved person is executed, and in Twain's novel the enslaved person is sold down the river, Williams finds a way out of the destruction of the nineteenth-century novels.

Critics have discussed Melville's use of the gothic in *Benito Cereno*, but Twain's use of gothic devices has received scant critical attention, and Williams's use of the gothic has received none. Reading *Dessa Rose* alongside *Benito Cereno* and *Pudd'nhead Wilson* highlights how the gothic can expose the constructed nature of laws defining race and property. Moreover, putting these three texts together allows Williams to stake a property claim to the con game that her predecessors play; she declares in her preface, "Maybe it is only a metaphor, but I now own a summer in the nineteenth century" (6). In the previous chapter, I explored how formerly enslaved people found fiction a powerful tool for reconstructing their lives. Following their lead, Williams imagines a summer when the con game works.

GAMES OF CONFIDENCE

As Young's book illustrates, the enslaved people playing confidence games in these three novels join a long line of hucksters and confidence artists plying their trade in American fiction.[3] Gary Lindberg explains that the term "confidence man" came from a man in New York City in 1849 who would ask a stranger if he had enough "confidence" in human nature to leave his watch with him for what supposedly would be a day (6). Although the term is an American invention, the con artist certainly has cousins in the trickster figures found in many cultural traditions. What is American about the con artist is not his or her deceitful behavior per se, but the specific context in which he or she works. As Johnson Jones Hooper's character Simon Suggs declares, "It is good to be shifty in a new country" (8). The newness of America bespeaks a lack of established traditions, stable hierarchies, and known communities, allowing a stranger to appear as an honorable pilgrim instead of a questionable outsider. William E. Lenz explains that an American con artist "relies not on supernatural powers or charms or courts but on the fluid nature of society in the New World with its unique opportunities for self-government, self-promotion, self-posturing, and self-creation" (1).[4] As I noted in the introduction, the prime model of this self-made person is Benjamin Franklin, the Enlightenment figure promoting the American dream in his autobiography. Although Franklin does not play games on the level of three-card monte, he certainly betrays his shrewdness about playing off the confidence of an unsuspecting audience. For example, at one point in his autobiography, he explains that even after he had achieved some success in his printing business, he still wanted his customers in Philadelphia to perceive him as industrious, so he "sometimes brought home the Paper I purchas'd at the Stores, thro' the Streets on a Wheelbarrow" (66).

What Franklin describes in his narrative is a performance to elicit the confidence of an audience in order to acquire some financial gain: the very essence of a con game. In Franklin's fabrication of an industrious man and in the New York watch-stealer's presumption of a trusting spirit, the con game, as Lindberg explains, "creates an inner effect, an impression, an experience of confidence, that surpasses the grounds for it. In short, a confidence man *makes belief*" (7). While one might think that making beliefs would be discouraged in a budding society, Lindberg argues that "the confidence man is a covert cultural hero for Americans" (3). The heroics stem in no small part from the promise inherit in the American dream of self-making and remaking. Figures such as Franklin and Barnum can be essentially "American" while also being adept at constructing illusions, or perhaps even because of those very skills of deception.[5]

While people held in slavery may be powerless to overthrow a vast system that makes them property, by working a con, they too can use deceit within the system to gain an advantage.[6] Lindberg differentiates trickster figures from con artists by arguing that tricksters "break boundaries" but that con artists do not "disrupt the social boundaries" (8). This is largely true of these con games, as the enslaved people use society's own construction of racial codes to hide their agency. However, the fact that they can so easily manipulate these fictional constructs results in a larger subversion, a haunting of the system. Ralph Ellison recognizes the potential for subversion from within when he explains that black performers wearing masks are just following American tradition:

> Americans began their revolt from the English fatherland when they dumped the tea into the Boston Harbor, masked as Indians, and the mobility of the society created in this limitless space has encouraged the use of the mask for good and evil ever since.... Masking is a play upon possibility and ours is a society in which possibilities are many. When American life is most American it is apt to be most theatrical. ("Change" 61)

Ellison not only depicts multiple con artists in *Invisible Man* from Trueblood and Dr. Bledsoe to Brother Jack and Rinehart; he also chooses as an epigraph for his book the quote from *Benito Cereno* when Delano asks Cereno, "What has cast such a shadow on you?" Cereno's answer is "the Negro" (107). The shadow is cast through subversion within the system, namely, the use of theatrics to mimic racial categories, thus exposing their tenuous nature.

In the confidence game played in *Benito Cereno*, the enslaved people must use theatrics to perform the role of property.[7] They thus create a safe illusion for their white audience while they simultaneously exert agency in a number of ways: disguising the true reason for the ship's dismal plight, concocting a story of storm and plague, forcing Cereno and the remaining white sailors to go along with the bluff, and devising a plot to take Delano's ship. This tall order requires not just superb acting but also coordination between all those on board who were held in slavery. The boat thus becomes the stage, and the crew becomes the cast, with Babo as the lead actor.[8] Even the dupe of the con at times perceives the performative flavor of what he witnesses on the *San Dominick*. At one point, while ruminating about Cereno's bizarre behavior, Delano feels an "uneasiness" and surveys the ship "as from a stage-box into the pit, upon the strange crowd before and below him" (67). He senses his outsider status as a kind of audience in a theater box, but he cannot discern the nature of the performance. Later, Delano even detects that the people around him are "acting out, both in word and deed . . . some juggling play before him" (76). This juggling scene takes place in Cereno's cabin, as Babo pretends to follow his master's strict orders to shave him every afternoon at the same time. Babo serves "his master's good pleasure," and Delano is deceived, thinking that "negroes are natural valets and hairdressers" because of their "docility" (73). However, the second reality known only to the insiders is also operating. The powerful Babo wields a sharp blade and causes his victim to "nervously [shudder]" at the "close sight of the gleaming steel" (74). Even the dullard Delano spies some hint of the con as he dreams that "in the black he saw a headsman, and in the white, a man at the block," an image straight from the pages of revolution (74). He dismisses this "vagary" though, continuing to be hoodwinked even when Babo draws blood.

Babo's doubled performance as fawning servant and menacing executioner is augmented by his manipulation of Cereno. Michael Rogin, who also labels this scene a "confidence game," describes Cereno as a "marionette" who is "forced to speak the lines that once seemed his by nature" (323). Jason Richards, in reading the novel as a kind of "burlesque," likewise sees Cereno as "puppet" and discusses how Babo "enacts his masquerade by deploying

Cereno's body as a white mask" (77, 74).⁹ As these critics point out, Babo performs whiteness through Cereno. He also, however, critiques it. He uses the Spanish flag to drape Cereno's body during the shaving, much like a costume. The flag points to the origin of Cereno's initial power to traverse an ocean and enslave the inhabitants of other nations. Babo's indecorous use of the banner indicates the insiders' knowledge that this sign of whiteness, though useful to the con, has lost its meaning.

To keep the con going, though, what Babo and crew must actually perform is blackness, which is channeled not just through their superficial groveling but also by the actors wearing the costume of property. At the tolling of the ship's bell, Delano witnesses yet another scene where two realities exist. The "gigantic" figure of Atuful approaches Cereno: "An iron collar was about his neck, from which depended a chain, thrice wound round his body; the terminating links padlocked together at a broad ban of iron, his girdle" (51). Atuful personifies property. His seeming powerlessness, despite his physique, is performed when Cereno demands that he ask for pardon. Cereno's role as owner of this property is symbolized by his wearing the key to Atuful's padlock around his neck, part of his master's costume (52). This scene becomes a mockery of the legal system of crime and punishment. Although Delano understands the sequence of events to be a "scene," he remains an outsider to the con game the formerly enslaved people play in their performance of property.

Whereas Babo and crew sustain their performance for a matter of hours, in *Pudd'nhead Wilson*, Roxy must keep her con game going for years, requiring a performance of elaborate lengths, a "long con" as it were. As in *Benito Cereno*, the con depends upon the characters' acting abilities as well as their use of costumes and masks. The idea to switch the babies is in fact sparked by Roxy's attention to clothes.¹⁰ She is on her way out the door with her baby, preparing to "jump in de river" to prevent the child from being sold when she "caught sight of her new Sunday gown" (70). Sad that she has not had the chance to wear the new dress, Roxy dons the outfit of "gaudy colours and fantastic figures" and proceeds to "make her death-toilet perfect" (70). She dresses for the role of the suicide, imagining "everybody lookin' at me" (70). While thinking of her final performance, she notices her baby's shabby tow-linen shirt and decides to dress Chambers in one of Thomas's fancy gowns. Chambers's costume causes the "strange light" in Roxy's eyes and initiates her plan for fooling everyone. However, before she gives a performance to the audience of the town, Roxy, as a good actress, must practice. She spends the rest of the night changing her "speech and manner," so that her son is now called "Marse Tom" and is coddled, while the other child gets a "real pat" and a curt tone (73). Roxy's passing of black for white and white for black succeeds in fooling everyone, so that the novel, as Myra Jehlen puts it, "builds its plot upon a plot" (39). Roxy's con is a simple change of clothes, but the confidence people have in outward appearance allows the con to work.

What Roxy discovers in time, though, is that her con works too well, so that her son sees her only as property. Hence she loses the son she sought to save. Vidar Pedersen argues that "Roxana thus becomes the victim of her own cleverness; she is caught in her own game almost from the beginning" (179). Roxy's cleverness, however, also leads her to a way to regain her son without exposing her con: she tells Tom who he truly is. By this point in the text, Roxy's character has become less sympathetic, and her revelation is not the heart-felt declaration of a mother's love but a way to blackmail her son. Nonetheless, by making Tom an insider to the game, the con is extended. Tom is already an actor himself, masking as a girl to conduct thieving raids on the town. While Roxy's announcement disturbs him for a time as he contemplates his racial identity, he soon realizes that no one detects it.[11] Tom then dresses as Roxy to conduct his raiding; he has in more than one way become his mother.

In time, though, Tom proves to be even more of a con artist than Roxy, as he perpetuates his own con game when selling the free Roxy to an unsuspecting planter. Roxy has devised the scheme, telling Tom to go "up de country a piece, sell me on a farm" and then to buy her back in a year (174). Roxy consequently plays the part of property though supposedly retaining agency. Tom, however, commits a "treachery" in selling Roxy to an Arkansas cotton planter who lives "down the river," a location that signifies throughout the novel a more brutal practice of slavery. Tom thus cons both the outsider and the insider.

When Roxy returns to confront him after escaping, she is disguised as a black man, and later when Tom attempts to steal from his uncle, he is disguised as a black girl. Both characters wear the mask of property while they are asserting agency. They don costumes in what Linda A. Morris describes as "masquerading" in order to create illusions for their outsider audiences (37). That these passing-white characters can become black and that they can both change gender certainly points to the fluid dynamics of identity, as many critics of the novel discuss, but it also demonstrates the vulnerability of their audience to a confidence game. The town, much like Amasa Delano, takes sheer appearance—a baby's gown, a dress, light skin—at face value.

Just as in *Benito Cereno* and *Puddin'head Wilson*, the enslaved people in *Dessa Rose* must put on a good performance for their con game. To devise the plan, Harker draws from the years he spent assisting his former master working Mississippi riverboats, hinting at what Williams perhaps borrows from Melville's *The Confidence Man*. Until his master got caught with five aces in a card game, he ran many successful cons, including one where he would sell Harker and then help him escape. The plan is for the white mistress, Rufel, to pretend to sell an enslaved person, who would then escape in a few days with help from the group. Nathan explains to Rufel that if they ran a similar scheme three or four times, they would net up to ten thousand dollars. Although Rufel is interested in the money, she also wants to help the runaways, particularly Nathan because of their affair. Dessa is skeptical and aghast that enslaved people are willing to put their "freedom at the mercy of a crazy white woman" (182). Rufel, though, performs beautifully, as she understands how to play the role of white female in distress. She uses her baby, Clara, as a kind of prop and, according to Dessa, knows when to "smile," "giggle," and "bat the eye" (207). Ashraf H. A. Rushdy argues that Rufel's participation "marks her revolutionary tendencies, her understanding that any act which decimates the system is a worthy one" (*Neo-Slave* 384). Moreover, her act inducts her into the association of con artists as she can perform "white" and "lady" while disguising the second reality known to insiders.

The enslaved people, on the other hand, must perform blackness, which again means acting the role of property without agency. Dessa explains, "We was slaves; wasn't posed to know nothing nor do nothing without first being told" (194). If anyone was caught escaping, they were to "act dumb and scared and show the pass from Miz Lady" (194). Added to their slavelike behavior are the makeup tricks Harker uses to disguise them as they escape, a kind of costume. Keith Byerman explains that the plan works because Harker's "special skill is understanding white thinking" (*Remembering* 59). A white audience is not suspicious of a desperate white woman selling docile enslaved people; thus, the confidence game works.

In all three works, however, the con games are actually quite ridiculous. In true slave narratives, runaways are tracked by dogs, followed by a posse of white men or a hired slave catcher. The little face paint and new names in a different town employed in *Dessa Rose* are measures surely too small to counter the difficulty of escaping a plantation undetected and of travelling to the next town while being hunted. And the idea in *Benito Cereno* that a ship's worth of people can act as if a revolt did not take place is hard to believe. The formerly enslaved people furthermore have to maintain that it just happened to be the white sailors who died in the ship's calamities. This alone should sink the con, as a seasoned mariner such as Delano should be attuned to any hint of mutiny.[12] And the assumption in *Pudd'nhead Wilson* that no one, not even Tom's father, could tell the two babies apart is so hard to believe that more than one of my students has insisted that the babies must be related and that Percy Driscoll is the father of both boys, despite Roxy's story about Cecil Burleigh Essex being Chambers's father. Admittedly, these works are all fiction, and the reader must suspend disbelief, but they all depict these cons as this dubious for a particular reason: to reveal how the legal system that defines people as property is equally absurd.

PROBLEMS OF PROPERTY

In each novel, the nonsensical con game exists because it works off of the legal system of property that governs slavery. Defining, acquiring, and maintaining property are central activities in the narratives, but these pursuits are complicated by the need to justify enslaving people as part of that property. In the eleven texts I examine in this larger study, property comes in various forms: houses, bodies, family, and narratives. For these three particular texts, enslaved people as items of property are depicted as animals. Depicting humans as animals was one way slaveholders tried to rationalize the line drawn between black and white that resulted in free and slave. David Brion Davis analyzes the language used by slaveholders in the "animalizing of African Americans, as a way of denying their capacity for freedom" and finds that this form of "dehumanization" acted to "[sever] ties of human identity and empathy and made slavery possible" (9). This conflation of people and animal is mocked in each of these works: in *Benito Cereno* by revealing the ignorance of Delano's views, in *Pudd'nhead Wilson* by exposing the underlying stupidity of the town, and in *Dessa Rose* by applying the imagery to a white man. The construction of enslaved people as property on the level of animals, though, shields white audiences to the agency of those held in slavery and accounts for how con games of such magnitude and absurdity can occur.

In *Benito Cereno*, the *San Dominick* has as its *raison d'être* the transformation of people into property, as enslaved people are stolen from their homeland and transported to be sold elsewhere. Approaching the vessel, Delano perceives the "true character of the vessel," by which he means its origin (Spanish) and its class (merchantman), but its character also exists in its cargo: "carrying negro slaves, amongst other valuable freight" (37). Delano again thinks of the enslaved people as freight, though modified by the adjective "living," when he reflects on how the multitude of enslaved people are "as little troublesome as crates and bales" (43, 44). Because Delano is invested in this system of property as a seaman himself, he can only see the enslaved people as freight, and all irony about the "true character" of the ship is lost on him. When he asks Cereno if he is the owner of the ship, Cereno answers, "I am owner of all you see . . . except for the main company of blacks, who belonged to my late friend, Alexandro Aranda" (50). The "living freight" has no living owner. Delano reveals his desire to be an owner when he offers to buy Babo. Babo interjects: "Master wouldn't part with Babo for a thousand doubloons" (60). At this point, the "master" of Babo is Babo himself.

Delano's ignorance manifests in his use of animal imagery for enslaved people.[13] When Delano first meets Babo, he immediately reads him as a docile animal: "By [Cereno's] side stood a black of small stature, in whose rude face, as occasionally, like a shepherd's dog, he mutely turned it up into the Spaniard's, sorrow and affection were equally blended" (40). The layering of the image of a dog onto Babo renders him as not just nonhuman but also as nonthreatening. Delano continues this layering as he imagines a "slumbering negress" as a "doe in the shade" exhibiting "naked nature" (62, 63). Picturing enslaved people as animals allows Delano to feel superior and "benign" as he "took to negroes . . . just as other men to Newfoundland dogs" (73).

In the insiders' second reality, though, Delano's conflation of enslaved people and animals leaves him the dupe to the con game being played out before him. His guesses about what might be amiss on the ship are all centered on Cereno. At one point, he debates between Cereno's "innocent lunacy or wicked imposture" and later suspects Cereno of "piratical character" (53, 57). He never detects what Cereno subsequently testifies: "Babo was the plotter from first to last; he ordered every murder, and was the helm and keel of the revolt" (102).[14] Here, instead of being imaged as an animal, Babo becomes "helm and keel," the entire ship. As David Andrews explains, "Delano does not perceive this peril because he believes that blacks, due to their stunted intellects, are incapable of calculated malice, a trait he perceives as distinctly human, differentiating man from animal" (90).

Yet another motivation, however, may be driving Delano's blindness. If he can profit from the system where enslaved people are property, it helps him to see people who are enslaved as animal-like, so seemingly benign ignorance may in fact be willed. In William Blackstone's famous *Commentaries on the Law*, he claims that "there is nothing which so generally strikes the imagination and engages the affections of mankind, as the right of property," but the result is that "pleased as we are with the possession, we seem afraid to look back to the means by which it was acquired, as if fearful of some defect in our title; or at best we rest satisfied with the decision of the laws in our favor, without examining the reason or authority upon which those laws have been built" (37). Questioning the slave system would dispute Delano's cherished view of himself as a good man since he benefits from the system and wishes to be part of it, as evidenced by his desire to buy Babo. Paul David Johnson identifies Delano's "blindness to potential evil within himself," an evil evident in his decision to see those enslaved as animals (428). Rather than interrogate his own character or the larger legal system, Delano remains duped by an outrageous con until the end.

In the world of *Puddin'head Wilson*, the problems associated with property affect everyone, but the white citizens of Dawson's Landing choose not to examine the laws that allow them to enslave others. The novel begins with a description of the town as a "snug collection" of houses with pretty flower gardens out front and in many instances a cat "stretched at full length, asleep and blissful" (55). The animal proves vital to the property as "testimony" that a "house was complete" because without a cat "how can it prove title?" (53, 56). While the image of a sleeping and "blissful" cat suggests domestic contentment, the language of "title" signals ownership of property. Paula Harrington connects the animal to the enslaved person in arguing that "owning another being—whether cat or slave—thus becomes a requirement of domestic life" (93). In the larger narrative of the American dream that I explore in the introduction, the path to success is indeed evidenced by the ownership of property, most often a house like the town's "snug" flower-decked homes. However, as the narrator eventually reveals, despite its quaint appearance, "Dawson's Landing was a slaveholding town" (57). The town "holds" people in slavery because it considers them property on the level of animals, choosing to remain blind to that "defect in the title."

While the town's cats may be content, it is the town's dogs that end up providing a metaphor for the position of enslaved people. David Wilson earns the nickname of "Pudd'nhead" on his first day in Dawson's Landing when he remarks about a barking dog: "I wish I owned half of that dog ... because I would kill my half" (59). All irony is lost on his audience as they then seriously debate why a person could not kill half a dog. Wilson's animal quip, however, illuminates the society's problematic accounting of people held in slavery as legal property, especially in relation to the central character of Roxy. Roxy's speech patterns identify her as an enslaved woman, but the narrator indicates that her skin color appears fair: "Only one sixteenth of her was black, and that sixteenth did not show" (63). Although she is 15/16s "white," she is "by a fiction of law and custom" considered to be "black" and thus enslaved and "saleable as such" (64).[15] Roxy cannot be only half-owned, although she is only a fraction "black," any more than a dog can be half-killed. She is wholly enslaved, which relegates her in this narrative to the status of a dog. When Roxy realizes that in executing her con, she has lost her son, she bemoans that he sees her as "merely his chattel, now, his convenience, his dog, his cringing and helpless slave" (81). Likewise, when Tom grasps his own racial position relative to the man he thought was his uncle, he understands that "I am his chattel, his property, his goods, and he can sell me, just as he could his dog" (119).

The conflation of people with animals hides Roxy's con game from the town, as dogs do not have human agency, but it also serves to highlight the absurd "fiction of law and custom" that undergirds the system of racial categories. Not only is Roxy 15/16s "white," but her description of her lineage, a model of Twain's comic exaggeration, shows her "whiteness" to be made of an interesting mix. She brags to Tom that her "great-great-great-gran'father" was "Cap'n John Smith, de highest blood dat Ole Virginny ever turned out," but she then posits his ancestors as Pocahontas and a "nigger King outen Africa," so that her "whiteness" descends from "blackness" through a Native American ancestor (57–58). As Chambers declares, Roxy is "imitation white," a designation that is doubly ironic as he includes himself in the category as well. As Percy Driscoll's biological son, he is what the community would define as "white," though he is living in the guise of "black" (103). It is thus only in this tangled mess of racial designations that something as preposterous as Roxy's exchanging of the babies can work because the system is equally as absurd as the con.

Roxy's initial inclination to fool everyone is actually sparked by a conundrum that exemplifies the irrational nature of the system, namely, the question of whether an enslaved person can steal property. At the beginning of the novel, Percy Driscoll discovers that he is missing some money. Although he was "a fairly humane man toward slaves and other animals," he "could not abide" theft and threatens to sell the guilty slave (66).[16] All of those enslaved, except for Roxy, are actually guilty of stealing small household items (though not money), but the narrator insists that to an enslaved person, taking a "trifle from the man who robbed him daily of an inestimable treasure—his liberty" was no great sin (67–68). Twain's narrator echoes the reasoning that Eugene D. Genovese explains that enslaved people historically used: "The slaves made a distinction: they stole from each other but merely took from their masters. Their logic was impeccable. If they belonged to their master—if they were in fact his chattels—how could they steal from him?" (602). This question reveals a flaw in the logic of slavery: If people can be held as property without agency, how can they then be considered as agents for stealing property? When Driscoll threatens to sell them all "DOWN THE RIVER," the enslaved people confess, and Driscoll does the "noble and gracious thing" of selling them locally (68). His threats, though, cause Roxy to fathom for the first time the vulnerability of her child as property, so she plans to kill him before she comes up with the idea to switch him with Driscoll's own son. What this episode demonstrates is nothing less than the illogical basis of the legal definition of people as property if at times they are conveniently considered agents.

Though innocent when accused, Roxy later commits a theft in devising her con. She steals whiteness for her son. Cheryl I. Harris explains that in slavery "whiteness was the characteristic, the attribute, the property of free human beings" (1720). That this property of whiteness can be stolen shows that it is not an innate quality. It can be faked in a confidence game. By stealing whiteness, Roxy allows her son protection from being sold as well as the ability to own property, in essence to be a full agent in the society.

Roxy's theft takes place against the novel's larger depiction of the vast problems of property.[17] All property in the narrative becomes pirate's gold and curses everyone. After Percy Driscoll accuses the people he holds in slavery of theft, he travels for seven weeks to see about a land speculation deal, leaving Roxy without supervision and free to switch the babies. His early death subsequently results from his being "worn out" from the failure of this land deal (82). Tom later doubles his "father" with his own property problems because he has to steal from his neighbors to pay off his gambling debts so that his uncle will not discover them and disinherit him. Although Twain devotes much of the novel to playing through the nature versus nurture debate with respect to the defects in Tom's character, all of Tom's decisions stem from his desire for property and the problems of obtaining it. Even when Roxy returns to Dawson's Landing and blackmails Tom, it is because the money she saves up during her time as a riverboat chambermaid is lost when the "bank had gone to smash" (101).[18]

Despite the many problems with property, the town remains blind to the pitfalls of its system as well as to Roxy and Tom's manipulations of it. That charming opening description of the "snug" houses sitting side-by-side identifies the town as "sleepy," connecting it to another town that gets duped by a confidence scheme, Washington Irving's Sleepy Hollow. Although when the citizens fail to understand Wilson's joke about the dog, they designate him a "pudd'nhead," by the end they realize that "we're elected" for the position. They miss the rather ridiculous con games conducted under their noses because of their confidence in their society's legal constructions of race and property that separate white from black, human from animal, and free from property. As long as the townspeople profit from these categories, they believe in them, but the framework of race ends up being solely a "fiction of law and custom."

Adam Nehemiah in *Dessa Rose* shares with Amasa Delano and Percy Driscoll the desire to believe in the law's constructions of racial categories because of a personal desire for profit. While Dessa is in prison for attempting to escape the confines of being property, Nehemiah interviews her for a book he is writing on how to prevent slave uprisings. Nehemiah is a social climber who believes in the narrative of the self-made man. He imagines that his book will earn enough money to propel him into the "planter class." As in the other two novels, this belief is bolstered by his use of animal imagery for Dessa; if she is more animal than human, then her status as property is justified. This belief, however, also makes him a good mark, in that he remains blind to Dessa's agency.

Adam Nehemiah seeks out Dessa primarily because of her role in destroying property. When she and the other people enslaved on a coffle revolt against a slave dealer, "thirty-one slaves had been killed or executed; nineteen branded or flogged: some thirty-eight thousand dollars in property destroyed or damaged" (22). Nehemiah sees the human loss strictly in monetary terms, as a financial opportunity that allows him to write his how-to guide for avoiding slave revolt. Nehemiah has been convinced by a publisher that "a book on slave uprisings, touching as it must upon the secret fears of non-slave holder and slave holder alike, should be an immediate success" (25). The book's popularity would be due to its ability to help sustain the system that makes Dessa property, although Nehemiah ironically needs Dessa's insight to write it. The book itself becomes a way for Nehemiah to make Dessa into a secondary form of property; by writing her story, he can own it. Andrée-Anne Kekeh explains that Nehemiah's "status as a historian is not unlike the slave trader's. He does not sell slaves per se: he writes them down and sells them as books" (221). His claim on Dessa is signified by his renaming her as "Odessa." Mary Kemp Davis points out that Adam Nehemiah's name alludes to the biblical name-giver. She argues that Nehemiah "replicates the acts of European enslavers and explorers who, in an act of aggression and subjugation, stripped the Africans of their names and renamed them" (548).[19]

Echoing these explorers, he claims Dessa as his territory and her story as his property.

His claim is supported by the use of animal imagery. He scoffs at the slave dealer's labeling of Dessa as a "she-devil," a designation that gives her supernatural agency. He decides instead that Dessa is "more like a wild and timorous animal finally brought to bay, moving quickly and clumsily to the farthest reaches of the cellar allowed by her chains" (22–23). He repeatedly refers to her "stench" and ignores any evidence of higher-level behavior or thinking. At one point, flustered by her silence, he thinks she had fallen asleep "much as a cow would in the midst of a satisfying chew" (36). He then catches Dessa, however, "flicking her eyes up at him," and although he thinks "this was a damnable business," he does not question his assumptions about her lack of intelligence. His insistence on society's construction of race, though necessary to support his own financial gain, leaves him blind. He is thus completely surprised by Dessa's escape.

Just as Roxy and Tom understand that their condition as property renders them the equivalent of dogs in their society, Dessa understands how the dynamics of slavery work to fashion her into an animal. Part of the punishment for her role in the uprising is confinement for hours in a small box. Dessa admits, "I was like an animal; whipped like one; in the dirt like one. I hadn't never known peoples could do peoples like this" (191). Though her oppressors try to make her into an animal, she only admits to being "like an animal" and still identifies herself and others held in slavery as "peoples" (191). She has learned both how white people see her as property and how she nevertheless retains personhood. Understanding both points of view will help her later to participate as the insider in the con game.

Unlike the enslaved people in Melville and Twain's texts, Dessa is ultimately able to reverse the direction of the animal imagery. When Adam Nehemiah locates her and her fellow con artists, the town sheriff is suspicious of Nehemiah's claims that Dessa is the runaway girl he has been seeking, but the sheriff puts Dessa in a cell until he can find her owner. Nehemiah taunts her in her cell, saying, "Caught you" and "Got you now" (224). Mae Gwendolyn Henderson points out that the use of the word "track" to describe Nehemiah's hunting of Dessa indicates that "Nehemiah *tracks* Dessa in an attempt to establish ownership—that is, the colonization—of her body" ("Speaking" 131). However, when Rufel claims, "This girl mines," Nehemiah can only counter, "This gal belong to the state" (227). Nehemiah cannot actually claim personal ownership of Dessa because he never held her in slavery. He relies instead on that secondary ownership that he thought he had established: "I got her down here in my book" (231). When Rufel and the sheriff look at his papers, though, the sheriff only sees "some scribbling," while Rufel finds a lot of pages that are just blank. His writing and his tracking do not result in a successful property claim of Dessa; they only cause him to become the Other he posited when he wrote about Dessa, a human reduced to an animal. Dessa now thinks of him as a "crazy white man" whose tracking makes him "a bloodhound on my trail" (225). When Nehemiah finally realizes that he has lost her and is "down on his knees, scrambling amongst them papers," Dessa concludes, "He'd tried to play bloodhound on me and now some bloodhound was turning him every way *but* loose" (232). Nehemiah's initial blindness to Dessa's human agency is fed by his desire for property but ends with his own loss of agency.

WHAT TO FEAR

With far-fetched con games played on comically blind audiences, all three narratives have elements of dark humor though the stakes are serious: escape or imprisonment, life or death. That the con games are performances may mask how truly dangerous they are. Enter the gothic. Each of these works contains standard gothic markers that alert the reader to impending peril. However, these gothic markers reflect a split in point of view as to what the narratives ultimately teach the reader to fear. The first answer, deriving from the point of view of the enslaved people, is the fear of losing personhood. While it might seem odd to say that an enslaved person could fear losing personhood since that person is property at birth, the absence is depicted as a loss over time, as certain moments trigger a new understanding of what it means to be property. When Amasa Delano offers to buy Babo in a casual manner as if he were purchasing a pet dog, when Percy Driscoll threatens to sell those he holds in slavery and perhaps separate Roxy from her baby, and when Dessa is left in a box for hours, the vast impact of the loss of personhood generates terror. While this fear is specific to slavery in its transformation of people into chattel, these moments of terror tap into a larger fear of losing self that is depicted in many gothic narratives. Louis S. Gross explains that "if there is one central area of fear the Gothic novel exploits it is the fear of losing one's sense of self as a human being in relation to the family, the state, and God" (8). Slavery presents this fear in its starkest form, and in these texts the presence of markers, such as haunted houses, enclosed spaces, and monstrous villains, underscores the import of losing personhood.

However, in revealing that the legal designations of race and property are merely constructions, these texts also undermine claims of legal ownership. In essence, the con games convert the enslaved people's fear of losing personhood into white society's fear of losing these boundaries of race and property, which becomes the second answer to what the narratives teach the reader to fear. In *Benito Cereno* and *Dessa Rose*, this fear manifests in the dupes of the con games, who are anxious that they are missing something, an anxiety that festers through gothic portents. In *Pudd'nhead Wilson*, Wilson perceives disturbing signs of something amiss only towards the end. Applying Sedgwick's theory that gothic narratives use spatial cues to indicate that the self is "massively blocked off from something to which it ought normally to have access," we can see that in these texts what the white outsiders would normally have access to is knowledge, an unobstructed reading of the world around them from their position of power (12). Their situation instead mirrors someone watching three cards whirling around but not knowing where the queen is, which leaves these outsiders fearing the unknown. Fred Botting explains that "Gothic terrors activate a sense of the unknown and project an uncontrollable and overwhelming power which threatens not only the loss of sanity, honour, property or social standing but the very order which supports and is regulated by the coherence of those terms" (7). In the known world, the categories of white and black neatly separate free people with agency from those who are deemed property. If a hidden reality exists where enslaved people have agency, the "very order" of society may be in peril.

With these two possible loci of fear, the question is which the texts promote. If a reader shares the white outsiders' fear of the loss of boundaries, the texts do the conservative work the gothic often performs of reinforcing the status quo by providing helpful warnings of trouble. If, however, a reader shares the black insiders' fear of the loss of personhood, the texts have subverted the system using the gothic's potential for transgression.[20] Critics have certainly debated whether *Benito Cereno* and *Pudd'nhead Wilson* are critical of slavery. The quandary lies in which point of view the texts ultimately value. Williams's narrative, although it offers various points of view, is easier to parse, given the con game's ultimate success. For all three texts, I will argue that the gothic markers reveal that in the end, the two fears are intertwined. As long as the law haunts those enslaved, the fear that the law is simply a fictional construct continues to haunt slaveholders. In Melville's and Twain's texts, the intertwining leads to overall destruction, and everyone loses, as a system built on constructions of race crumbles. In her twentieth-century rewriting, Williams finds an escape route when characters acknowledge and confront their fears. While the key to any con game is who can see both realities, the key for gothic texts is who can see the ghosts.

Benito Cereno traffics heavily in gothic markers, and for most of the novel, the narrator stays close to the point of view of Delano, so that the main fear communicated is that something is amiss. In discussing the con in the novel, I posited Delano as too invested in the structure of slavery to perceive that the con game was even taking place. Strangely enough, Delano *is* able to perceive the presence of the gothic, but the markers still do not help him, as he fails to detect the correct source for the terror. From the first, Delano surmises that the *San Dominick* is a "ship in distress" (37). With fog obscuring his view, he imagines the ship looks like a "white-washed monastery" with dark moving figures that represent "Black Friars pacing the cloisters" (37). Although Delano is an American from Massachusetts sailing on the southern end of Chile, the boat conjures for him an image of an Old World gothic church. The Old World associations continue with an allusion to castle architecture: "Battered and mouldy, the castellated forecastle seemed some ancient turret, long ago taken by assault, and then left to decay" (38). Yet another part of the ship contains "tenantless balconies hung over the sea as if it were the grand Venetian canal" (38). Displayed on a coat of arms is a picture of a "dark satyr in a mask, holding his foot on the prostrate neck of a writhing figure, likewise masked" (38). In borrowing European gothic tropes, Melville employs the strategy that other early American writers use of layering Old World gothic settings on top of a New World topos as a shorthand for announcing a haunted tale. Edgar Allan Poe's "The Fall of the House of Usher," for example, depicts its narrator approaching an apparently ancient and crumbling family mansion next to a tarn. When Delano imagines the *San Dominick*, which is literally a ship in the Pacific Ocean, as a monastery, a castle, or a European canal complete with a devil-figure, the architecture signals a gothic tale.

Other descriptions evoke death. Delano thinks the keel and ribs make the ship look like it "launched from Ezekiel's Valley of Dry Bones," which in the biblical vision take flesh and come back from the dead (38). The *San Dominick* thus appears to be ghost ship: "The ship seems unreal; these strange costumes, gestures, and faces, but a shadowy tableau just emerged from the deep, which directly must receive back what it gave" (39). When Delano boards, four of the seemingly enslaved people are humming a "low monotonous chant" like a "funeral march" (39). Everything about the setting and the ship signals foreboding, fear, and death.

Delano's subsequent encounter with the ship's captain echoes the experience of Poe's narrator in entering the Usher mansion. Both characters meet the men they propose to save and notice strange maladies. While Poe's narrator finds Usher to be suffering from an "excessive nervous agitation" that gives him a "ghastly pallor" (203), Delano finds Cereno to be experiencing "nervous suffering" and later notices a "cadaverous aspect" (41, 48). Both narrators are suspicious but not alarmed enough to flee for their lives. Characters often make stupid decisions in gothic narratives because they do not perceive that they are in a gothic narrative; that is, they are not adequately attuned to the dangers of a dark monastery, a ghostly ship, or an overly nervous stranger. Delano, though unaware that his situation parallels a Poe story, does seem aware of the general gothic clues. Peter Coviello, in reading *Benito Cereno* as "relentlessly gothic," explains that Delano does indeed "[imagine] himself at the center of a gothic tale" (161). Delano, however, dismisses his fears. When he ponders Cereno's strange and suspicious behavior, he "began to feel a ghostly dread of Don Benito," an anxiety that is aided by the noise of the men striking hatchets "as in ominous comment on the white stranger's thoughts" (57). But he changes his mind, concluding that these misgivings are absurd, and "began to laugh at his former forebodings" (59). These forebodings recall creations from gothic narratives, but now the thought of Cereno as a "hobgoblin" seems silly (59). Coviello argues that Melville is critiquing the sentimental mode and that Delano is a "bad reader" because he decides to be a "sentimental reader" (163). Yet another possibility, though, is that Delano continues to be a gothic reader, as he repeatedly feels "uneasiness," even though he tries on multiple occasions to talk himself out of it. The problem, then, may not be one of genre as much as one of discernment. Delano assumes the wrong source of his unease: Cereno is not a "hobgoblin," but Babo is.

As a character who is indeed in a gothic plot, Delano is, to borrow Sedgwick's words, "massively blocked off from something," namely, the answer to the conundrum posed by the *San Dominick*'s captain and passengers. His anxiety is manifest through his pondering of "four curious points"; this listing and numbering betray his need to master the unknown before him, an unknown that is perfectly represented by the puzzle of a knot. Delano comes across a white sailor tying a knot of such intricacy that Delano asks, "What is it for?" (65). The sailor replies, "For some one else to undo" and then in a low voice, "Undo it, cut it, quick" (65). The sailor tries to communicate that the ship is a tangled puzzle, but as Delano continues to focus on Cereno as the source of his continuing uneasiness, he does not untie the mystery.

His assumption that enslaved people have only the intelligence of animals continues to blind him. When Babo attempts to kill Cereno, Delano finally has that "flash of revelation" (88). With "the scales dropped from his eyes," he sees the ship's figurehead revealed, a skeleton of the original captain, and realizes that the *San Dominick* is indeed a ship of death. He is in a gothic tale, and the answer to the conundrum is the loss of stable boundaries defining "master" and "slave."

Only after Delano's "flash of revelation" does *Benito Cereno* acknowledge the fear felt by those held in slavery of losing personhood. Even then, the reader has to glean the view indirectly through Cereno's deposition. Through his testimony, the reader learns that the blacks' first step in trying to stop their loss of personhood is taking control of the ship.[21] The blacks then insist that Cereno take them to "any negro [country]" and then specifically to Senegal (94). Jeannine Marie DeLombard points out that in directing Cereno to take them to Senegal, Babo and crew want to go "not simply back to a particular place but to their previous condition of self-ownership" (55). Yet the logistical problems of the distance to Senegal and the dwindling supplies of food and fresh water result in their being marooned off the coast of Chile. Even more problematic is the larger legal question of asserting (or reasserting) personhood. DeLombard explains that *Benito Cereno* "probes the limits of legal personhood by demonstrating the impossibility of pinpointing the moment of transformation from subjection to the will of another to liberated, responsible autonomy" (36). Babo decides to kill his master "because he and his companions could not otherwise be sure of their liberty" (95). His logic here is understandable; property is tied to an owner. The black rebels also decide they need a contract giving them "the ship, with the cargo." If the contract were viable, they would then own themselves. The situation is as convoluted as Twain's paradox of whether an enslaved person can commit theft: to wit, can property (or former property or ownerless property) have the agency to enter into a contract to own itself?

The crew's various attempts to claim self-ownership through killing their master, changing their location, and creating a contract betray their fear of losing personhood completely. This motivation drives the grand con game, justifying the narrator's designation of Cereno's revealing deposition as "the key to fit into the lock of the complications which precede it" (105). But since the blacks' fear is filtered through Cereno's words, we do not hear from Babo or anyone else directly. After Babo is captured, he "uttered no sound, and could not be forced to" (107). Furthermore, Cereno's deposition alternates between describing the blacks' actions to gain personhood and revealing their violence towards the white sailors. Cereno in fact notes ten different times that Babo and his crew either killed whites or threatened to do so, allowing the whites' fear to punctuate the text, much like the hatchet-polishers' chants punctuate Delano's narrative. Whereas Delano cannot understand those chants, Cereno's description of the white sailors' terror is palpable. Hence, even in this ending section, the weight of the text still focuses on the whites' fear of losing the boundaries of race and property that structure their world.

Given this focus, critics have understandably debated whether the text actually critiques slavery. Sidney Kaplan, in outlining the two schools of thought in his 1957 article, argues, "It must be ventured that the image of Melville as subtle abolitionist in *Benito Cereno* may be a construction of generous wish rather than hard fact" (12). He contends that even if "the duped Delano was meant to be simple, even stupid," the problem is that "for Melville, in his story, Babo was a victor in the malign sense only" (16–17, 26). Recent critics acknowledge Kaplan's problem but tend to disagree with his conclusion. Robert S. Levine explains that "Melville offers his readers virtually no clear guidance on how to read the novella as antislavery" ("Reading" 146). He finds, though, that "Melville subtly and quietly presses his most canny readers to read from the point of view of Babo" through the reader's awareness of Delano's use of racist stereotypes. James H. Kavanagh points to the use of irony to break "the seductive grip of identification between the reader and Amasa Delano," while Ezra F. Tawil asserts a "tipping point" that happens when "the cognitive weight finally shifts and skepticism towards Delano's perspective rather than trust becomes the norm" (360, 51). What these critics are describing is what narratologist Dorrit Cohn labels "discordant narration": when the reader must decide "that the *author* intends his or her work to be understood differently from the way the *narrator* understands it: in a way that can only be discovered by reading the work against the grain of the narrator's discourse, providing it with a meaning that, though not explicitly spelled out, is silently signaled to the reader behind the narrator's back" (307). This process, however, is difficult: "The severance of narrators from their authors is not an easy step to take; it is a move that even highly educated readers tend to resist" (Cohn 312). Melville makes it especially challenging given that there is no silent signal or "clear guidance." Covielle even calls the text "a kind of trap" that "[*hates*] its readers" (175).

Reading against the grain is possible, however, if we consider the dynamics of the con game. The con game does not seek to destroy the system but to hide within it. Babo and crew pretend to be property to conceal their agency instead of directly denouncing slavery in the presence of Delano.

Yet the con game makes what the outsider perceives as reality to be simply a performance. If slavery is a performance, and if "whiteness" and "blackness" can be masks to be put on or, more significantly, taken off, then the legal construction of race as innate is false. Consequently, although the con game does not seek to overturn the legal system, it reveals the system to be simply a creation, thereby subverting it.

Benito Cereno may not offer a direct condemnation of slavery, but the con game's attacks on its underpinnings reveal its faulty structures. While the text continues to give weight to Delano's view, his reasoning is impaired by all he cannot see as he remains in this created structure. In their ending conversation, Cereno reflects on how Delano could not see the con: "you were with me all day; stood with me, sat with me, talked with me, looked at me, ate with me, drank with me; and yet, your last act was to clutch for a monster, not only an innocent man, but the most pitiable of all men" (106). Cereno concludes that the situation was simply beyond reason: "So far may even the best man err, in judging the conduct of one with the recesses of whose condition he is not acquainted" (106). He and Delano thus ascribe their survival to "God," "Providence," and the "Prince of Heaven" (106). They seek supernatural explanations because their worldly structures of race and property do not elucidate all that has transpired.

Delano and Cereno's reach to other-worldly agents, however, attests to the haunting that remains at the end of the narrative. The fear of disrupted boundaries is superficially assuaged by Delano's control of the *San Dominick*. The resulting trial and execution of Babo suggests that the legal system has worked to regain order, but the gothic markers continue to announce fear. Delano tries to get Cereno to shrug off his gloom: "But the past is passed; why moralize upon it? Forget it. See, yon bright sun has forgotten it all, and the blue sea, and the blue sky; these have turned over new leaves" (106). Even after his experience, Delano still cannot perceive the ghosts. When Cereno declines to join in Delano's sanguine mood, Delano asks the infamous question, "What has cast such a shadow on you?" (107). As Cereno answers "the negro," the text abounds with gothic signals: Cereno declares the winds "waft me to my tomb" while he gathers his mantle "as if it were a pall" with his sword only a "ghost" (107). Babo, the "negro," may have been killed, but he becomes a haunt. His head mounted on a pole in the plaza faces both the church with his master's bones and the monastery that houses Cereno. The narrative's initial gothic markers of church, monastery, and pervading death reappear here at the end, signaling that the haunting has not abated even with the resumption of law and order. Frederick Busch explains that Babo "began as a man and became a curse" (114).[22] For Delano, though, Babo is never a man; he is an animal, freight, cargo, property. The curse is that Delano cannot see Babo as a man even in death. When Delano first boards the *San Dominick*, he is greeted by a "clamorous throng of whites and blacks" who "in one language, and as with one voice, all poured out a common tale of suffering" (39). What Delano fails to see at the beginning is what he is still blind to at the end: everyone is in the ghost ship of slavery, and the fears of losing personhood and boundaries are intertwined. The con game thus exposes how the legal construction that conflates of people with property ultimately haunts and destroys everyone.

In *Pudd'nhead Wilson*, Mark Twain explores the fear of losing personhood first, reversing the order of *Benito Cereno*. Although this fear is depicted sympathetically through Roxy's words and actions, the question of whether the text gives ultimate weight to this fear over the white town's fear of the loss of stable boundaries still remains difficult to answer. The text seems to shift midway to favor the town's point of view as Roxy moves from victim to culprit. In trying to make sense of the shift, Shelley Fisher Fishkin explains that *Pudd'nhead Wilson* is a "flawed" book that "sometimes veers in one direction, sometimes in another" (2). Jehlen discusses a "turnaround" that "seems to start the story over" (44). Hershel Parker just declares the novel "patently unreadable" (136). Leonard Martinez, however, seeks to defend the book by comparing it with *Benito Cereno*, acknowledging that the "dominant claim" of critics of both books is that they "flinch from saying much beyond expressing repressed national fears or anxieties about race" (116). Martinez claims that Twain's book differs from Melville's because Melville's ending is simply stock gothic and "not unrelated to the turning over the shoulder of a frightened character in an earlier gothic text" (119). Whereas Martinez sees the use of gothic in *Benito Cereno* as a conservative move, I read the gothic in both texts as revealing the haunting lingering after the supposed resolution. In *Benito Cereno*, as in *Pudd'nhead Wilson*, there is no answer as to which fear the text validates because the fears are intertwined, and with con games revealing society's construction of people as property, everyone loses.

Early in *Pudd'nhead Wilson*, the narrator follows Roxy's point of view as she is struck with fear because of Percy Driscoll's threats to sell those he holds in slavery down the river. When he sells everyone but Roxy, he does so locally, and for this supposedly kind gesture, "the culprits flung themselves prone, in an ecstasy of gratitude, and kissed his feet, declaring that they would never forget his goodness and never cease to pray for him as long as they lived" (68). The text drips with sarcasm, imaging Driscoll as a kind of "god" who had "closed the gates of hell against them" (68). To Roxy, though, he now plays the role of gothic monster, the agent who threatens her life and that of her son. While Driscoll sleeps well that night, content with this generosity, Roxy becomes the gothic damsel in distress: "A profound terror had taken possession of her. Her child could grow up and be sold down the river! The thought crazed her with horror" (69). As she contemplates her child's possible fates, Roxy decides that she has to kill him. The fear that Roxy expresses because of the trap she is in echoes that of the enslaved women I analyze in chapter 1, who at times also contemplate infanticide. Just as Jacobs and Crafts use their characters' desperate circumstances to appeal to their readers' emotions, Twain posits Roxy as the sympathetic frantic mother who wants to save her child from the monster of slavery represented by Driscoll. Only after Tom's "snowy long baby-gown" makes her son, Chambers, into a look-alike for Tom does Roxy change her plan to the con game of switching the babies. Even then, her action is made under duress. Jehlen argues that Roxy "can jump in the river with her baby or live in daily peril of its being sold. Given those alternatives, her stratagem appears righteous and even fair, despite its concomitant enslavement of the white boy" (40). The switch furthermore appears fair at this point in the text because the narrator is only following Roxy's point of view. Roxy, as a gothic damsel shrewder than most, has found a way to hide the thing most precious to her in plain sight. Her son, now known as "Tom," grows up pampered, educated, white, and free. Roxy herself is freed by the dying Driscoll, who never dreams that she had stolen his son in saving her own. All should be well, but in making her son "white" she, in Porter's words, "makes him free but no longer hers" (134). He grows up to be her master. Thus in the end, Roxy did not have a choice that would allow her to keep her son: he can either be killed, sold, or white.

The sympathy the narrator elicits for Roxy's predicament halts, though, when her baby becomes a "white" man, and the text shifts to focus on the fear of the boundaries that are crossed with the new "Tom" passing as white, a shift reflected by gothic markers. Before Tom is even aware of his true racial identity, the fear of crossed boundaries presents itself through the gothic trope of doubling. When Tom returns to Dawson's Landing from Yale, he wears "Eastern fashion, city fashion" (85). His fine clothes offend the town's sense of its own worth, and the town gets even by making an "old deformed negro bell-ringer" follow Tom "tricked out in a flamboyant curtain-calico exaggeration of his finery, and imitating his fancy Eastern graces as well as he could" (85). Linda A. Morris writes, "We might wonder why this scene has such a haunting quality about it" (43). The answer is the fear stemming from crossed boundaries, specifically of black becoming white. What the town and Tom do not know yet is that the racial boundary has already been crossed; the double acts as a kind of gothic warning of peril.

With the double as foreshadowing, Twain introduces a haunted house. Though a clear marker of something to fear, the house has received scant attention from critics. This lack of notice is surprising, given the significant role the haunted house plays in American literature; Eric Savoy proclaims it as the "most persistent site, object, structural analogue, and trope of American gothic's allegorical turn" (9). Perhaps the critics' lack of attention stems from this house's odd history—odd because it has none. In gothic tales, architecture usually becomes haunted because of the dreadful actions that have taken place within it, so that the walls (the turrets, the gargoyles) absorb the terror and make it manifest in their forbidding appearance. Though the house in *Pudd'nhead Wilson* has acquired "the reputation a few years before of being haunted," there is no reason given for the reputation; there is no terrifying history or tale of property struggle or ghostly apparition (111). The proverbial cart goes before the horse because only after the house is labeled "*the* haunted house" does the house show signs of being haunted: "It was getting crazy and ruinous, now, from long neglect" (111). The building's isolation bothers the town with its "snug" houses set together: "It stood three hundred yards beyond Pudd'nhead Wilson's house, with nothing between but vacancy. It was the last house in the town at that end" (111). In a town with such a communal identity that "the town" seems to think and speak in one voice, distance and differentiation are dangerous. As gothic marker, the haunted house becomes a repository for fear.

The house first becomes a manifestation of Roxy's fear of losing personhood because she goes there when she has nowhere else to go. Her identity as a person in this society is conflicted: as a free person, she cannot live with the enslaved people; as a black person, she cannot live with the whites; as a person without money, her options are limited. When Roxy tells Tom to meet her there, she explains, "I'se a-roostin' in de ha'nted house 'cas'e I can't 'ford to 'roos nowher's else" (109–110). Haunted by her placelessness, Roxy's only place is a haunted house, echoing the damsels I discuss in chapter 1 who find refuge in haunted property. Harrington points out that the only two people to enter the house are Roxy and Tom (95). These two characters, a formerly enslaved woman and a black man passing as white, fall outside the society's conception of "people," which leads them to need the secrecy afforded by the house. The haunted house is thus the appropriately dark, gothic place where Tom learns the secret that he is Roxy's son. He reacts with a "whirlwind of disorganizing sensations and emotion" and a "cold panic," and he later "came to have a hunted sense and a hunted look" (113, 119). The house labeled "haunted" becomes haunted with Roxy's and Tom's fears of losing personhood.

The house, however, becomes the launching point in turn of Roxy and Tom's haunting of the town and the resulting disruption of boundaries. Roxy may seek the isolated building because she has nowhere else to "roost," but once there, she reasserts the level of agency she had when she switched the babies. Harrington argues that Roxy's abode is described in "the most impoverished, dehumanized terms," but the description actually shows that Roxy has claimed the house as home: "She had a pile of clean straw in the corner for a bed, some cheap but well-kept clothing was hanging on the wall, there was a tin lantern freckling the floor with little spots of light, and there were various soap- and candle-boxes scattered about, which served for chairs" (112). The room is not grand by any means, but the fact that she has made this house hers by arranging her "well-kept" belongings in it gives her the power of a property claim. Although property is fret with problems in this text, Roxy still partakes in the larger dynamic I explore throughout this study that only free people can claim property and that property ownership then brings power. Tom recognizes her power, as he sees her "above him like a Fate" (114). As she talks to Tom, "She went and sat down on her candle-box, and the pride and pomp of her victorious attitude made it a throne" (114). The town is not yet aware of her power, but in adding Tom as an insider to her game of confidence, Roxy creates a kind of gothic monster haunting the town, as Tom becomes the very essence of crossed boundaries.

When Roxy reveals Tom's true parentage, she makes him "black" by claiming that she is his mother, but she also makes him "white" by claiming his father was Cecil Burleigh Essex, one of the town's patriarchs. In a rather disturbing passage, Roxy seems to have internalized the society's racist assumptions about black inferiority by being aghast that Tom shies away from a duel, thereby breaking the white gentlemen's code of honor he should uphold as Essex's biological son. Roxy claims, "You has disgraced yo' birth," fussing that the fraction of black blood in Tom's genealogy makes him a coward (157). Although Roxy's con game exposes the myth of racial distinctions, she seems to support that very structure. Whether or not he should have participated in the foolish duel, Tom is clearly portrayed in the text as a bad character. He gambles, steals from everyone, enjoys embarrassing Wilson and the Italian twins, tricks his mother into slavery farther down the river, and finally murders the "uncle" who has adopted him after his father died.

Whence the evil? By including twins in the narrative in addition to the plot of switching babies, Twain creates a virtual incubator for a nature-versus-nurture argument. Fishkin's explanation of Tom's character counters Roxy's: "The book doesn't make the argument that a black child raised as a white will be as good as a white: it argues that a black raised as a white will be as bad as a white" (17). However, as Roxy's absurd genealogy including John Smith and Pocahontas demonstrates, even Tom's "white" line is mixed, and he simply does not fit into the categories that the society would like to believe are neatly segregated.[23] Tom instead stands in the intersection of both fears generated by and through the con game. Raised as white, he fears the crossing of racial boundaries, so the shadow of a black double haunts him. Revealed as black, he then proceeds to live in fear of losing personhood. When he kills Judge Driscoll, "he drove the knife home—and was free" (195). While Tom is immediately free from his worries about property as he will inherit the Judge's estates, he is moreover free as an enslaved person who has killed the most obvious person to have claim over him. Roxy and Tom begin as haunted and filled with fear, but they move to being haunts with the potential to create the fear of crossed boundaries.

The question, then, is do Roxy and Tom actually evoke fear? Unlike *Benito Cereno*, where Delano spends most of the text afraid of what he does not know, in *Pudd'nhead Wilson*, the outsiders to the con do not suspect they have been duped and do not know to be afraid. Roxy's con game is so beyond anything comprehensible that, as Carolyn Porter points out, "The law cannot forbid it because the law cannot imagine it" (126). Only Wilson begins to suspect something late in the narrative, and even then, he is not afraid as much as curious. Twain includes the most clichéd marker of the gothic, a haunted house, in a novel where the surrounding town is seemingly not haunted. The novel thus seems to raise the question of whether someone can be haunted if they are not aware of it. The narrative, however, does not pause long enough for this question to be answered. As in *Benito Cereno*, a quick, superficial restoration of order is seemingly produced by a legal trial.

Even though the town may not be able to see its haunting, the reader can. The reader has been in on Roxy's con from the beginning and then follows the text's shift in point of view to witness Tom's many failings. For the reader to perceive the town as haunted by the possibility of someone who can mask as white, though, he or she has to separate from the valorization of Wilson. Wilson, who has been the nerdy underdog since his bad dog joke, finally seizes victory in using fingerprints to reveal Tom's true identity. John S. Whitley writes that Twain's "tragic novel about a slave-owning society" is "hopelessly crossed" with an "optimistic detective plot" (63). The detective plot promises a resolution with Wilson as detective providing a simple answer to "who done it." The legal system appears to provide finality, but the case does not enact justice for the murder. Tom is not imprisoned or executed. He is instead claimed as property, as if the murder did not occur because property cannot be a culpable agent. Malcolm Bradbury points out, "When Tom is sold down the river at the end, what happens to him is what probably would have happened even if he had not committed the murder" (24–25). Despite Wilson's theatrics at the legal trial, the possibility of a Tom—of a character whose race is mixed, indeterminate, passing, and not subject to boundaries—still exists and still haunts a society who pretends otherwise. A reader who, as Cohn says, "[reads] the work against the grain of the narrator's discourse" can see the lack of justice in the legal trial (307).

What the trial clearly demonstrates is the limit of the law. Although Wilson reveals the con game Roxy has played, even he does not see that the existence of that con game questions the foundation of a "slaveholding town." Barbara Ladd contends that "one of the most serious tragedies" in the book is that Wilson is implicated in the "moral morass of slavery" (*Nationalism* 111). Wilson and the legal system he employs become a subject of farce, which Twain foreshadows in his opening "Whisper to the Reader," claiming his "law chapters" are accurate because they were overseen by someone who "studied law part of a while in south-west Missouri thirty-five years ago" (53). Both Melville and Twain take aim at the very legal system that makes people into property by showing the impotence of legal trials to contain fears about the disruption of boundaries. In his whisper, Twain clues the reader to see how Roxy's con and Tom's existence question the "fictions of law and custom" and haunt the town, even if it is not aware of it.

The initial fear driving the con, the loss of personhood, also lingers after the end of the text, but, as in *Benito Cereno*, the two fears are intertwined, so that they feed off of each other. When the creditors of Percy Driscoll's estate claim that Tom was not just "lawfully their property" but "had been so for eight years," the law's conflation of people with property negates Tom's agency in killing Judge Driscoll. At the same time, the law vacates Judge Driscoll's personhood as well, as if his death did not happen because no person was there to kill him. In claiming that the "guilt lay with the erroneous inventory," the creditors suggest it was simply an accounting error, and the system of property wins.[24] Just as in *Benito Cereno*, however, every person loses. The fear of the damsel in distress that her son would be sold is fulfilled, and "Roxy's heart was broken" (224). Tom's fear of losing personhood is also fulfilled, as he is treated as merely property, like a dog. Even Chambers, the character now freed from slavery, who in the accounting of property is now the credit to Tom's debit, remains haunted: "His manners were the manners of a slave. Money and fine clothes could not mend these defects or cover them up, they only made them the more glaring and the more pathetic. The poor fellow could not endure the terrors of the white man's parlour" (225). Pudd'nhead Wilson is now seen as the savior of a town made up of fools. No one wins.

In both texts, the legal system that defines people as property is corrupting to the extent that Melville and Twain leave no survivors, and even the victims of the system become tainted by it: Roxy and Tom turn unsympathetic in their deceit, and Babo becomes monstrous in his violence. The stark similarity of devastation depicted in these two texts is made even sharper by adding a third text, *Dessa Rose*, to the conversation. From her twentieth-century vantage point, Williams constructs a con game that succeeds, and a whole new possibility emerges.

Sherley Anne Williams may cover the same ground as Melville and Twain do in constructing her con game, but by the late twentieth century, that ground has shifted significantly. Williams benefits from the modernist exploration of multiple points of view. Whereas Melville is able to reveal the point of view of enslaved people only tangentially, and Twain is not able to sustain his exploration of it, Williams begins with Dessa's view and then intersperses her view first with that of Adam Nehemiah and later with Rufel. Williams also benefits from the postmodern interrogation of the shaping of history. Kekeh explains that *Dessa Rose* is a "polyphonic text in which each participant in turn is allowed to speak up and to assume the responsibility of the making of the story/history" (220). In contrast to the legal documents in *Benito Cereno* that try to put the revolt into a safe box and the trial in *Pudd'nhead Wilson* that purports to reveal the true story, history in *Dessa Rose* is not solely the purview of the legal establishment. With multiple viewpoints in play, history is up for grabs.

The interspersed multiple viewpoints change the reader's relationship with the text. The reader of the nineteenth-century novels had to read against the grain to glean the enslaved person's point of view, but in *Dessa Rose*, the reader's task is to weigh and compare differing viewpoints. Despite Williams's contemporary approach, these multiple viewpoints are again marked by gothic conventions revealing the same two loci of fear. In the first section, entitled "Darky," the reader has to balance Dessa's fear of losing personhood with Nehemiah's fear of the unknown. What clearly distinguishes *Dessa Rose* from the earlier narratives, though, is the later sections of the book where Rufel replaces Nehemiah as white observer. Rufel and Dessa actually confront their competing fears. By crossing the boundary of fear, Dessa and Rufel are able to work together in a con game. Tracing the gothic markers reveals how Williams thus rewrites the story of race and fear. When the text returns at the end to Nehemiah's point of view, Rufel and Dessa's alliance prompts the reader to deny his voice, and the con game succeeds.

In the first section, the balance between Dessa's and Nehemiah's voices is not exactly equal because the reader hears more from Nehemiah. Kekeh argues, however, that using Dessa's view in both the prologue and the epilogue gives her "narrative authority" as her voice "encircles the narrative, showing her full control over her tale" (225). Additionally, Dessa's view comes from direct access to her dreams and thoughts in addition to what she says aloud to Nehemiah. For Nehemiah's point of view, as Ana Nunes points out, the reader must rely on his journal entries and a third-person narrator, so that "it is the omniscient narrator who discloses the white man's hesitation and thoughts about his own text" (100). Nonetheless, the reader must compare the two versions. For example, when Nehemiah strikes Dessa, the reader learns from Nehemiah that he is disgusted that he lowered himself to violence and from Dessa that she did not know the reason for his outburst but could read anger in his face. Shifting between views, the gothic markers signal to the reader that something is amiss, but the two points of view signal two different fears.

The most obvious gothic marker signaling danger is the setting: a dark jail cell in the cellar of a house. Physically imprisoned in a white person's house, Dessa is not only trapped; she is literally lower than its occupants. Gothic architecture, as Eugenia DeLamotte explains, communicates "literal or metaphysical boundaries" (20). Dessa in her jail cell is clearly separated from society. Surprisingly, Nehemiah is more bothered by this setting than Dessa is. While she references the chains, which "rasped, rubbed hatefully at her ankles and wrists," she does not show fear of the jail cell itself (14). Nehemiah, however, is "fearful of being drawn into the shadows" of the cellar with the "darky," as if Dessa and the gothic space are conjoined (30). Finding that "being closeted with the darky within the small confines of the cellar was an unsettling experience," Nehemiah convinces Hughes, the jailer, to let him chain Dessa to a tree, so he can meet with her in the "fresh air" (23, 35). The situation does not markedly improve outdoors, as Dessa seems to bring the shadows with her: "Her dark hair seemed to merge into the deeper shades cast by the low-hanging branches of the tree" (44). His conflation of her darkness with shadows suggest that it is Dessa herself that sparks his unease.

Nehemiah is anxious around Dessa because he fears the unknown she represents. He imagines himself as intellectually superior, even to the white people with whom he interacts. With Dessa, however, he knows he is missing something: "Lurking behind the darky's all too often blank gaze was something more than the cunning stubbornness which, alone, he had first perceived" (42). What he is missing is her agency. Dessa begins conning him during their interactions in the jail cell, long before the elaborate con game she performs with the other formerly enslaved people and Rufel. Just as Delano recognizes the performative flavor of the people's behavior on the *San Dominick*, Nehemiah acknowledges that Dessa's story was an "entrancing recital, better in its way than a paid theatrical" (20). Her snippets of narration hardly ever answer his questions directly; he finds her "random manner, a loquacious, roundabout fashion" to be "exasperating to the point of fury" (23). At one point, he even has Hughes put her on a diet of heavily salted water to get her to cooperate. For her part, Dessa talks to him to break the tedium and in hopes that he would "tell her something she didn't know" about her friends' fates (56). She does not give him the information he wants, but she enacts a "game" by "playing with words" (60). Dessa cons Nehemiah by pretending to be daft and ignorant. He has a sense that he is being played but is afraid to get too close to the "shadows" around her; he simply remains fearful.

This fear of her shadows is couched in supernatural terms, as if she has some unknown and frightening power. He is "held spellbound" by her talking, "fascinated, forgetting to write" (18). The dark skin that he repeatedly notes is paired with the whites in her eyes that cause him to think of the "devil's stare" (20). When Dessa admits that she wanted to kill her mistress, Nehemiah is shocked and thinks, "Truly the female of this species is as deadly as the male" (43). Although her mysterious powers render her unknown and scary, Nehemiah uses the animal imagery to deny her agency and convince himself of her inferiority.

In fighting off the suspicions that Dessa is evil, Nehemiah completely misses the signal of her agency, her humming. Nehemiah notes repeatedly that Dessa hums what sounds like a "dirge" (29). He is irritated by her "moaning" and finds it "absurd" (35). He dismisses Hughes's assertion that the singing signifies that the enslaved people are "happy," but he cannot decipher it (29).[25] At one point, he asks her to sing the words: "Gonna march in the gold band/ In the arms by'n by" (51). To Nehemiah, this is a "quaint piece of doggerel," but when the narrative shifts to Dessa's view, Dessa reveals that the songs are her way of communicating with the others who are enslaved (52). The message is that she will soon be freed. Nehemiah is right to fear the unknown, but like Delano on the puzzling ship, he imagines the wrong source. Instead of gothic shadows or supernatural power, he should fear Dessa's agency. Dessa's escape confirms the disruption of boundaries, as Dessa dares to be free.

Nehemiah's fear alternates with Dessa's, as her stories about Kaine reveal her fear of losing personhood. The prologue opens with Dessa dreaming of a past intimate moment with Kaine before she wakes up to the reality of chains in a jail cell. In addition to grieving the loss of her love, Dessa grieves the way the loss of Kaine is the loss of her selfhood, so the moments she dreams or remembers are considerations of what it means to be property. Dessa brags that Kaine "chosed me. Masa ain't had nothing to do wid it" (19). She remembers Kaine talking about being property: "Niggas just only belongs to white folks and that be's all" (37). Dessa understands that he makes a banjo in order to own something, as only people own property. She recalls her fear when she heard that Monroe would be sold because he chose a woman that his master did not approve, and she knew Kaine's rebelliousness might get him sold as well.

These fears are increased by Dessa's pregnancy. Although Kaine had urged her to abort the baby, Dessa resists because "this baby, ours, us's" (46). Even as Dessa tries to assert possession through language, "fear had eaten at her insides" because "she would never be able to save [the baby] if Master wanted it" (48–49). Dessa knows that when children are old enough, they are sold away, and "even in dreams that threat had haunted her" (57). The first time she answers one of Nehemiah's questions directly, a question about why she escaped the coffle, she asks, "Was you slave, you want to be sold deep south?" (41).

The anxieties of being sold, being separated, and being property continue to frighten Dessa even with Kaine already dead and her fate supposedly sealed. She is haunted by "dreams and ghosts of dreams" (48). All of the ghosts of those gone "sat with her in the cellar" (54). She thinks also of the people who died in the revolt on the coffle and the high costs of that action, "so much for it all to end in this hole" (54). Nehemiah thinks Dessa's stories about Kaine and her past are a distraction; what he misses is that they are expressions of her fear of not having personhood. They are in fact the very answer to his question about why she turned to violence.

In the second and third sections of *Dessa Rose*, Williams pushes the exploration of the dual tracks of fear further by forcing Dessa and Rufel to confront their respective fears and then to understand each other's viewpoint. Although the narrative returns at the end to Adam Nehemiah and to the split in point of view between insiders and outsiders, in this middle section, Rufel has to comprehend the terror the fugitives feel to become an insider to the con game. In turn, Dessa has to learn to trust someone who bears the skin color of those who have terrorized her. The setting for this process is Rufel's unfinished plantation house. While a plantation house often plays the role of the haunted house in southern gothic narratives (see chapter 3), this one is different.[26] Rufel's husband has been absent long enough for her to suspect that he will not be coming back. Most of the enslaved people have run away, and those who remain start hiding runaways from other places. Rufel acquiesces because the farm work needs to be done. Kelly Lynch Reames points out the importance of the setting: "The fact that the house is unfinished and the patriarch absent opens the possibility for the remaining characters to change the story" (118). Dessa and Rufel first have to confront their dual fears of losing personhood and facing the unknown; these fears are centered on bodies and families.

In depicting the journey Dessa and Rufel take towards trusting each other, Williams starts with fear on a physical, concrete level: their raced bodies. When Dessa finally regains consciousness after her escape from jail and the birth of her son, she is confused to find herself in a luxurious feather bed. She is even more confused and frankly terrified by the white woman who tends her; in the course of two paragraphs, Dessa thinks "the white woman" eight times, trying to process what seems like a "dream" with a white face that "seemed to float toward her" (82). She then recalls an earlier dream of a white woman, which now seems premonition. She had tried to tell her mother about the dream, but every possible reading Mammy has of the dream promises bad luck, so Dessa drifts back to the present. But the white woman with her hair "the color of fire," her face that "seemed to radiate a milky glow," and her mouth "like a bloody gash," terrifies her (86). When she later wakes up to find the white woman in bed with her, Dessa thinks the hair "seemed alive," and she "almost suffocated in her terror" (114). Rufel's white body, which Nunes argues represents "the established standards of Western beauty," is "repulsive" to Dessa (115). Reames explains that the novel "reverses the metaphorical moral meanings attributed to whiteness and blackness," so that Dessa "feels trapped" by the color white (117). Dessa's reaction to "the white woman" also, however, speaks to a gothic marker of paralyzing whiteness. In *Playing in the Dark*, Toni Morrison analyzes depictions of blackness and whiteness in American literature, and in a close reading of Edgar Allan Poe's *The Narrative of Arthur Gordon Pym* discusses how scary images of whiteness are "found frequently, but not always at the end of the narrative.

They appear so often and in such particular circumstances that they give pause. They clamor, it seems for an attention that would yield the meaning that lies in their positioning, their repetition, and their strong suggestion of paralysis and incoherence; of impasse and non-sequitur" (33).[27]

Williams, though, rewrites gothic whiteness by placing the image at the beginning of Dessa and Rufel's relationship. The image springs from Dessa's knowledge of other white people. She comments, for example, on Nehemiah's light blue eyes that made her "shiver" because of their "emptiness" (49). Her memory of attacking her mistress contains images of the woman's white skin and red mouth that then resurface when Dessa sees "the white woman." Because Rufel looks like the mistress and Nehemiah, her presence is terrifying and ghostly. The whiteness taps into Dessa's fear of being paralyzed to the point of losing her self, but this whiteness does not end the text; it begins their story.

If Rufel's body, however, is terrifying in its very essence, what she does with it further feeds Dessa's fears. When Dessa first sees Rufel nursing the baby, she screams. Although Rufel started feeding the baby "almost without thought" because he was crying, to Dessa, the sight of her black baby being nursed by a white woman sparks the fear of her baby being taken away. Rufel's action "went against everything [Dessa] had been taught to think about white women but to inspect that fact too closely was almost to deny her own existence" (117). It is as if Dessa will lose personhood if a white woman takes her place as a mother to her child. Dessa reacts again when she sees Rufel in bed with Nathan. She realizes that "something inside me was screaming. Can't I have nothing?" (163).

Dessa's body in turn triggers Rufel's fear of the unknown. Nathan tells Rufel the gut-wrenching story of Dessa's whipping and confinement in a box. At first Rufel is sympathetic; she "could see the scene as he described it" and exclaims, "That vicious trader" (134–35). Yet Rufel does not want to believe the story because it questions the life she has lived based on white superiority. Rufel fears the story may cause her to confront cruelty in her own life. She remembers that when she heard screams from a person her husband was beating, she made him promise to stop, but she suspects that he simply moved the beatings farther away from the house. If she cannot deny the physical abuse of enslaved people, Rufel then wants to think they did something to deserve it, so she thinks Dessa "must have done something pretty terrible" (139). Her twisted thinking aligns her with Nehemiah, who asserts Dessa's scars "bespoke a history of misconduct" instead of evidence of torture (21). Rufel wants to see the physical evidence of Dessa's story. When she walks in on Dessa changing clothes and catches a glimpse of the scars, however, she regrets it. The fearful unknown is made known, as Rufel realizes Dessa "had a right to hide her scars, her pain" (154).

Rufel's fear of the unknown battles with Dessa's fear of losing personhood in yet another intimate arena, the conception of family and the identity of "Mammy." When Rufel starts idly reminiscing about her Mammy and the clothes she made, Dessa "lashed out" at her: "You ain't got no 'mammy,'" as she remembers her own mother (118). As Ashraf H. A. Rushdy explains, "Neither Dessa nor Rufel is confused; each realizes that the other is talking about a different person," but each senses a "disruption in her narrative and her life" by the other's memory of a Mammy (*Neo-Slave* 375). For Dessa, Mammy represents her memory of her family and her origins, but this memory also comes with loss and displacement. She exclaims to Rufel that "Mammy gave birth to ten chi'ren that come in the world living," but as she lists them, she remembers how many died or were "sold away" (119). By claiming that Mammy can only be hers, Dessa is trying to counter the loss of personhood that resulted from the sale of human property and the splitting of families.

For Rufel, Mammy represents what is left of the world she knows. Ostracized by her Charleston family because of her husband's shady dealings and left alone by his absence, Rufel clings to the memory of Mammy not as someone she held in slavery, but as the only one who cared for her. Repeatedly, she exclaims, "She loved me. And no darky can tell me different!" (125). Dessa's questioning of Rufel's narrative indeed causes a "disruption" because it plays right into Rufel's fear of the unknown. Dessa initially challenges Rufel to say Mammy's name. Rufel eventually comes up with "Dorcas" but soon faces the truth that she does not even know if Dorcas had children of her own before being bought by Rufel's parents. Rufel bemoans that Dessa has now "taken her beloved Mammy and put a stranger in her place" even as she continues to insist on love (128). After seeing Dessa's scars, Rufel is the one who admits aloud that there are two women named Mammy.

Because Rufel confronts the unknown she had feared, she is capable of crossing a rather large boundary in helping the fugitives conduct their con game. Dessa's fear of "the white woman" takes longer to overcome, which is understandable given the vast harm she has suffered from white people in the past. To take this step to understanding, however, a step Melville's and Twain's texts do not take, the characters must perceive the haunting. The turning point for Dessa comes when they have begun the con game, and she and Rufel are staying at a plantation house. When Dessa awakes to find Rufel struggling to get the white man who owns the house out of her bed, they join forces to push him out of the room. Dessa is shocked that "the white woman was subject to the same ravishment as me" and admits, "You can't do something like [fighting off a potential rapist] with someone and not develop some closeness, some trust" (201, 206). That Rufel can also be in danger of being treated as object rather than person changes their dynamics.

For her part, Rufel's knowledge of the workings of slavery becomes rather stark. She understands that it is the conflation of people with property that fuels the horrors of slavery; white people like her husband are driven by "seeing how much money you could make if you owned other people" (211). When Rufel gets angry at Dessa for not wanting her to go West with them and claims that "I'm talking friends," Dessa tries to deny the statement's meaning but then admits, "I wanted to believe I'd heard the white woman ask me to friend with her" (219).

With a nice narrative punch, it is at this very moment of revelation that Adam Nehemiah rejoins the plot by calling "Odessa" as he sees her on the street. When Dessa is put in a jail cell again, she is back to the gothic confinement of the beginning, and all of her initial fear returns: "I felt almost like I hadn't never left that first jail or this last white man" (223). The brand that marked her as someone's property starts itching. Skilled from her work with the con game, Rufel puts on a good show of being astounded by Nehemiah's claims, while Nehemiah brings back the traditional gothic coding, claiming "the blackness of the darky heart" (227). Nehemiah keeps claiming that if the sheriff will undress Dessa (or let him do it), her scars will prove his story that she is property.[28] Dessa's fear of losing personhood thus seems to rise from the dead to haunt her in yet another jail cell. But the intimacy the women have created works for them, as Rufel demands that the sheriff have a woman undress Dessa, and the enslaved woman brought to do so claims there are no scars. The insertion of a legal remedy in this jail cell ends differently than those in Melville's and Twain's novels because here an enslaved person gets to be witness. Aunt Chole, surely alluding to Clio, the muse of history, claims that Dessa has no scars, proving that the past has no hold on her, the brand does not equate her to property, and her ghosts are vanquished.

Unlike *Benito Cereno* and *Pudd'nhead Wilson*, the haunting lingering at the end of this narrative is thus not that of people denied personhood; Dessa and the fugitives head West to freedom. What does remain is Nehemiah's fear of crossed boundaries. Although he continually repeats, "I know her" to claim Dessa, he still does not know her, certainly not the way Rufel has come to know her, and he is left, as Dessa says, "low" (232). After denying Nehemiah and the horrid past he represents, Dessa and Rufel agree to call each other by their given names, signifying both personhood and equality. William crafts a con game that works because Rufel and Dessa understand each other's fears and are able to craft a narrative together.

※ ※ ※

Teresa A. Goddu argues against the conception of gothic narratives as "escapist," claiming instead that the gothic is "intensely engaged with historical concerns" (*Gothic* 2). When Melville, Twain, and Williams use the gothic conventions of ghosts, haunted houses, or dungeons, they are not simply adding literary flair; they are pointing to moments of fear. These fears are revealed through specific con games, but in each text the fear has a larger target: America writ large.

In *Benito Cereno*, the ending legal deposition reveals that Babo had affixed the captain's skeleton as figurehead on the front of the ship in place of "the ship's proper figure-head, the image of Christopher Colon, the discoverer of the New World" (97). Columbus only "discovers" the New World from the Europeans' viewpoint, and this discovery leads to the massive slave trade gobbling up African lives and depositing them in the Americas. The crudely scrawled message under the figurehead to "Follow Your Leader" thus has the doubly ironic meanings of showing the white sailors the fate that awaits them and of putting Captain Alexandro's body in place of Columbus as one more who followed in the wake of Europeans exploiting enslaved people to conquer the New World. The skeleton figurehead is a fitting gothic signal of the haunting of this New World.

Twain's nod to the larger historical concern is likewise dripping with bitter irony. Throughout the novel, the chapters are headed by quips from Wilson's calendar. The selection that heads the concluding chapter is "*The Discovery—It was wonderful to find America, but it would have been more wonderful to miss it*" (224). What would be missed in not "discovering" America, and to whom would its absence be "more wonderful"? Surely not the self-satisfied residents of Dawson's Landing with its "snug" houses. The answer can only be those who lose their freedom in a land that is "wonderful" in its promise of freedom.

Dessa Rose with its successful con game and happy ending likewise reaches for the larger depiction of America. In aiming to go West, the fugitives tap into a standard narrative of the American West as promising freedom. From the Mormons searching for religious freedom to the Dust Bowl refugees searching for economic freedom, the West as golden promise is a consistent drumbeat in the music of American identity. Even the recent novel *The Underground Railroad* has its protagonist headed West at the end to find freedom. In *Dessa Rose*, Harker has chosen the West because "it's not slavery there" (186). While "America" in *Benito Cereno* and *Pudd'nhead Wilson* is a dream of discovery that becomes a nightmare, in the epilogue of *Dessa Rose*, Dessa reveals that the group was able to settle in the West and find that elusive freedom. By imagining Dessa's friendship with Rufel, her escape to the West, and her recording of the story for her grandchildren, Williams is able to "own a summer in the nineteenth century," as she rewrites the destruction of the nineteenth-century novels.

Melville and Twain point to the moment of America's discovery as the source of haunting, yet Williams's ending strikes a different fear: the haunting of lost opportunity. In reality, the pregnant runaway did not meet the white woman harboring fugitives; she was instead executed for attempting to escape. Arthur Redding explains that "American haunts are also figures of another potential history and another potential America; they conjure up not only a forgotten history, but a more ghostly history that has never been allowed to happen" (7). For Dessa's historical model, no white woman understood her fear, no one intervened to save her, and no golden West existed as escape path. *Dessa Rose* allows a con game to work and a different America to exist, if only in the imagination.

- CHAPTER THREE -

Specters on Staircases in William Faulkner's *Absalom, Absalom!*, Eudora Welty's *Delta Wedding*, and Toni Morrison's *Song of Solomon*

In Toni Morrison's 1977 novel *Song of Solomon*, the African American protagonist Milkman Dead enters a house that has every sign of being haunted, even though he recalls how Hansel and Gretel's desire for candy led them into the house of a witch. Milkman has been lured to this house by the promise of gold that was buried in a cave nearby. His father and his aunt discovered the treasure years earlier when they were hiding in the cave after the white family who owned the house murdered their father. As in Hansel and Gretel's story, Milkman's desire results in a confrontation with a witchlike character. He climbs the stairs of the house and encounters Circe, the African American woman who was already a hundred years old when Milkman's father was a boy and is somehow still living in the house. In sending her character into a haunted house to be confronted by a specter, Toni Morrison does not just echo the standard gothic story of the sins of the past haunting the present. She instead rewrites two earlier iterations of this specific gothic scene in William Faulkner's 1936 novel *Absalom, Absalom!* and Eudora Welty's 1946 novel *Delta Wedding*. Both of these novels contain houses haunted by their previous owners' sins, both contain scenes where characters enter the houses seeking information, and both have these characters confronted on the stairs by mysterious African American women. Morrison may be intentionally rewriting both Faulkner and Welty.[1] My primary concern here, though, is what is at stake in this repeated portrayal of an African American specter standing on a staircase and impeding other characters' desire for knowledge. I will argue that slavery's conflation of people with property causes these women not just to haunt the houses but to haunt *as* houses, as the status of property they were assigned because of their race. While this status renders the women powerless in one sense, each uses her fusion with property to assert a different kind of possession, thereby becoming powerful specters.

Treated as property, the women testify to the horror of slavery's paradigm of race and property, a paradigm that reaches into the twentieth century.

The women's conflation with houses reveals the problems with the acquisition of property requisite for the American dream. As Nathaniel Hawthorne warns the reader in *The House of Seven Gables*, a beautiful house with expensive furnishings may contain "some low and obscure nook" with a "corpse, half-decayed, and still decaying" (229–30). Beginning with Edgar Allan Poe's "The Fall of the House of Usher" in 1839, the haunted house has a rich tradition in American literature, causing Eric Savoy to proclaim it as the "most persistent site, object, structural analogue, and trope of American gothic's allegorical turn" (9). Carol Margaret Davison adds that while the house in northern gothic works "assumes the role of a church," in southern gothic, it "regularly assumes the form of the slave plantation house" (56).² In their recreation of plantation houses, Faulkner, Welty, and Morrison are thus firmly planted in the American literary tradition. Dale Bailey explains, however, that "more than half the fun" of reading haunted house novels is seeing how writers can "deploy their conventions in startling ways" (6). He finds that the best novels "provoke our fears about ourselves and our society, and, at their best, they present deeply subversive critiques of all that we hold to be true—about class, about race, about gender, about American history itself" (6).

That is certainly the case here, as Faulkner, Welty, and Morrison interrogate slavery and its aftermath through the vexed concept of property. The haunted houses in their works are built in that American dream tradition of using monetary fortune to establish identity, but they become haunted with the horror of slavery's fusion of people with property. Even though Faulkner's character Clytie is the daughter of the white patriarch Thomas Sutpen, her black blood deems her to be the family's property, and as their property, she becomes one with the house. Aunt Studney and Circe live after the Civil War, but they too are threatened with being considered as property on the level of a house because the dispossession based on race continues. In each text, however, the women's conflation with property connects them with the houses in a way that allows agency; housekeeping becomes not just servitude but a "keeping" that signals ownership. In the staircase scenes, the specters use their possession to thwart or redirect other characters wanting to enter the houses to access the past. Clytie, Aunt Studney, and Circe as haunts from the past act as gatekeepers to it.

William Faulkner as a white man writing in the 1930s certainly has different motives in portraying this haunting than Eudora Welty as a white woman writing during World War II or Toni Morrison as an African American woman writing decades later. Faulkner's interest is in the tragedy of the white man's sin and fall, so Clytie represents this tragedy in becoming fused with Sutpen's property to the point of actually speaking in the voice of the house. As property, Clytie acts as a barrier to outsiders and consequently defines the family. Welty's interest lies in showing the blindness of the white Fairchild family to their dependence on African American labor in a system that mimics slavery even though the story is set in 1923. Her version of the specter is almost the opposite of Faulkner's in that Aunt Studney's entire existence is rooted in her disengagement from the family. Aunt Studney denies the family's assumption of ownership and asserts a different claim to property enacted through the practice of conjure. Morrison's interest is in what part of the past can be claimed as legacy by African Americans, and she creates a character in Circe whose motive in inhabiting the house is explicitly to gain revenge for being treated as property. Her employers, like Welty's Fairchilds, assume the continuation of slavery's conception of property. Circe's assertion of an owner's right to destroy the house becomes her property claim.

Written in different time periods for different purposes, the three scenes nonetheless align in their depictions of how people treated as property can in turn haunt that property and claim it as their own. Although critics have connected the depiction of Circe to Clytie, and one critic has connected Circe to Aunt Studney, no one has put these three works in conversation.[3] While critics generally read Circe as powerful, they usually deem Clytie as powerless and Aunt Studney as simply enigmatic.[4] Reading the three scenes together, though, reveals how all three women are powerless when conflated with property and powerful in becoming specters. Identifying the tension between power and powerlessness in each novel is a matter of reading through a gothic lens. Many critics have read *Absalom, Absalom!* as gothic, although Clytie is generally read as a passive ghost rather than an active specter. Ruth D. Weston provides a gothic reading of *Delta Wedding*, arguing that the scene depicting Marmion uses "gothic conventions," but she does not analyze Aunt Studney (102). And critics who want to write about Morrison and the gothic have thus far focused on *Beloved* instead of *Song of Solomon*.[5] The gothic traces of a specter in a haunted house, however, signal what evokes fear in these texts. Together, these specters standing on staircases reveal both the horror and the danger of conflating people with property.

THE PURSUIT OF PROPERTY

In all three novels, characters actively seek to acquire property, but because that property includes people, it contains hidden corpses and becomes haunted. In *Absalom, Absalom!*, Thomas Sutpen reenacts the American dream narrative of going from rags to riches. Rosa tells the story of Sutpen's mysterious entrance into the town of Jefferson and then his seemingly maniacal drive to build an estate. Sutpen along with the people he holds in slavery and a French architect spend two years building a house of "grim and castlelike magnificence," which is the key element of Sutpen's carefully executed plan to amass property so that he can have a particular identity (29). Sutpen grew up in an area in the mountains of West Virginia where there was no conception of private property: "where he lived the land belonged to anybody and everybody and so the man who would go to the trouble and work to fence off a piece of it and say 'This is mine' was crazy" (179).[6] It is only when Sutpen is turned away from the door of a rich man's house that he creates a design that centers on the accumulation of property: "I had a design: To accomplish it I should require money, a house, a plantation, slaves, a family—incidentally, of course, a wife. I set out to acquire these" (212). All of Sutpen's other actions in the book, including his decision to go to Haiti, his building of Sutpen's Hundred, his marriage to Ellen, and his refusal to acknowledge Charles, are propelled by his desire for property.[7] Rebecca Saunders adds that even the telling of the story is presented in terms of property when Rosa tells Quentin he will find the story useful later if he becomes a writer because he can sell the story to buy his wife a gown or a chair (69).[8]

Property is likewise central to Welty's novel *Delta Wedding*, although the white Fairchild family living off the labor of their black servants prefers not to think about the vulgar material realities of money and property. Nonetheless, their very town is called "Fairchilds," indicating their ownership of the entire area. The material possessions owned by the Fairchilds are detailed in the novel, from paintings and books to furniture, silverware, and glasses, almost as if someone were taking a careful inventory. The family, though, does not want the taint of money touching their world. Aunt Mac even washes the payroll, so the money will not be dirty. Brannon Costello points out that "the Fairchilds want to downplay the crass fact of money and its formative capacity in their privileged life" (22). The source of their money, the cotton fields harvested by servants, remains in the background, but it still exerts a power, as the visiting cousin Laura notices at tea: "The throb of the compress never stopped. Laura could feel it now in the handle of her cup, the noiseless vibration that trembled in the best china, was within it" (105).

The wedding at the center of the novel brings to light the complex questions of property: who owns which houses. When Dabney decides to get married, she asks her father, Battle, if she can have Marmion, a large but abandoned house on the Fairchild land. When Battle explains that the house is owned by Maureen, the mentally disabled cousin who lives with them, Dabney protests, "Marmion can't belong to Maureen!" Battle explains, "Yes—not legally, but really" and acknowledges that it is "complicated" (119). The house was supposedly inherited by Annie Laurie, Laura's mother, who moved out of the Delta and then gave the house to her brother Denis, Maureen's father. Denis died in the war, his wife now appears to be mentally unstable, and his only heir is Maureen. Later in the novel, Battle and Ellen tell Laura that when she grows up, she will have Marmion, although Aunt Tempe scolds Battle for bringing up the complicated property rights, saying, "You let Dabney have Marmion now, she wants it!" (326). The family's seemingly casual attitude towards property in the way they transfer houses back and forth derives not only from having an overabundance of everything, but also from their reliance on the unacknowledged labor of African Americans.

In *Song of Solomon*, Milkman grows up with a father obsessed with property. Macon Dead becomes a rich man by buying houses and leasing them to African American families. He carries the keys to all of the properties he owns in his pocket, so he can "[fondle] them from time to time" to make himself feel secure and "calm" (17).[9] When Milkman travels to Danville in search of gold, he realizes his father's obsession originated in the loss of his father: "As the son of Macon Dead the first, he paid homage to his own father's life and death by loving what that father had loved: property, good solid property, the bountifulness of life" (300). Milkman's grandfather had arrived in Danville "as ignorant as a hammer and broke as a convict," but in the course of sixteen years, he had acquired "one of the best farms in Montour County" (235).[10] In setting off on his journey to seek gold, Milkman simply follows in the family line of pursuing property. The possibility that the desire for property could be the positive search for home with its connotations of warmth, love, and family is evident, as Milkman visits the hometowns of his father and then his grandfather when he travels to Shalimar. He even becomes homesick for the comforts of Pilate's house when he realizes that his father's "distorted" drive for money was "a measure of his loss at his father's death" (300). *Absalom, Absalom!* and *Delta Wedding* also contain glimpses of the potential for property to equal home. Part of Thomas Sutpen's design in owning the grand house is so that "now he would take that boy in where he would never again need to stand on the outside of a white door and knock at it" (210). And the conversations about who owns Marmion are prompted in part by Laura's current need for a home now that her mother has died. Although Laura lives in Jackson with her father, Ellen sees Laura's need for a mother-figure and ponders giving her a home with them in Fairchilds.

The longing for house as home in all three works is surpassed, however, by the equation of property with power. Macon Dead holds his keys because they give him power. He tells Milkman to "own things. And let the things you own own other things. Then you'll own yourself and other people too" (55). In buying into the myth of the American dream, Macon Dead ironically occupies the original place of the white slaveholder and finds power in not just "owning" himself, but in owning other African Americans as well. Sutpen's design has power as its end goal as well. To counter the powerlessness he felt as the poor boy turned away, he thought he needed land, slaves, and "a fine house to combat them with" (192). The house is a weapon of power. In *Delta Wedding*, even Robbie Reid, the outsider who marries the family's favorite son, George, reveals a desire for power. When she sets off on a long walk to the Fairchilds' house in the heat of the day, she kicks the servant Pinchy out of a shed, so she can rest in the shade during her walk. Robbie muses over who might own Marmion while she is in the shed that she has claimed.

Sutpen's Hundred, Marmion, and the Butler house do not become sites of power or homes to provide the characters security because they instead become haunted. That it is houses that signal the gothic tension in these narratives is no accident. In addition to being the most visible marker of a person's success, houses also signal the connection of the home to the uncanny, according to Sigmund Freud. In his study of the uncanny, Freud examines the German word for uncanny, "unheimlich," and discovers that its root word means "homely." He explains that "the uncanny is that class of the frightening which leads back to what is known of old and long familiar" (220). It is not, therefore, the strange and alien that sparks the uncanny, but the reoccurrence of the familiar or homely. Although the characters' need for a home gets perverted by their desire for power, each of the houses is connected to the familiar and specifically to the characters' families. These connections intensify the problem that what was supposed to be a home becomes a haunted house.

And the haunting shows. Just as Hawthorne's successful man is depicted as a beautiful house with a decaying corpse hidden in some lower room, these houses contain the metaphorical corpses of their owners' sins, sins that signal the intertwining of property and racism.[11] In *Absalom, Absalom!*, when Faulkner crafts his haunted house, he borrows the materials directly from Edgar Allan Poe.[12] In "The Fall of the House of Usher" the narrator explains Usher's belief in the "sentience of all vegetable things," which over time has come to include "the gray stones of the home of his forefathers" (209). Mr. Compson tells Quentin the story of Sutpen's Hundred and likewise imagines that "houses actually possess a sentience, a personality and character acquired not from the people who breathe or have breathed in them so much as rather inherent in the wood and brick or begotten upon the wood and brick by the man or men who conceived and built them" (67). The house thus personifies the character of the man who built it, so that even before knowing the full story of Sutpen, Quentin can sense the house's sentience. He recalls as a boy being dared by other children to approach the house that they all knew must be haunted, not only because strangers from Arkansas who stopped there unawares had fled in fright, but because of its sheer decay: "the rotting shell with its sagging portico and scaling walls" (173).[13] Martin Kreiswirth points out that Faulkner first entitled his narrative "Dark House," indicating that from the very beginning he was imagining a haunted house.

Sutpen's Hundred becomes this haunted house because of the hidden corpse of Sutpen's racism and greed. He gains the money to build the house from his time as an overseer of enslaved people in Haiti, which includes his quelling of a bloody slave rebellion. The method by which he overcomes a force of enslaved people armed with machetes and vastly outnumbering his side remains mysterious.[14] He then supposedly buys the land from Indians with the Spanish gold he acquired in Haiti, although the town is convinced that the deal is not completely legitimate: "that hundred miles of land which he took from a tribe of ignorant Indians, nobody knows how" (10).[15] He uses more slave labor to build the house; for two years he has the men he brought from Haiti work nonstop building.[16] He also seemingly enslaves a French architect who tries to escape but is captured by a posse of white men with dogs and forced back to work as if he were a runaway as well. The house is then built in sin: possible theft from the Native Americans and the labor and blood of enslaved people.[17]

While Faulkner's depiction of haunting is overt and dramatic, the haunting in *Delta Wedding* is more subtle, as Welty focuses more on what the white characters do not want to acknowledge and depicts the house through the point of view of children. When Laura and Roy see Marmion, Laura first perceives it as a "wonderful house in the woods," but then she notices that "it was all quiet, and unlived in, surely; the dark water was going in front of it, not a road" (262). That "dark water" is the Yazoo River, the "River of Death," alluding to the River Styx and a journey into the underworld (283). The children see an estate overrun by vegetation with tiny leaves "taking the posts" and the bad omen of a dead mockingbird on the steps (263–64).[18] Although Dabney is older than the children, she too is unaware of the potential problems with her new house, instead picturing it as a "magnificent temple-like, castle-like house" (211). Her image eerily echoes the description of Sutpen's Hundred as a house of "grim and castlelike magnificence" (29). When thinking of her "eagerness" to live in Marmion, she thinks, "How sweet life was, and how well she could hold it, pluck it, eat it, lay her cheek to it—oh, no one else knew. The juice of life and the hot, delighting taste and the fragrance and warmth to the cheek, the mouth" (209). The problem is which fruit she may be contemplating. When Dabney rather flippantly asks Maureen for the house, "Look, honey—will you give your house to me?" Maureen responds, "You can have my house-la, and a bite-la of my apple too" (119). Marmion may very well be the forbidden fruit, a house haunted by its past.[19]

Although Marmion's past does not have the explicit racial resonances of Sutpen's Hundred or the Butler house, it was surely built with African American labor. The Fairchild fields in 1923 are still being worked by African Americans living in pseudoslavery conditions. Constructed by James Fairchild in 1890, the house was abandoned that same year because Fairchild was killed in a duel with a neighbor. Fairchild's wife then died of a broken heart, and two maiden aunts took the children to another house to raise. The duel James Fairchild engages in reflects the stereotypical Southern code of honor, and the architecture signals its link to the old South. Elizabeth Christine Russ comments that "deliriously hubristic, like the Tower of Babel or the romantic legend of the South, Marmion is doomed to fail on a grand scale" (92).[20] Even romantic Dabney realizes that the house's past "had lately come to horrify her" (210).

In *Song of Solomon*, the Butler house is haunted by its previous white owner's sins, but Morrison changes the dynamic by depicting an African American protagonist encountering the house. While Thomas Sutpen assumes his house will establish his power, and the Fairchilds seem mostly oblivious to any problems with their ownership of property, Milkman Dead is primed to see the Butler house as haunted because he hears the family's history before he visits the house (238). In his search for its location, he runs across Reverend Cooper, who tells him the story of his grandfather's death. Cooper explains that "everybody knew" who killed Macon Dead: "Same people Circe worked for—the Butlers" (232). When Milkman naively asks why no one did anything, Cooper responds, "White folks didn't care, colored folks didn't dare ... Besides, the people what did it owned half the country. Macon's land was in their way" (232). The Butlers are now all dead, however, and only the rotten house remains, a house that "looked as if it had been eaten by a galloping disease, the sores of which were dark and fluid" (220). Knowing the history, Milkman necessarily sees the house as "dark, ruined, evil" (238). From Faulkner's "Dark House" to Welty's "dark water" flowing in front of Marmion to Morrison's "dark, ruined, evil" house, the darkness points not only to the sins their owners committed in acquiring the houses, but to the "dark" race who worked, suffered, and even died because of these houses. It is little wonder that at the heart of each of these houses stands a "dark" mysterious presence.

SPECTERS AND PROPERTY

The specters standing in the houses harken back to earlier portrayals of African American women treated as property, beginning with the damsels in distress that I examine in chapter 1. Clytie, Circe, and Aunt Studney are linked to the houses of white families. Clytie and Circe have spent their entire lives housekeeping, and although Aunt Studney's job is not clear, certainly the other African American women in *Delta Wedding* who work as domestic servants employ their lives maintaining the Fairchild houses.[21] Without the agency to choose other pursuits, the women are depicted only in relation to these houses. We do not see them in their own homes, and none of them has children. While earlier in life Circe acted as a midwife, when Milkman encounters her, she has withdrawn from the community into the house. The resulting traumas the women may have experienced because of their stations in life are also not narrated. In particular, the threat of rape is left unexamined, although its menace is certainly present, as Clytie's mother must have been raped by Thomas Sutpen to produce Clytie. The women are depicted instead as appendages to the white families' properties; thus the conflation of these women with property is doubled in narratives that depict them only in relation to that property. That Aunt Studney's and Circe's circumstances echo Clytie's attests to the endurance of slavery's structure of property relations. The past conflation, in gothic fashion, does not die.

In Faulkner's version of the specter, Clytie occupies a tenuous position in the Sutpen household as both daughter and enslaved person, both family and property. This ambiguity creates her mystery, as she does not fit neatly into the bifurcated black and white worlds on which this southern society is founded. Keith E. Byerman explains that she "exists as almost pure cipher. All the terms associated with her—'inscrutable,' 'sphinx,' 'Cerberus'—suggest not so much a being as a condition entirely outside of time" ("Untold" 130). As a "condition," Clytie has no "will" in Byerman's assessment and therefore no power of her own. Although the secret existence of Thomas Sutpen's mixed-race son, Charles Bon, destroys the Sutpen family, Sutpen's mixed-race daughter, Clytie, simply lives in the house with the family. Her gender seemingly negates her danger, as she does not threaten to inherit or to produce a family line of mixed-race Sutpens. However, the inscrutable "condition" that renders her powerless and "outside of time" also ironically makes her seem supernatural. In Quentin's memory of meeting her when dared as a boy to approach the house, he imagines that she "might have been any age up to ten thousand years" because she had "grown old up to a certain point just like normal people do, then had stopped" (174). Clytie then "might well have been the ghost if one was ever needed" (175).

A ghost is indeed needed for a house to be haunted, and when Rosa enters the house and finds Clytie blocking the stairs, the full characterization of Clytie emerges as both powerless property in the eyes of the law and powerful specter through the lens of the gothic.[22] As Rosa details her meeting with Clytie at the base of the stairs, she does not describe Clytie as a person. Instead, Rosa refers to her several times as simply "the face" or the "coffee-colored face" and later as "the body." Rosa can seemingly only handle Clytie in parts, thus dehumanizing her. Those parts have strange power, though, as Rosa imagines the "face" had "known to the second when I was to enter, had waited there during that entire twelve miles behind that walking mule and watched me draw nearer and nearer and enter the door at last as it had known" (109). Rosa later describes Clytie as a "something," a "force" that stops Rosa's forward motion, and a "brooding awareness." The "brooding" links Clytie to the house, which is also "brooding," and as Rosa describes Clytie's voice, the specific source of Clytie's mysterious power becomes clear.

As Sutpen's property, Clytie takes on the voice of the house. Rosa's reduction of Clytie to the "Supten face" leads her to see Clytie as a "replica" of Supten, a kind of gothic double left "to preside upon his absence" (110). When Clytie finally speaks the words, "Dont you go up there, Rosa," Rosa imagines, "it had not been she who spoke but the house itself that said the words" (111). Alia C.Y. Pan argues that this conflation occurs because "Rosa refuses to recognize Clytie but instead collapses Clytie's subjectivity with the space of the house, so that Clytie's voice becomes Sutpen's and her body becomes an '*instrument*' of the master's will" (428). Clytie can become one with the house because she is already an article of property. Even as Sutpen's daughter (and his double), she is not granted full personhood. She is not free to leave the house because she in effect *is* the house. In this fusion of property, however, Clytie becomes a speaking specter, and it is her "coffee-colored face" that takes on the agency of the house to speak. If the house became haunted because Sutpen used the bodies and blood of those he held in slavery to build it, it now correspondingly speaks through the body and voice of an enslaved person. Thus, while Pan is correct that Clytie's voice becomes Sutpen's, the reverse is also true: Sutpen's voice and that of the house he builds to manifest his identity speaks in Clytie's voice. Though the family possesses her, she possesses the house, the emblem of Sutpen identity.

Unlike Clytie, Aunt Studney in *Delta Wedding* refuses her society's paradigm, which extends the racial divide of slavery with African American servants remaining as subordinates bolstering the white family's wealth. The Fairchild family's obliviousness to their servants, however, is matched by Aunt Studney's refusal to engage with them. Laura describes her as "coal-black, old as the hills, with her foot always in the road; on her back she carried a big sack that nearly weighed her down" (262). Aunt Studney's indefinite age, as old as "hills," gives her an air of mystery. Aunt Temple earlier asks Ellen, "Is old Aunt Studney dead yet?" suggesting that Aunt Studney, much like Clytie, has seemingly lived longer than is usual (200). That Laura further describes Aunt Studney as "coal-black" suggests that she has no white blood. Unlike Clytie, whose very face signals her mixed parentage, Aunt Studney's skin color represents her separation from the white family. Her distance is confirmed by the only verbal response she gives throughout the narrative: "Ain't studyin' you" (262). This distance becomes her entire identity, as her name "Aunt Studney" is a simplified version of her phrase.[23] Aunt Studney is "inscrutable," as David McWhirter labels her, so the full mystery of her character cannot be accessed and therefore cannot be controlled (119).

While this inscrutability may render her opaque, it also makes her powerful. Laura asks Roy, "Are you scared of Aunt Studney?" (263). Although Roy is hesitant about admitting that he is, "No. Yes, I am," he is quick to add, "Papa's scared of her too" (263). In a reading of Welty's female characters in *A Curtain of Green*, Susan V. Donaldson argues that in contrast to Faulkner's grotesque women, Welty's women who make "spectacles" of themselves are "outrageous and boundary-breaking" ("Making a Spectacle" 583). Aunt Studney's odd behavior isolates her in a way that strangely makes her even more visible and thus more powerful. Roy issues Laura a "double-dog-dare" to look into Aunt

Studney's sack. Daring would indeed be required, as that "big sack that nearly weighed her down" confirms her power. Roy's comment that "nobody knows what she's got in the sack" is telling, in that Aunt Studney is not included in his conception of people. Nonetheless, Aunt Studney herself knows what is in her sack, and in claiming property, she is claiming that she is a person herself, despite Roy's logic, for only people can own property.

What she might carry inside the sack amplifies her power. From Roy's comment that Aunt Studney's sack is "where Mama gets her babies" (263) to the "masculine sexuality" that Suzan Harrison identifies in her name, Aunt Studney's character is linked to fertility and birth (55). Once Laura and Roy follow Aunt Studney inside Marmion, Laura notices bees flying in the house and guesses that they are coming from Aunt Studney's sack. The bees spread everywhere until Laura thinks, "The place was alive" (266). Laura hears "a hum everywhere, in everything," suggesting that Aunt Studney's connection to fertility gives her the power to control life and death. This power renders Laura "electrified" (266). Then Laura realizes the perils of what else Aunt Studney might own: "It occurred to Laura that Aunt Studney was not on the lookout for things to put in, but was watching to keep things from getting out" (266). Peggy Whitman Prenshaw links her sack to Pandora's Box, and indeed there may be both good and ill lurking inside (57). Laura receives an ominous clue later about those "things" when Roy throws her into the river. The scene underwater fulfills Laura's imagination of what the inside of the bag would look like: "As though Aunt Studney's sack had opened after all, like a whale's mouth, Laura opening her eyes head down saw its insides all around her—dark water and fearful fishes" (267). Aunt Studney's sack becomes the "dark water" that signals the haunting of the house. That the inside of the sack is "like a whale's mouth" suggests that like the biblical Jonah, Laura is swallowed because she has gone where she is not supposed to be.[24] Aunt Studney's sack is full of fear; her property makes her powerful.

In the Fairchild family view, however, she is just another black servant, even if she is a bit eccentric. When Laura "fearfully" asks Roy, "Where does she live?" Roy is a bit unsure and answers, "Oh, back on our place somewhere. Back of the Deadening" (262, 263). The vagueness of "somewhere" indicates that, unlike Clytie, who does not seem able to leave Sutpen's Hundred, Aunt Studney is not easily placed into a specific and thus knowable and controllable space. Roy's assertion that Aunt Studney lives on "our place," however, signals ownership of Aunt Studney in that she becomes included in and conflated with the family's property. This claim is undercut, however, by his guess that she lives "back of the deadening." The "Fairchild Deadening" is the land "where the old Fairchilds had started, deadened off the trees to take the land a hundred years ago" (233). Land that was cleared was claimed by the Fairchilds, but Aunt Studney lives "back of" or beyond the territory they have claimed, so she is not part of their property. That she lives in a place beyond the "deadening" further hints at her supernatural quality, as she exists somehow beyond death. Roy later points to "a dot of cabin," which was "exactly like the rest" as where he thinks she lives (268). Donnie McMahand takes the "ruinous state of her dwelling place" as an indication that "her poverty and implied degradation override her uniqueness" and thus diminish the depiction of her power. He argues, "That she opens and closes her bag as she chooses and controls her verbal exchanges with the Fairchilds indeed confers agency to her character, but such agency is so diminished that it doesn't disrupt in any genuine way the habits and routines of the people she scorns" (179). The Fairchilds indeed do not perceive her power, and Welty depicts a child audience for her actions, but the reader can certainly discern what the characters are missing. In her refusal to engage, Aunt Studney denies that she is their property.

Moreover, Aunt Studney even makes her own claim to property. When Roy and Laura see her enter the house, Roy cries, "She's going into Dabney's house!" (263). They follow her inside, and Laura notices: "There was an accusing, panting breathing, and the thud of a big weight planted in the floor" (264). Aunt Studney "planted" the sack that signifies her ownership of property right in the middle of Fairchild property, suggesting that the bag will root and grow. The "accusing" reaction signals that it is not "Dabney's house" and that Roy and Laura are the ones trespassing. Legal property rights run up against Aunt Studney's mysterious gothic energy.

In *Song of Solomon*, the character of Circe echoes Clytie in the fusion of her identity with the haunted house and echoes Aunt Studney in her resistance to becoming reduced to property. Like her fellow specters, Clytie's position reflects a tension between agency and captivity. Her powerless state in life has rendered her powerful in specter form, signaled by her impossible age. Reverend Cooper tells Milkman that Circe "was a hundred when I was a boy"; since Milkman's father is now seventy-two and is four or five years older than Cooper, Circe would now have to be around one hundred and sixty. Milkman therefore does not expect to see her at the Butler house and is very confused when he does. The woman he meets is "so old she was colorless. So old only her mouth and eyes were distinguishable features in her face. Nose, chin, cheekbones, forehead, neck all had surrendered their identity to the pleats and crochetwork of skin committed to constant change" (240). He then has to ask, "You're Circe, aren't you?" (241).

Impossible as it may be that she is still alive, she admits, "My name is Circe" (241). Her name is further indication that she is not merely human. Judith Fletcher traces the parallels between Morrison's character and the mythic Circe, finding that the "lush greenery" and "inaccessibility" of the Butler house "makes it a veritable island" comparable to Circe's island (412). Fletcher adds that "Circe is a strange combination of appalling decrepitude and sexual power. Like the ancient tale she is in decline, but still possessed of a compelling allure" (412). Milkman in fact is confused about her age and her status as a mortal being because she has a "face so old it could not be alive," but at the same time she has "the strong, mellifluent voice of a twenty-year-old girl" (240). Just as the mythic Circe is a fertility goddess, this Circe is a midwife (Fletcher 413). Milkman realizes she is a "healer, deliverer," and "in another world she would have been the head nurse at Mercy" (246).

In this world, however, she seems trapped in a haunted house playing the part of a specter and perhaps even a witch. A second literary allusion woven into the scene is the fairy tale "Hansel and Gretel." Milkman walks towards a "crumbling house," as if it were made of cookie dough, and becomes a child driven by hunger. Whereas Hansel and Gretel are driven by candy, Milkman is driven by gold supposedly hidden in a cave, a story equally implausible as the fairy tale, but Milkman's hunger for property leads him to believe it. His greed further compels him to enter the decrepit house. Even though he becomes suffocated at first by a "hairy animal smell," he pushes forward and begins to smell "ginger root," connecting the Butler house with the gingerbread house of the fairy tale. He then sees Circe at the top of the stairs and can only think of every witch from every dream he ever had: "dreams every child had, of the witch who chased him down dark alleys, between lawn trees, and finally into rooms from which he could not escape" (239). Circe is clearly powerful, and Milkman cannot flee. He realizes that "there was no way for him to resist climbing up towards her outstretched hands, her fingers spread wide for him, her mouth gaping open for him, her eyes devouring him" (239).

Although Milkman at first feels completely "helpless" to resist Circe and overwhelmed by her impossible age, as she talks about her life, he suspects she cannot leave. He asks, "Is this your house now? Did they will you this? Is that why you have to stay here?" (242). Raised by the father who worships property and on a single-minded quest for gold, Milkman does not understand Circe's relationship to the Butler house and asks the wrong questions about property. He tells her, "You should leave this place" and offers her money (246). She refuses his help and answers, "You think I don't know how to walk when I want to walk?" (246). He still does not understand her position and asks if she loved the Butlers "that much." Milkman appears to be correct in reading Circe as somehow stuck in the house; not only can she not leave, but she apparently cannot even die. He is wrong, however, in assessing the reason. She is not Clytie becoming the voice, agent, and property of the white master when he is gone, and she is definitely not staying out of love. Circe explains that once Mrs. Butler sold everything and let all of the other servants go, she "killed herself rather than do the work I'd been doing all my life" (247). Like Aunt Studney, Circe refuses at the end to be regarded as a pseudoslave and simply someone's property. Mrs. Butler sold all the property that gave the family its identity, but she did not want to lose Circe. When Reverend Cooper wonders if Milkman has come to exact revenge on the Butler family for the murder of his grandfather, he assures him that "any evening up left to do, Circe took care of" (233). Circe remains in the house and in the world to complete the "evening up" and to oversee the destruction of the Butler house, their final piece of property. She may not "want to walk" or perhaps even cannot flee, but within these walls, she exists as a supernatural specter.

ASCENDING STAIRCASES

All three women take on the identity of specters, impossibly old and mysteriously powerful, and stay behind in these houses as the ghostly residue of the sins that the white owners committed in the name of obtaining property. They are not defying death, however, just to scare the other characters. The women inhabit the houses to block the other characters from their particular quests. Rosa (and later Quentin), Roy and Laura, and Milkman enter the houses seeking connections to their families, not fully realizing the complexity of those links and the trauma of those histories. In entering the haunted houses, they seek to travel back in time, a movement depicted as nothing less than dangerous. The specters seemingly still exist from these pasts, so the confrontations are not just between humans and specters. They are also between the present and the past, between the desire to understand history and the need to keep secret memories that are painful. Thus, the specters must thwart or at least warn the other characters against their quests. While the existence of a ghost or specter already signals a rupture in time, as it indicates that the past exists in the present, these three narratives (unlike the postmodern narratives I analyze in chapter 5) resist the idea of a reversal of that rupture, the present going back into the past, because of the dangers lurking there. In each case, when the outside character barges into a haunted house desiring to enter the past, the specters must act as barriers to prevent this rupture. By being gatekeepers, the specters' connection to the property of the houses allows them a gothic possession of property and the power to guard it. The job of housekeeping shifts from servitude to a form of ownership.

In each book, the confrontation happens at the base of a staircase. Gothic works use architecture as a prime way of communicating meaning. What is locked in the dungeon or the closet is representative of what characters fear or wish to hide. Eugenia DeLamotte points to an "anxiety about boundaries" as the driving source of gothic terror: "all the major Gothic conventions involve either literal or metaphorical boundaries and sometimes both. Most obviously this is true of the architectural settings. Castle walls isolate an inside world from an outside world, preventing intrusion from without and escape from within" (20). The boundaries between the inside world and the outside are figured in these works as between what knowledge may be hidden in the houses and the characters who enter to acquire that knowledge. The desire to climb the stairs not only reflects the spatial metaphor of ascent to achieve this higher level of knowledge; it also reflects the need to enter the private areas of a house. As American houses, Sutpen's Hundred, Marmion, and the Butler house do not have castle walls, keeps, or dungeons, so the closed doors and private spaces of the upstairs rooms reserved for family members and intimates of a house signal the crossing of boundaries. The characters want to cross the boundaries because they seek connection to their families. In these three works, however, that boundary is not a door or a wall but the specters in their role as ghostly reminders of the entanglement of race and property.

In *Absalom, Absalom!*, when Rosa traverses the twelve miles between her house in town and Sutpen's Hundred in the country, she is ostensibly responding to the "summons" she receives via Wash Jones. But her haste comes from her desire to be needed by someone and to be connected to family. Rosa was, as she puts it, "born too late" (15). Her mother was "at least forty" and died in childbirth, making Rosa "the price of her mother's life and never to be permitted to forget it" (46). She was then raised by her aunt and her father, but her aunt skips town with a horse trader, and her father shuts himself in the attic protesting the war and then dies, leaving Rosa a "pauper and orphan" (66). Although Rosa lives vicariously through the tales of Judith's romance, she is mocked by the family at Sutpen's Hundred. When Ellen and Judith visit her as they prepare for Judith's wedding, they laugh at Rosa's offer to help Judith learn to "keep house." The possibility that she might actually be useful to her family propels her those twelve miles into the barrier of Clytie.

Since Rosa's role in life has been as housekeeper, her confrontation with this house's keeper is a battle over possession of space. In her study of "haunted housekeeping," Holly Blackford analyzes the tension between "heroines" who wish to command a household and their female servants who intercede. She finds that "tragically, the heroines do not understand the servant's implied message warning them against trying to take possession of a house, which in the end only takes possession of women" (237). In imagining that the family needs her, Rosa indeed posits herself as a heroine who already knows how to keep a house. Clytie, however, understands too well the dangers of this particular haunted house and its current possession of a murdered corpse, so she acts as barrier to the outsider.

Entering the house only to find that she was not needed, to find, "I had come, not too late as I had thought, but come too soon," Rosa is also unknowingly replaying the incident that first caused Thomas Sutpen to create his design to acquire property (108). As a boy when he is sent to deliver a message to the large house of the man employing his father, he is turned away by a black servant and is thus baptized into the world of class differences where he is not the equal of the white man who owns the house. Thadious Davis, in a convincing close reading of the staircase scene, points out the parallels: "Clytie's presence reminds Rosa that she is cut off from significant areas of life, particularly from family participation, just as the Negro, symbolically represented by the 'balloon face' and the 'monkey nigger,' serves to remind Sutpen of his poor-white origins. It is not only that Rosa is not a wife, but that finally she is not sister, daughter, aunt, or niece. She is and remains an outsider" (*Faulkner's* 208). Although Rosa also hints at a legal claim when she repeatedly refers to Sutpen's Hundred as her sister Ellen's house, Clytie's presence questions Rosa's claim to blood ties.

With her "coffee-colored face" speaking from within the house literally and metaphorically, Clytie marks the line between Rosa as outside without a valid claim and the family as inside possessing the house. Clytie actually plays this role of barrier throughout the narrative. She prevents Wash Jones from coming any further than the kitchen door, even when he is bringing food to sustain the three women during the war. In one of Clytie's few utterances, she says, "Stop right there, white man. Stop right where you is" (226). Although she identifies him specifically as white and thus above her in racial status, she speaks in the voice of the family who owns her, shunning the social company of the lower-class character. Clytie likewise plays the barrier in the scene when Quentin and his boyhood friends approach the house. Her question, "What do you want?" sends them all running (174). Clytie, who seemingly has no agency as only property, uses her voice in the text to enact a barrier to Sutpen property, in essence taking the agency to construct the limits of the family.

Yet Clytie's voice, even as Rosa imagines it fused with the house and with the "demon" Sutpen himself, does not arrest Rosa in her drive to discover what is upstairs. Rosa registers Clytie's saying, "Dont you go up there Rosa" as Rosa's "still advancing body" reaches the stairs, but it is not until Clytie touches her that Rosa then "did stop dead" (111). The touch shocks Rosa because the "touch of flesh with flesh" is not only intimate, but it also brings Clytie back from the world of objects to the world of people.[25] She is not house but person. The problem for Rosa is that as legal property, Clytie is safely distant and powerless: she is a "face," a "body," and the "house itself." As a person, Clytie has a "black arresting and untimorous hand" that suggests agency, and Rosa responds by pointing to Clytie's race: "Take your hand off me, nigger!" (112). Rosa uses the ugly racial slur to distance herself from Clytie. As Masami Sugimori argues, that Rosa first mistakes Clytie for Henry suggests "Clytie's visual sameness," so Rosa must use language to separate herself from Clytie (10). I would argue that the language is used by Rosa to put Clytie back into the box labeled "property," but as a Sutpen family member Clytie has, as Davis puts it, a "natural place" causing Rosa then to cry, "And you too? And you too, sister, sister?" implying a kinship with someone she ironically refuses to acknowledge as fully a person (112–13). Rosa now hopes she is having a nightmare and that Henry will soon be telling her to wake up. Instead, she hears Judith at the top of the stairs ask, "Yes, Rosa?" as if it is Rosa who came to the house needing assistance instead of being called to help Judith (120).[26] Judith is also standing before "that closed door" of a room that Rosa never enters, so she never sees Charles Bon's body for herself, does not offer comfort to her niece, and in essence does not become family. Although Judith tells Clytie, "Miss Rosa will be here for dinner," she also adds, "Shall we go downstairs?" (121). As "Miss Rosa" who must remain downstairs, she is company, not sister and not family. She has no claim to the house. Clytie, though powerless as the family's property, is not just a "sister" but is also the keeper of the house and succeeds in keeping Rosa from the corpse that signifies the house's haunting.

In true gothic fashion, the staircase scene is doubled, although the second version is not an exact repetition of the first. This time, Quentin accompanies Rosa, and this time, she will not be stopped. The very reason Rosa summons Quentin in the first place and tells him the story of Sutpen is to persuade him to accompany her to Sutpen's Hundred so she can once again try to penetrate the secrets of the house. Her telling spawns the subsequent tellings by Mr. Compson, Quentin, and Shreve. Thus the whole book is driven by Rosa's need to repeat the staircase scene to try to thwart Clytie's power. In the second iteration, it is Rosa who seems to have mystic powers. Although she has not been to Sutpen's Hundred in years, she tells Quentin, "There's something in that house ... Something living in it. Hidden in it. It has been out there for four years, living hidden in that house" (140). Although Rosa is still scared of Clytie and whimpers, "She's going to try to stop me," she is determined to press forward, fussing at Quentin for neglecting to bring a pistol and handing him a hatchet to carry (291). Having heard Sutpen's story, Quentin also wants entrance into the house. He wants to cross into the past to get answers to his questions, but he can sense for himself the conflation of the house with the people who built it, as he smells "desolation and decay as if the wood of which it was built were flesh" (293).[27] This time, Rosa knocks Clytie down, thereby crossing through the barrier, and goes on up the stairs. In picking Clytie up, Quentin thinks, "Yes. She is the one who owns the terror" (295). The phrasing is significant here, as Quentin does not say Clytie is terrified, as if she were a person expressing a human emotion, or that Clytie is terrifying, as if she were only a specter warding off intruders. Her existence as property means she was owned, but here as still acting as the house itself, she "owns" one thing: she "owns" terror. Whatever legal claim that Rosa may have at this point to her sister's house dissolves in the face of Clytie's gothic possession, which allows her to be the boundary to knowledge.

Quentin, however, also breaks through the boundary, follows Rosa up the stairs, and meets Henry Sutpen. Neither Rosa nor Quentin, however, finds the connection they sought in forging up the stairs. Rosa returns with "eyes wide and unseeing" and a face with a quality of "bloodlessness" (296). Quentin's reaction is dire and echoes Poe's narrator in "The Raven," as Quentin thinks, "Nevermore of peace. Nevermore of peace. Nevermore. Nevermore. Nevermore" (298–99). In crossing into the past and meeting the dying Henry, yet another specter in the Sutpen house, Quentin sees further evidence of Sutpen's design and fall when he discovers that Henry killed his brother because of his race. Quentin is then stuck in the damned eternal past of Poe's narrator.[28] What Quentin encounters is the terror that Clytie owns, the full effect of turning people into property. He and Rosa should have heeded the specter's warning.

In *Delta Wedding* when Roy and Laura go to Marmion, Roy treats the outing as a kind of adventure where he will claim territory, while Laura, much like Rosa, is primarily motivated by her need to feel a part of the Fairchild family even though her mother has died. She frets about not being able to be a flower girl in the wedding because she is still in mourning. She clings at times to Ellen, wondering if there were "some unused love" in "Aunt Ellen's eyes" and "could she get it" (109). The games Laura plays with her cousins display this need for belonging but also her hesitation. She describes a circle game: "It was funny how sometimes you wanted to be in a circle and then you wanted out of it in a rush. Sometimes the circle was for you, sometimes against you, if you were It" (161). The children then move on to a game of tag, but when Laura returns to the tree designated as "home," no one is around to see that she has claimed her freedom and declared "home" (163). To Laura, home seems tenuous.

She consequently enters Marmion to claim the Fairchilds as her family, while Roy enters to claim Marmion as his legal property. The children are confronted, however, with Aunt Studney's spectral claim to Marmion. Laura initially responds to Marmion with awe; she is enchanted by the double staircase and the large chandelier in the entry with its "clusters of soft and burned-down candles, as though a great thing had sometime happened here" (264). Roy responds with a desire to control. Though he is only eight years old, he feels confident in his right as a male member of the Fairchild family to enter the house and claim ownership of the property. He cries to Laura, "Run up the stairs!" immediately assuming the privilege of entering the private family space of the house. Laura is less sure of her right, whispering "Aunt Studney" to draw Roy's attention to the woman in their path and asking the question of ownership: "Did you say this is *Dabney's* house?" (264). In addition to the foreboding Aunt Studney, Laura notices the "closed doors in the walls all around" (265). Although she does not comprehend the full import of the house's haunting, Laura intuits the gothic details. Roy, on the other hand, claims the house, telling Laura, "Make yourself at home. Run up the stairs" (265). And when Laura asks, "Is it still the Delta in here?" Roy answers, "Croesus, Laura! Sure it is!" as he "with a jump" begins to run up the stairs (265).

In the meantime, Aunt Studney has not only "planted" her mysterious bag in the middle of the floor, but she begins a performance of conjure, establishing her own claim to the house. While Roy is running up the stairs, Aunt Studney "[turns] herself in place around and around, arms bent and hovering" (265). Although Laura is too afraid to follow Roy up the stairs, she spies a beautiful little piano and touches a key. The sound has an echo: "And all at once Aunt Studney sounded too—a cry high and threatening like the first note of a song at a ceremony, a wedding or a funeral, and like the bark of a dog too, somehow" (265). Laura cannot discern whether Aunt Studney's cry is for good or ill. If the cry is for a wedding, the sound, along with the bees connoting fertility, may suggest that the conjure is beneficial.[29] Aunt Studney may actually be blessing the bride's future house. The other possibility, which is the cry is that of a funeral, and Aunt Studney is cursing the house, seems to fit better with the rest of her behavior displaying her separation or even disdain for this white family. The bride is marrying the overseer, a man who brags that he has figured out his job because "it is just a matter of knowing how to handle your Negroes" (183). Aunt Studney may therefore be countering the claims of both the Fairchild family and their overseer. Laura's reaction suggests that despite her confusion, she senses the danger Aunt Studney poses. She realizes that "she could not stand Dabney's house any longer" and tells Roy to "come down" and to "come back" (265–66).

Roy, however, is having too much fun asserting control over everything he sees. He not only claims the property as "home," but he is able to see out a window at the top of the house: "I see Troy! I see the Grove—I see Aunt Primrose, back in her flowers! I see *Papa*! I see the whole creation. Look, look at me, Papa!" (266). In seeing the "whole creation," Roy imagines that he is an all-powerful eye, a god of sorts. Even after Aunt Studney lets the bees loose in the house, Roy responds by mocking her. He laughs and repeats three times: "Why have you let bees in my house?" In changing the modifier of "house" from "Dabney's" to "my," Roy betrays his boyish claim to the property. Aunt Studney responds with conjure, as her bees become a weapon in the fight over property. Donnie McMahand in fact calls the bees "the most fanciful act of black aggression in the novel" (177). By unleashing bees to do her work for her, Aunt Studney echoes Aunt Peggy, the conjure woman crafted by Charles Chesnutt, who sends hornets to sting a racehorse's knees to facilitate the return of an enslaved mother to her baby. Aunt Studney's method of claiming works as she "saw [Roy and Laura] out of the house" (266). Roy surely does not admit defeat, managing to "swagger out," but he is stung in the process. Although Laura thought the visit to Dabney's future house would connect her more closely to the family, the unsettling encounter with Aunt Studney in the creepy house disappoints her aim to be a Fairchild despite her mother's death. Entering Marmion results in no more connection to her family than Rosa and Quentin felt after entering Sutpen's Hundred.

Unlike Roy, Laura, Rosa, and Quentin, Milkman is not warned or thwarted from climbing the stairs and entering the private family part of the Butler house. He is instead invited, a key distinction in this third iteration of the scene. After being rendered powerless by the sight of Circe on the stairs, Milkman is then pulled by Circe into a room: "She took his hand in hers—like a small boy being dragged reluctantly to bed" (240). As he tries to figure out if this witchlike character is Circe, she instructs him to sit on a gray velvet sofa. The difference between Milkman's being encouraged to make himself at home and the other characters' being hampered from doing so may be due to the other characters seeking connections to the white families whose sins had led to the haunting of the houses. Milkman's family is instead damaged by the sins of the Butlers. Not only do they kill Milkman's grandfather to acquire his valuable land, but they also use their capital and African American labor to make this house opulent. Circe explains, "They loved this place. Loved it. Brought pink veined marble from across the sea for it and hired men in Italy to do the chandelier that I had to climb a ladder and clean with white muslin once every two months. They loved it. Stole for it, lied for it, killed for it" (247). Milkman may be here because he is driven by his desire for gold and has bought into the pursuit of property, but his connection to the African American victims rather than the white perpetrators of violence allows him entrance into the upper rooms.

Milkman, unlike the other characters, also acquires what he initially seeks: the location of the cave where the gold is supposedly buried. Circe, though, will more importantly give him the information that will redirect his quest to a better end. She points him to the value of family and explains that Macon Dead's body was left in a cave. Milkman assumes it is the same cave where he hopes to find gold and lies to get directions, telling Circe that he wants to bury the body properly. Circe proceeds to give him the directions to find the cave on the face of the hills. Armed with this knowledge, Milkman pays little heed while he is in the house to Circe's true gift, insight about his family. He instead rushes out to follow the trail. That he is still acting like the children Hansel and Gretel is evident when he "gingerly" moves brush to head down the path and later smells money when he finds the cave: "It was like candy and sex and soft twinkling lights" (250–51). When he realizes the cave is empty, he discovers that he is gripped with "real hunger" (253). What Milkman will discover is that the hunger that drives him will not be assuaged with money. His journey will lead him to build off the knowledge Circe gives him and identify his family as the treasure he needs. Although Milkman misreads Circe initially as "merely foolish," she is able to tell him more about his family than his father did. She tells him that his grandmother was Native American and named Sing, that his grandfather was named Jake, and that they came from Virginia. He heads to Virginia, still on the trail of the elusive gold, but he instead finds his family's history. When he realizes that Macon's ghost has not been telling Pilate to sing all this time but was saying his wife's name, "Sing," Milkman moves from an obsession with property to a realization that he is haunted by the past: "Here he was walking around in the middle of the twentieth century trying to explain what a ghost had done" (294).

The result of Milkman's knowledge is that his conception of home changes from property to family, a redemptive turn none of the characters in *Absalom, Absalom!* or *Delta Wedding* are able to make.[30] As he listens to children sing, Milkman becomes "homesick" for both Pilate and his mother. When he eventually understands his family's story, thus reaching the end of the trail Circe sent him down, "he could hardly wait to get home" (329). Milkman drops the search for the gold because he has discovered the difference between property and home. In contrast to Clytie and Aunt Studney, Circe does not attempt to block Milkman's journey into the past as much as guide him to follow a different path.

FAULT LINES

Although Milkman gains something more valuable than property, he and the other characters racing into haunted houses find their encounter with the past to be unsettling. Clytie blocks Rosa the first time and then tries to warn Rosa and Quentin, Aunt Studney summons bees to drive out Roy and Laura, and Circe tries to steer Milkman into a nobler quest, but in addition to their role as gatekeepers, the specters signify the human cost of the white families' greed for property. All three live beyond their allotted life span to speak the truth of this cost. This truth, however, like the fault line evident in the House of Usher at the beginning of Poe's story, leads the reader to anticipate the destruction of the haunted houses by the end. Haunted houses cannot remain as emblems of the American dream because the corpse hidden in the basement threatens the whole construction. While Aunt Studney's presence does not cause obvious destruction, her claim has a clear effect on Laura and forebodes problems for Dabney. Although the Butler house is still standing, Circe promises to stay in it until the dogs succeed in tearing it apart. Only in *Absalom, Absalom!* does the specter actually destroy the house.

While this might lead to the conclusion that in the end Clytie reacts most strongly to being made property, the reason Clytie destroys Sutpen's Hundred is not entirely clear. After Rosa and Quentin encounter Henry Sutpen in the upstairs bedroom, Rosa takes three months to get over her initial shock and realize that Henry probably needed medical attention. She decides to send an ambulance to bring him into town. Shreve repeats Mr. Compson's guess that Clytie believed the wagon was "coming to carry Henry into town for the white folks to hang him for shooting Charles Bon" (299). The male narrators believe that Clytie displays her ultimate loyalty to the Sutpen family by killing Henry in a fire so he will not be hung. Killing Henry to save him from dying is odd logic, but since Rosa does not narrate this section, and Clytie does not narrate at all, the men's conjecture is the only explanation given. Clytie has certainly planned for the event by stocking up on tinder and kerosene, so the house is ablaze before Rosa can get to it. When the door is opened, "the entire staircase was on fire" (300). Although Quentin was not present to witness the events, the narrator indicates that Quentin's imagination is so vivid that "Quentin could see it" (300). What he sees is Clytie's "tragic gnome face" in the window of the "doomed house," "against a red backdrop of fire" (300). For Quentin, and for Shreve and Mr. Compson, the specter, who is conflated with the house because of her past position as property, remains fused with the building as it burns.

A different explanation, however, of Clytie's motivations may lie in an earlier version of the Sutpen story. John T. Matthews explains that in 1931 Faulkner wrote the short story "Evangeline," which has the kernel of *Absalom, Absalom!*: a haunted house, a proposed marriage between Judith and Charles Bon that is opposed by Henry, and an earlier version of the servant Clytie in the character of Raby (248). Raby tells the Sutpen story by answering the questions of a journalist investigating the haunted house. When the journalist realizes that Raby has been helping Henry hide in the house, he asks, "Why did you do all this for Henry Sutpen? Didn't you have your own life to live, your own family to raise?" (604). Raby simply answers, "Henry Sutpen is my brother," a declaration of shared blood more direct than any utterance in *Absalom, Absalom!* (604). Nancy Ellen Batty suggests that perhaps some "vestigial residue of Raby's character" exists in the novel, so that many critics read Clytie's actions as stemming from her loyalty to her family. This reading is certainly plausible, but Raby differs significantly from Clytie. Not only does Raby tell the whole story; she sits on the porch of her own cabin surrounded by her descendants. Clytie, remaining fused with the Sutpen house, does not have a cabin of her own and certainly not enough of her own life to have children and grandchildren. Raby is a speaking person who can directly claim Henry as a sibling, but Clytie seems stuck in the position of property, as her experience as an enslaved person seems to extend even into the twentieth century. Clytie may define the family, but her place in it is not as clear.

Yet another possible reading of Clytie's action is suggested by Donaldson, who acknowledges that Clytie keeps Henry from being arrested, but "her action also succeeds in preventing Henry from telling and retelling the story of the Sutpens" ("Subverting" 29). If Henry were to live, even if just long enough to stand trial or to tell more of his story than the bare circular conversation reported by Quentin, then not only would the story continue with new information, but Clytie might remain even longer fused with property, unable to leave the house or even to die. Clytie thus decides when the story is finished, again enacting her role as a kind of barrier. In the end she seizes enough agency to destroy the house, which confirms that she has power, but as she remains fused with the house, she is also destroyed.

In *Song of Solomon*, Circe has the opportunity to answer the question posed to Raby (although not to Clytie) of whether her actions stem from her continuing loyalty to the white family. Batty reads Morrison's writing of the Circe scene as an answer to the "arrogant assumption on the part of both Quentin and Faulkner's readers" that Clytie is motivated by a "powerful filial bond" (86). Milkman suspects that Circe cannot leave the house, and he offers to help her. When she rejects his help, his tone becomes more sarcastic: "You loved those white folks that much?" (246). This question could easily be asked of Clytie as well as Circe, as both women not only stay in the houses of their white oppressors but exist beyond their normal life span to haunt the houses for the next generation. Circe's answer contradicts Milkman's assumption that her motivation is love. When he quips "and you still loyal," she responds, "You don't listen to people" (247). After she explains why Mrs. Butler killed herself, she tells Milkman that she is remaining to make sure the property they did love, the house, "will crumble and rot" (247). She is taking care of the Butler's dogs only in order to let them destroy the house. Clytie's fire is certainly faster, but Batty argues that "unlike Clytie or Raby, Circe will never torch the Butler mansion: such as act, we might speculate, would be too humane, would amount almost to an act of forgiveness or mercy" (87). Circe clearly wants a slow destruction, so that every individual piece of property from the grand chandelier to the silk wallpaper is destroyed in turn. Fletcher, however, notices something perhaps even more profound that Circe destroys: she also "disrupts [the master] narrative, which is replaced by a deconstructive reading of a literary edifice, the hero's quest" (418). Of the three women, only Circe has a positive effect on her visitor. She gives Milkman important information about his family, which eventually replaces his clichéd quest to find buried gold. In this way, she helps to dismantle not only the hero's question, but also the destructive narrative of property.

McMahand, however, finds that Circe's "commitment to justice" leaves her with a life "rooted in destruction" and "committed to the white gaze" (181). He connects her situation to Aunt Studney's, arguing that their relationships with "white dominance" prevent them from "creating more productive, fulfilling lives" (181). McMahand thus persuasively outlines both characters' powerlessness, but the fixation on destruction McMahand finds as evidence of Circe's obsession with the dead white family can also be read as a source of her power. As I detail in chapter 4, only an owner has the right to destroy property, so in destroying the rooms she once had to "keep," she is making a property claim that counters the legal claim to property that gave the Butlers not just their power but also their identity. Although perhaps not as "productive" as constructing her own house, Circe does lay claim to property.

In *Delta Wedding*, the effect of Aunt Studney on Marmion's fate is not as dramatic, although there are hints of potential problems in the future. This foreboding is offset by the marriage, suggesting that the narrative is a comedy that has concluded happily. The novel is therefore less in line with "The Fall of the House of Usher" with its grand finale of destruction and more reminiscent of *The House of Seven Gables*, where the house remains standing, empty of life but with the residue of haunting lingering. Laura is the only Fairchild who perceives this haunting, though. As the outsider, Laura's distance from their world may allow her to understand better the house's creepiness. Her perception may also be aided by her mother's recent death. At one point, Ellen describes Laura as "insistently a little messenger or reminder of death" (151). As the visible emblem of her mother's death, Laura serves as a counterpoint to the family's happy marital festivities. When Dabney first greets Laura, she exclaims, "You be in my wedding! You be a flower girl!" but Laura must remind her, "I can't. My mother died," causing Dabney to fall back "as if Laura slapped her" and moan, "It's just so *hard*, everything's just so *hard*" (105). The family prefers to dwell on the wedding, the future, and life, but Laura's world is necessarily shaped by death.

After Laura witnesses Aunt Studney's conjure, she does not wish to return to Marmion. Ellen finally makes the offer Laura has been longing for, the invitation to live with them at Shellmound, and then adds, "until you go to Marmion perhaps." Laura answers that she wants to stay but adds with a cry,

"But I don't want to go to Marmion" (326). Aunt Studney may be enigmatic, and a conjure ritual may be opaque for a young white girl, but Laura senses the danger enough to realize that she does not want to claim her property rights over Marmion. She realizes in fact that she no longer wants to live with the family at all: "in the end she would go—go from all this, back to her father" (326).

The final scene in the book, a family picnic, hints that Aunt Studney's gothic claim through conjure has worked on Laura. As the family rides out to the river on wagons, some members begin singing "Loch Lomond": "Oh, you'll take the high road and I'll take the low road,/And I'll be in Scotland afore ye" (330). John Purser explains that the song depicts a "soldier awaiting execution [claiming that] he will reach Scotland before his companion as his spirit will get there first by the low road" (156–57). Although there are a myriad of other interpretations of the song's lyrics, each hinges on the "low road" being death and Scotland being the home or destination of the spirit. As they ride, India tells Laura the "secret" that she is going to have a little brother. Laura responds with a "secret" of her own, a different version of the song: "I've been in Marmion afore ye. I've seen it all afore. It's all happened afore" (330). In putting "Marmion" in place of "Scotland," Laura reveals that she perceives Marmion as the destination of the spirit. This image echoes the earlier allusion to the underworld when Laura and Roy reach the house by crossing over the "River of Death." Although Laura was initially uncertain about whether Aunt Studney's cry was for a wedding or a funeral, in the end she connects Marmion with death. While India's secret is about life and the continuation of the Fairchild family, Laura's secret is about what has "happened afore," the past and its toll on the present, as she indeed becomes a kind of "messenger of death." Aunt Studney's claim to the property has worked its spectral magic.

※ ※ ※

On the map William Faulkner created for *Absalom, Absalom!* of Jefferson and its surroundings, he adds, "William Faulkner, Sole Owner and Proprietor." Although the novel depicts the struggle of Thomas Sutpen to acquire property, the imaginary territory of the narrative clearly belongs to Faulkner. Walter Benn Michaels in defining the "romance" as a "kind of property" points out that Hawthorne initiates the abstract claim to property in *The House of Seven Gables*. In his preface, Hawthorne explains his project of "laying out a street that infringes upon nobody's private rights, and appropriating a lot of land which had no visible owner, and building a house, of materials long in use for constructing castles in the air" (3). While the book itself is, as Michaels puts it, "the text of clear and unobstructed title," within that book, and within *Absalom, Absalom!, Delta Wedding*, and *Song of Solomon* as well, is a story of the struggle for property. Faulkner may indeed be "sole owner" of the fictional Yoknapatawpha, and he may have inherited the right to his imaginary realm by writing in the gothic mode of Hawthorne, thus continuing an American gothic tradition. But that same gothic mode teaches the reader to expect doubling and repetition, a return to haunted places and the resurrection of haunted people. Faulkner cannot solely own the story of the female African American specter who embodies the conflation of people and property. Clytie may die in the fire that destroys Sutpen property, but she returns from the dead in the sister stories of Aunt Studney and Circe.

If the purpose of the gothic is to teach the reader what to fear, to indicate the source of the sin or the place of the decaying corpse hidden in the basement, these haunts reveal that the result of turning people into property because of their race is a gothic nightmare of haunting and destruction where the American dream of acquiring property becomes the American nightmare of acquiring property. Of the three, only Clytie is enslaved, but the interaction of race and property rooted in slavery continues into the twentieth century so that Aunt Studney and Circe can echo Clytie's experience of being treated as property. Reading the three together highlights key differences, such as Clytie's death versus Aunt Studney's defiance, Aunt Studney's conjure performance versus Circe's dogs, and Quentin's debilitating shock versus Milkman's redemptive turn from property. The significant common thread, however, is that the aftermath of slavery's conflation of people with property is destruction: Thomas Sutpen's grand design ends with a family torn apart by murder and an estate in flames; Dabney's dream of living in Marmion may be the equivalent of eating the forbidden fruit; and the Butlers all die, leaving a rotting house as their only legacy. Together Clytie, Aunt Studney, and Circe reveal that people fused with property can also possess that property by haunting it. Powerless and powerful, the specters stand on staircases to warn the present world about the horrors of the past.

CHAPTER FOUR

Claiming, Killing, and Haunting in Toni Morrison's *Beloved*

In William Melvin Kelley's 1959 novel *A Different Drummer*, the character Tucker Caliban starts a mass exodus of the entire African American population of a fictional southern state located east of Mississippi and west of Alabama. Caliban does not give political speeches, engage in marches, or even suggest that other people flee the state when he does. Instead, the June 1957 revolution is sparked by singularly odd behavior: Caliban spreads ten tons of salt on his fields, shoots his animals, and then burns down his house, thus destroying all of his own property. Although he has an audience of bewildered white men, he does not bother to explain his actions. Some clues, though, appear in a succession of characters' perspectives on the event. Caliban bought the land from his white employer, Dewey Wilson III, whose ancestor bought Caliban's ancestor off the boat from Africa. The slaveholder could not enforce his claim on the powerful African, so he ended up killing him instead. Caliban demonstrates his own claim to property by ruining the land owned by this original slaveholder, thereby exercising an owner's ultimate right of destruction. By subsequently quitting the state, Caliban not only opts out of the system of property that enslaved his ancestors; he also declares his freedom from that system. Hearing of his radical choice, the African Americans of the state likewise pack up their belongings and leave.

In Toni Morrison's 1987 novel *Beloved*, Sethe also flees the South, although her escape is fraught with more danger because she is a fugitive from slavery in 1855, five years after the Fugitive Slave Act was passed. Like Tucker Caliban, Sethe wants to be free from the system that declares people to be property, and like Caliban, she turns to destruction as a way to claim her rights, albeit with dire consequences. When her owner arrives in Ohio with a posse to capture Sethe and her children, Sethe makes the bold and horrifying decision to kill her children rather than let them be redeemed as property. In attempting to kill all of her children and succeeding in killing one daughter, Sethe tries to opt out of the slave system completely by moving her children "out, away, over there" where "they'd be safe" (192, 193). Her logic is quite simple: her owner, who is called in the book "schoolteacher," cannot claim them as his property if she kills them.

Critics have explored Sethe's unimaginable moral dilemma, which is specifically based on the life of Margaret Garner and more generally drawn from the lives of enslaved parents whose children were someone else's property.[1] What has not received adequate attention is that Sethe challenges schoolteacher's property claim by making one of her own.[2] Only an owner has the right to destroy property, so Sethe's action establishes her ownership while erasing schoolteacher's claim, a process that harkens to one of the key court rulings in American property law, *Pierson v. Post*. The death of Beloved signals Sethe as the rightful claimant, but Sethe simultaneously loses the very being she is trying to save. Sethe's loss and guilt beget eighteen years of haunting followed by the return of the murdered child in the flesh to devastate Sethe further with her complaints of abandonment. Sethe may have legal possession, but a system of property rooted in destruction leads to haunting.

Legal possession is thus confronted by spectral possession. As David Punter observes, although the law is powerful with its "imposition of certainty," ghosts have "armies" as well (2, 3). Reading Beloved's haunting as a bid for the property of her self illuminates her different personas. She seems to be Sethe's daughter returned from the dead, a survivor of the Middle Passage, and a runaway who has been kept locked up all of her life.[3] Evidence in the novel points to each of these three as a possibility or, given Beloved's supernatural qualities, perhaps to all three at once. This triple identity may seem puzzling, but each identity represents a specific moment when Beloved is considered someone else's property. When Beloved is killed by Sethe, she is the object of a property claim; when Beloved is on a slave ship, she is simply freight; when Beloved is imprisoned and raped, her very body belongs to someone else. To combat the reduction of people to property, Beloved dons these three particular guises, fighting legal possession with her gothic haunting.

This battle between spectral and legal possession focuses on the particular place of 124 Bluestone Road. Critics have discussed how the haunting infuses the house, so that it becomes a character seemingly acting out the rage of the ghost, but I will argue that Beloved haunts 124 not because she, in the guise of Sethe's daughter, was killed in the shed near the house or because Sethe, as the target of her haunting, lives there.[4] Beloved, as the victim of property claims, haunts the house because of who owns it. In the introduction, I explored the significance of Harriet Jacobs's claiming that even after she and her children are free from slavery, she feels that she still lacking the "dream of my life," which is to have a "home of my own" (156). A home signals both protection from the outside world and personhood for the owner. Beloved does not own the house, but neither do Baby Suggs and Sethe. Generations of women lack that key to identity in America of owning a safe place to craft personhood. Instead, 124 is owned by a white man, Edward Bodwin. Once we read the continued white ownership of the house as an obstacle for the formerly enslaved women to establish a sense of identity, Beloved's presence makes sense as a spectral claim to property. Sethe's attempt on Bodwin's life, in a near repetition of the scene where she kills Beloved, also looks less like a mistake made in her mania over Beloved and more like a second violent attempt to claim property. Once again, Sethe loses the child she tries to save, but Beloved's spectral claims likewise dissipate with her subsequent disappearance.

Those claims had become dangerous, as Beloved had begun to possess Sethe to the point of erasing her. Denver's intercession between them as well as her quick action in preventing Sethe's murder of Bodwin allow Sethe's survival. Critics have argued that Denver's "charmed birth," her relationships with both her mother and Beloved, and her interactions with the community all contribute to her ability to be a glimpse of hope in a very dark tale. Her power furthermore derives from the fact that she was never property. In escaping Sweet Home, Sethe succeeds in getting Denver "out, away, over there," but to a "there" different than the dark other world where Beloved is sent. Beloved and Denver as sisters thus represent two possibilities for claiming: Beloved as claimed property is destroyed, while Denver as claimed daughter survives. In chapter 2, I examine how in Twain's and Melville's works, the conflation of people and property leads to destruction, but Williams crafts a fictional rewriting of history events. Morrison rewrites a historical story as well, using Denver as the possibility of creation instead of destruction. In Kelley's novel, Tucker Caliban's destruction of property may end in his successful bid for freedom from his family's past, but Sethe's attempt to opt out of the problem of property through destruction does not work. Denver's understanding of her family's past leaves her, however, with the potential to claim personhood.

SCHOOLTEACHER'S LEGAL CLAIM

Schoolteacher's proper name is never revealed in *Beloved*. The enslaved people call him "schoolteacher" because he teaches his two nephews in addition to running his brother-in-law's plantation after his death. The lack of a name renders him a generic entity. He is simply a slaveholder and exists in the novel as his function, much as Mr. Trappe exists in Crafts's novel to entrap people attempting to escape slavery. This function is what he is teaching his two nephews. Late in the novel, Sethe tells Beloved a story about overhearing schoolteacher say when tutoring his two nephews, "I told you to put [Sethe's] human characteristics on the left; her animal ones on the right. And don't forget to line them up" (228). This glimpse into schoolteacher's mind lays bare to Sethe the true nature of her situation in his eyes. She is part animal and capable of being owned. When Sethe describes the violence that schoolteacher allows the nephews to commit, she repeatedly exclaims that "they took my milk" (19). The nephews also beat her with a cowhide so violently that her back is left with a network of scars, but Sethe focuses on the theft of her milk as the crucial offense. Barbara Christian argues that "Sethe itemizes her milk in much the same way the slave owners itemized the different parts of the slave's body, as if that is all she is, all that she is worth" (42). Sethe, however, does not diminish her own worth as much as she protests her treatment as a thing with parts that can actually be taken and characteristics that can be catalogued as animal and then owned.[5] What schoolteacher thus teaches Sethe is the workings of legal possession.

Schoolteacher's legal possession of people creates a world in which people and property are conflated. Caught in that world is Paul D, whose story of slavery at Sweet Home and later in Alfred, Georgia, is so painful that he imagines his heart as a tobacco tin where he can lock away his memories. Although Paul D suffers physical torture during slavery, even at one point having to wear a bit in his mouth, his status as property is what continues to haunt him. In rehashing his memories, he always asks himself whether he is a man or simply property, and even in a postslavery world, he is unsure of the answer: "concerning his own manhood, he could not satisfy himself on that point" (260). He has "never told a soul" about his experience with the bit before, and he tries to explain to Sethe that the pain was not the contraption in his mouth but what it signified (85). Paul D reveals his meaning by telling the tale of Mister, a runt of a rooster who grew up to be the "king" of the yard (86). When Paul D with the bit in his mouth sees Mister, who looked "free. Better than me. Stronger, tougher," he thinks he is "something [that] was less than a chicken" (86). He is not a man at Sweet Home; he is a thing. When schoolteacher sells him, Paul D learns that he indeed can be exchanged for $900.

Sixo is the only enslaved person at Sweet Home to challenge schoolteacher's ownership. Made in the pattern of men such as Tucker Caliban,

Sixo does not acquiesce to a system that reduces him to property. He retains his own culture by going to the woods to dance, and he stops speaking English because "there was no future in it" (30). He organizes the escape and is able to get his pregnant "Thirty-Mile Woman" to safety, ensuring his progeny will survive. Sixo even tries to negotiate some amount of power by working within the system. When schoolteacher accuses him of stealing a shoat, Sixo admits to killing, butchering, cooking, and eating the pig, but he tells schoolteacher that he was not stealing the meat but "improving your property, sir" (224). Sixo's witty response to schoolteacher reveals a logical flaw in the slave system: to be enslaved, blacks were considered property, and property cannot commit crime because crime requires agency.[6] Despite Sixo's cleverness, schoolteacher controls the discourse that labels Sixo as property and as a thief, even if it is illogical. Sixo's only choice to retain personhood is to opt out. When he is caught escaping, he refuses to go back to slavery, laughing and singing until schoolteacher decides that "this one will never be suitable" and kills him (266).

While Sixo's death may provide him a kind of freedom, schoolteacher's killing of him confirms schoolteacher's legal claim to the property of Sixo's person because in American law the right to own and the power to destruct are tightly linked. Andrew Fede, in examining the slave codes of colonies in the seventeenth and eighteenth centuries, finds that the law "legitimized all slave killings perpetrated while the master was correcting his slave for any offense the slave may have allegedly committed" (117). In the nineteenth century, a white stranger (not the owner) had some criminal liability for killing a slave, but the southern states continued "the master's almost unlimited right to kill his slaves with impunity" (Fede 118).

It is not just that the law allowed an owner to kill an enslaved person; it was the killing of that person that solidified the right to own people as property, as evident in the infamous 1829 case *State v. Mann*. In this case, John Mann had rented a woman named Lydia, but while he was whipping her, she tried to run, so Mann shot and killed her. To legal historians, the case represents "the acceptance among southern jurists that the law gave slaves virtually no recourse from a master's punishments and decisions" (Hadden 2). Thomas Ruffin, the judge in the case, writes that in slavery, "the end is the profit of the master," which requires complete obedience on the part of the enslaved person: "such obedience is the consequence only of uncontrolled authority over the body. There is nothing else which can operate to produce the effect. The power of the master must be absolution, to render the submission of the slave perfect" (*State*). The ruling in *State v. Mann* was that enslaved people were, in Hadden's words, "pure property" (17). An owner (or in this case a renter) could destroy this property because the absolute power of the owner over the enslaved person not only included but was made manifest in the power to kill. Schoolteacher thus has the legal right to kill Sixo, sell Paul D, capture Sethe and her children, and return them to slavery.

SETHE'S LEGAL CLAIM

To combat schoolteacher's legal claim, Sethe decides to make one of her own. In choosing to kill her children, Sethe uses the only strategy she has to get them away from schoolteacher permanently, since the Fugitive Slave Act of 1850 made the free state of Ohio not exactly free. Sethe moreover takes the owner's place in claiming the right to kill. Her action thus speaks directly back to slavery's construction of people as property and the subsequent sanctioning of murder. As extraordinary as Sethe's decision may seem, she is not alone in concluding that the death of her children is preferable to slavery. In *The Bondwoman's Narrative,* Lizzie tells of a young mother who kills her infant and then herself when they are about to be sold. In *Pudd'nhead Wilson,* Roxy plans to jump in the river with her baby before she realizes that she could switch her child with the master's child. And in *Dessa Rose,* Dessa and Kaine discuss killing their baby so their master will not sell the child away from them. These repeated depictions of infanticide reveal that in the "peculiar institution" of slavery, death is an escape from an unbearable life. For Sethe, the death of her children is furthermore an escape from schoolteacher's claim. To save them from being his property, she must claim them as her own.

Although Sethe frames her action as a property claim when explaining it to Paul D, he does not understand her. Paul D describes Sethe as "spinning" when she tells him the story of killing Beloved and "circling him the way she was circling the subject" (189). He only catches "pieces of what she said" because he is not really listening to the "circling"; he is waiting for the "main part" (189). Paul D, however, misses Sethe's description of motherhood, which for her is crucial to that "main part." Sethe explains that she did not have another woman to talk to at Sweet Home and had to figure out how to take care of her babies by herself. Despite the dehumanizing experience of slavery, Sethe "got us all out" and reveals that after escaping, she felt that her children were now "mine to love." She then stops circling and directly announces: "I took and put my babies where they'd be safe" (193). The words "mine" and "took" signals that Sethe is claiming them as hers, and her role as their mother compels her actions. Paul D realizes that "what she claimed" scares him and protests, "It didn't work, did it?" Sethe answers, "It worked" because "schoolteacher ain't got em" (194). In Sethe's description, the action is deliberate and comes out of her larger experience as a mother, but many critics read the line "if she thought anything, it was No. No. Nono. Nonono" to indicate that Sethe's action is not a choice but simply an impulse. Sharon Decker, for example, points out that "the word 'decision' never appears, and the implication is that Sethe is forced to kill her child" (257). Critics understandably do not want to blame the victimized and traumatized Sethe for the tragedy of Beloved's death, but in shifting the blame completely to the institution of slavery, what they miss is Sethe's agency. She is not a passive victim. While the specific horrific action Sethe takes is certainly forced by the institution of slavery, Sethe's full explanation places the momentary impulse into a larger narrative of claiming. In Sethe's construction of events, she actively chooses to get her children "outside this place." To do this, she must claim her children as her own.

Critics have further discussed whether this claim leaves her confined within the system that presented her with the horrible choice between slavery and murder or whether she indeed opts out of the system of property. Dean J. Franco analyzes the many valences of the word "claim" in the novel and argues that while Sethe may seem trapped, her action is "an injury to the law" (422). Christopher Peterson, on the other hand, sees Sethe as still within the system because of the correspondence between kinship and ownership: "Although property relations that obtain between parent and offspring and those between master and slave are certainly not equivalent, they are both property relations nonetheless" (549). Peterson argues that *Beloved* asks "whether Sethe's maternal claim on Beloved might not in some way repeat the master's (paternal) violence that it seeks to prevent" (551). Once we see, however, that Sethe has to use the master's language of ownership to defy the master's claim, the answer to whether Sethe is within or without the system is that she has to be both, much like the con artists in chapter 2 have to negotiate two levels of reality. Although Sethe's action "works" in getting her children away from schoolteacher, thus allowing Sethe to negate slavery and thwart the system completely, her action "works" because she uses the language of American laws on slavery and property.

Sethe's action speaks directly to the law's construction of property rights, specifically to the foundational 1805 case *Pierson v. Post*. This case involved a hunter named Post, who was pursuing a fox on unclaimed, vacant land, when Pierson, though aware of Post's pursuit, killed the fox and claimed the trophy. The original court found in favor of the initial pursuer, Post, since he was hunting the fox when Pierson intervened. The Supreme Court of New York, though, overturned the verdict, arguing that pursuit was a slippery slope because it is difficult to ascertain when a pursuit begins, but the killing of the fox, although impolite to the initial pursuer, made for clearer title. Contemporary readers may wonder why two men and two courts spent time and money determining the ownership of one fox pelt. One answer may be found in William Blackstone's *Commentaries on the Laws of England*, which served as the authority on law in colonial America, where he explains that "there is nothing which so generally strikes the imagination and engages the affections of mankind, as the right of property" and that "pleased as we are with the possession, we seem afraid to look back to the means by which it was acquired, as if fearful of some defect in our title" (37). Establishing the means of ownership of the dead fox is crucial because property rights were, as I have argued throughout this study, the foundation of the American dream. Although initially *Pierson v. Post* established legal precedent concerning the hunting of animals, which is admittedly not a trivial subject in an undeveloped country, over time, the case's influence expanded. According to Angela Fernandez, it "became a staple of twentieth-century theorizing about property" (116). The case's influence is also evident in literature, such as James Fenimore Cooper's *The Pioneers* and William Faulkner's *Go Down, Moses*, although no one has yet connected the case to *Beloved*.[7]

The link between fox hunting and Sethe's murder of Beloved may indeed seem slight, but the relationship springs from two implications of *Pierson v. Post*. The first is that possession is most clearly indicated by the ability to destroy property; as Carol M. Rose explains, "The metaphor of the law of first possession is, after all, death and transfiguration; to own a fox the hunter must slay it, so that he or someone else can turn it into a cost" (16). The second is that killing the object wins over pursuing the object because of the clarity of title: "Possession as the basis of property ownership, then, seems to amount to something like yelling loudly enough to all who may be interested" (Rose 16). Considering this legal precedent, Sethe must destroy her children to make her claim superior to schoolteacher's, and she must do so in a manner that clearly and loudly communicates her property rights.

The murder scene depicts Sethe accomplishing both of these tasks in language that harkens to the hunting context of *Pierson v. Post* and to the need to communicate ownership. The scene begins with the point of view of the audience for Sethe's actions: schoolteacher and his posse of white men. Critics argue that Morrison begins with the white men's perspectives to underscore the oppressive context for Sethe's actions, with Klaus Brax arguing that the point of view "reveals and emphasizes that many European colonists see Africans as primitive and irrational beings" (259) while James Phelan explains that this point of view makes the reader feel "jarred by seeing [Sethe] from what is such an alien perspective" (324). After building the backdrop whereby the reader sees slavery through the eyes of Sethe and others held in slavery, the white men's perspectives are indeed shocking, but when we read Sethe's actions through the lens of the law, Morrison's choice of point of view takes on new meaning. These men, especially schoolteacher with his claims on her life and family, are the target audience for Sethe's property claim.

The first perspective is that of the slavecatcher, who is hunting enslaved people just as one would hunt a fox. He stays "in the saddle, his rifle ready, his eyes trained away from the house to the left and to the right" ready to capture an enslaved person but careful to "keep back a pace, leave the tying to another. Otherwise you ended up killing what you were paid to bring back alive. Unlike a snake or a bear, a dead nigger could not be skinned for profit and was not worth his own dead weight in coin" (173–74). The slavecatcher plays the part of Post in pursuing what he sees as an animal in order to claim it, although he must capture his prey alive. Sethe answers with the part of Pierson in claiming through destruction. The horrific scene of what appears to be three dead children does the job of "yelling loudly" to communicate Sethe's right to the property of her children and herself. When the text moves to schoolteacher's point of view, the conflict is clearly over property: "Right off it was clear, to schoolteacher especially, that there was nothing there to claim" (175).[8] He does not think of the horror. Instead, he understands that his claim has been challenged. Admittedly, he does not see logic and reasoning in Sethe's action, thinking she had "gone wild" and "something was wrong with her" (176). Saturated with racism, he does not perceive Sethe as claimant because he cannot conceive of her as being on his level, but he still gives up his property claim and rides away. If her only goal is thwarting schoolteacher, Sethe succeeds.

In mirroring the *Pierson v. Post* case, Morrison rewrites the history of the actual legal case of Margaret Garner that inspired her to write *Beloved (Conversations* 206).[9] She alters this history significantly by making Sethe's action a valid property claim. In 1856, Garner, her husband, her in-laws, and her four children escaped from Kentucky across a frozen river to the free state of Ohio. The Garners' owners, however, obtained a warrant under the Fugitive

Slave Act and discovered the Garners hiding at a relative's house. As the white men approached the house, Margaret Garner killed her two-year-old daughter Mary by slitting her throat. This action sparked a legal battle between the state of Ohio, which charged her with murder (as a way of saving the family from slavery), and the federal government, which defined her as property, although ironically as property that had also somehow committed the crime of theft in escaping and "stealing" her child. The federal judge upheld the Fugitive Slave Act and ordered that Garner and her family be returned to their owners. Avery Gordon explains that legally Margaret Garner was "only what a property contract promises, a transaction of exchange value" (160). Although Toni Morrison explains that she "did not do much research on Margaret Garner other than the obvious stuff, because I wanted to invent her life," her fictional Sethe closely follows the script of the real Margaret Garner, with the signal difference being the outcome of their actions (*Conversations* 248).[10] Garner remained property and was sold to another owner, while Sethe remains "free" in Ohio. With this change, Christopher Peterson suggests that Morrison shows "a certain abolitionist spirit of divine motherly love," and he cautions that the changes make *Beloved* less about "historical recovery" and more about "historical invention" (553). However, this desire to invent, as this study shows, puts Morrison in good company. Harriet Jacobs and Hannah Crafts turn their lives into narratives to shape them, and Sherley Anne Williams imagines a different outcome for an enslaved woman who revolts and escapes from a coffle. In her fiction, Morrison gives Sethe the power Margaret lacked, and the crucial "invention" is that Sethe is able to make a claim through killing that works, if not in making her a person in schoolteacher's eyes, then at least in rewriting or unwriting his property claim. She speaks the language of property, using the discourse of the very legal system she aims to overthrow.

BELOVED'S SPECTRAL CLAIM

Beloved, however, is killed as the object of Sethe's claim, and legal possession ends in destruction. While Beloved dies because she is property, she haunts because she is also human. Unlike Tucker Caliban's salt-encrusted fields, Beloved is not simply a thing to be destroyed, not a field or a fox. Beloved's return to life, however, challenges Sethe's legal claim in that if Beloved is in fact undead, Sethe did not retain the owner's power to destroy, and Beloved's spectral power negates Sethe's legal claim.

The different facets of Beloved's persona amplify her power. She is somehow Sethe's daughter returned from the dead, a survivor from the Middle Passage who witnessed her mother's death, and a local girl who escaped a life of imprisonment, all at the same time. Critics have analyzed how these different personas exist in one body. Deborah Horvitz, for example, sees in the book "many Beloveds—generations of mothers and daughters—hunted down and stolen from Africa" (157). A. Timothy Spaulding explains that "by infusing Beloved with complex and ambiguous dimensions, Morrison retains traditional elements of the gothic but prevents us from understanding her through any one interpretative thread" (66). These "many Beloveds" are certainly "complex," but they are linked by the experience of becoming property. Although in certain instances the law had to acknowledge those held in slavery were people in addition to being property, the transfer of people into pure property becomes absolute at specific times. Tim Armstrong points to two moments when "the value assigned the slave is realizable": "the point of purchase or sale, the point of an insurance claim" (40). In two of her three guises, Beloved is the subject of an insurance claim; in the third guise, her very body is not her own. As a ghost, Beloved returns to Sethe, to 124, and to the community to claim the personhood that she was denied in her previous existences.

In her identity as Sethe's daughter returned from the dead, Beloved is the age the "crawling already?" baby would be had she lived, and Denver indicates that Beloved has a scar where her throat would have been cut. Beloved claims multiple times that she returned because she remembers Sethe's face from long ago and that she and Sethe have the same face (252). Beloved seems to know about the earrings that Sethe received from Mrs. Garner when she asks for their story: "Tell me your diamonds" (69). However, the most convincing evidence for Sethe that this person is her dead daughter is when Beloved hums a tune Sethe made up to sing to her babies. Sethe hears the "click" of truth (207).

What is significant about Beloved in the guise of Sethe's daughter is the reason she haunts Sethe. Sethe initially assumes that Beloved's return means that her daughter is not "mad" at her: "And now I know that if you was [mad], you ain't now because you came back here to me" (217). She imagines that Beloved understands her actions: "I don't have to explain a thing. I didn't have time to explain before because it had to be done quick. Quick. She had to be safe and I put her where she would be. But my love was tough and she back now" (236). Sethe further concludes that Beloved's returning signifies that her claim worked because now "she mine" (236). Beloved, however, has come back to haunt and to claim her identity as a family member. She is demanding, threatening, and punishing. She repeatedly accuses Sethe of "leaving her behind" (284). Denver thinks that "Sethe was trying to make up for the handsaw; Beloved was making her pay for it," but although Sethe begs for forgiveness, she does not in fact admit that her actions were wrong (295). Instead, she tries to make Beloved understand that being property in the slave system meant "that anybody white could take your whole self for anything that came to mind" (295). Although Beloved may accuse Sethe of the handsaw and may haunt to reclaim her personhood, Sethe is actually not haunted by killing Beloved.

What haunts Sethe instead is that she had to work within the system of slavery and property to do so; it is not the violence but the complicity with white law that troubles her. When schoolteacher instructs the nephews to make the lists, Sethe understands that he sees her and her children as solely property, but the white men are able to write this list, in addition to deeds and warrants and everything else that allows their legal authority as owners, because Sethe makes the ink they use. Early in the novel, Sethe tells Denver that she made the ink that schoolteacher used to write a "book about us," and late in the narrative, Sethe admits to Paul D, "I made the ink, Paul D. He couldn't have done it if I hadn't make the ink" (320).[11] The pronoun "it" refers to schoolteacher's agency to write the slaves' lives and to declare them his property. By "making the ink," Sethe contributes to the master's language of claiming, and this complicity haunts her.[12] When she confronts schoolteacher's legal claim with one of her own, she then perpetuates the system of property. Beloved's ghostly reappearance points both to the ongoing harm Sethe did in her attempt to thwart schoolteacher and to her ultimate failure as Beloved is more than claimed property.

She is also more than Sethe's daughter. In her second identity as an enslaved person in the Middle Passage, Beloved is again conflated with property, with the same results: death and haunting. In this iteration, Beloved is either a human survivor of a recent slave ship or the ghost of a survivor of a slave ship from long ago. Although America outlawed the importation of slaves in 1808, slave ships continued their commerce until the Civil War, so Beloved could have been on a slave ship as a child in the late 1850s.[13] However, since she is a ghost in her first identity as Sethe's daughter, it is certainly plausible that she is a ghost in this second identity and that she refers to a slave ship from an earlier time. Whether Beloved as Middle Passage survivor is human or ghost, her role remains the same: she is a gothic figure who brings this horrific experience to bear on the text.[14] Morrison explains that in crafting the character, she was thinking of two kinds of dead; the first is Sethe's "child returned to her from the dead" and the second is "another kind of dead which is not spiritual but flesh, which is, a survivor from the true, factual slave ship" (*Conversations* 247). Beloved as haunt brings these two kinds of dead into the world of the living. Morrison adds that the "language of both experiences—death and the Middle Passage—is the same" (247). This language reflects the trauma of losing personhood and even life when murder is constructed as simply destroying property.

Beloved's own descriptions of the Middle Passage signal this trauma and loss. In loosely connected phrases, Beloved tells of "crouching" in a hot, crowded hold of a ship where people are sick and "thrashing" (248). The conditions are so bad that Beloved reveals that suicide is desirable: "we are all trying to leave our bodies behind" (248).[15] Later, she stands on deck and watches the "men without skin" (fair-skinned sailors) push dead people into the sea, including "my man," perhaps her father. Her mother, identified as "the woman with my face," goes into the sea as well, but the white men "did not push her. She went there. She was getting ready to smile at me and when she saw the dead people pushed into the sea she went also and left me there with no face or hers" (253). Elizabeth B. House argues that because the mother "escaped into the ocean" that "in the girl's eyes, her mother willingly deserted her" (18). Her distress at being left behind then connects her with Sethe's daughter, who felt abandoned when Sethe pushed her out of slavery by killing her. Horvitz suggests an even closer connection: since Sethe's mother is the only character in the book to experience the Middle Passage, Horvitz identifies Beloved as Sethe's mother come back to haunt her (163–65). While this connection is intriguing, it does not explain why Sethe's mother would haunt her or how the death of her mother on the ship and the murder of her daughter are linked.

The connection between the Beloved who is Sethe's daughter and the Beloved who is in the Middle Passage is property. Just as the murdered daughter is killed by Sethe to supersede schoolteacher's property claim, the survivor Beloved is captured and her mother is killed because they are claimed as property. Morrison alludes to a "true, factual slave ship" in crafting Beloved's second persona. Although she does not identify a particular ship, the infamous case of the *Zong* fits in terms of the specific images Beloved relates of a "little hill of dead people" pushed with poles into the sea with a woman jumping in afterward (249). In 1781 the *Zong* was traveling from Africa to Jamaica when the ship's supply of drinking water was too low to sustain the sailors and the enslaved people on board. The ship's captain ordered 132 people thrown overboard to their deaths. Deaths on slave ships were routine from overcrowding, lack of sanitary conditions, suicide by desperate captives, and even the murder of enslaved people too unfit or openly defiant. In *Beloved*, two of Baby Suggs's daughters die on a ship before it even leaves harbor. What made the deaths on the *Zong* notable, though, was that the Liverpool owners of the ship sued their insurers to receive payment for their loss. They won their case, and the dead Africans became an insurance claim.[16] James Walvin explains the impact: "The very name—the *Zong*—quickly entered the demonology of Atlantic slavery, and came to represent the depravity and heartless violence of the entire slave system" (2). Ian Baucom argues that the *Zong* case "can be seen to exemplify the advent and triumph of an abstract, speculative, hypercapitalized modernity" (33). The case becomes significant because it defined people as solely property and allowed their death to be a loss that can be claimed for money. The enslaved human can then be exchanged for money, alive or dead, and when the claim is filed, legal ownership is made manifest by death.[17]

The case of the *Zong* thus illustrates the horror in Beloved's Middle Passage experience. The "little hill of dead people" Beloved describes are enslaved people who perhaps died from the brutal conditions on board or were killed by the crew when supplies ran low or committed suicide to escape. Dying, they can be the object of a property claim. Surviving, Beloved is also property. The Middle Passage has stripped her not only of mother and father but of her personhood as well: "there is no one to want me to say me my name" (251). She is simply freight on a ship, in the same condition as the enslaved people in *Benito Cereno* before they revolt. Just as Paul D discovers the bald truth of his worth when he hears the dollar amount for which he is sold, the survivor Beloved is also destined to be traded for money. Her parents, on the other hand, are subject to being listed as part of an insurance claim. Beloved in her guise as Sethe's daughter likewise becomes the product of an insurance claim; before schoolteacher rides away, he stops in town to "[file] a claim" (216).[18]

Beloved thus exists as an embodiment of both Sethe's murdered daughter and a survivor from a slave ship because it is in these specific experiences that the human who is supposed to be loved becomes a thing to be claimed. Beloved in her spectral form haunts to combat the previous legal possessions. If, however, Beloved as daughter is back in specter form to punish Sethe for participating in the system of property, whom is Beloved as survivor haunting with her tales of death and horror? One possible answer is found in the epigraph to the book: "Sixty Million and more." Morrison dedicates the book to the unnamed masses of people who lost their personhood during slavery. William R. Handley explains that the number "suggests a loss of such magnitude that no sufficient accounting can be made of it: these spectral italics cannot literally represent the dead, give a reality to the Middle Passage, or reincarnate its victims" (688). As part of the prefatory material, the epigraph's direct audience is the reader of that unaccountable number. While Sethe is haunted by Beloved for her specific actions and moment in time, Morrison enlarges Beloved's identity to encompass the Middle Passage in order to expand the reach of this haunting to the reader. Morrison explains, "I thought this has got to be the least read of all the books I'd written because it is about something the characters don't want to remember, I don't want to remember, black people don't want to remember, white people don't want to remember. I mean, it's national amnesia" (*Conversations* 257). The gothic as a tool teaches readers of *Beloved* to remember the death and destruction that happen, on the personal scale of a lost loved one and on the massive scale of the enslavement of millions, when people are claimed as property.

The third iteration of Beloved's identity points to yet another moment when a person becomes pure property: sexual exploitation. Early in the novel, Sethe guesses that Beloved "had been locked up by some whiteman for his own purposes, and never let out the door" (140). Sethe's guess matches the story of Ella, who tells of being held by a white man and his son for their perverse desires, the story of Amy Denver with its hints at her own possible sexual exploitation in being confined in the root cellar, and certainly that of Amy's mother, as Amy admits that the man she worked for was rumored to be her father. House points out, "Beloved's own words suggest that she has been confined and used sexually" (20). Beloved tells Denver, "In the dark my name is Beloved" and later tells Sethe that "one of the [white men] was in the house I was in. He hurt me" (88, 254). Sethe's initial conjecture aligns with specific evidence when Stamp Paid reveals that there "was a girl locked up in the house with a whiteman over by Deer Creek. Found him dead last summer and the girl gone. Maybe that's her. Folks say he had her in there since she was a pup" (277).[19]

Suffering sexual exploitation is the physical consequence of not owning your own body, an issue that reoccurs throughout the book, ultimately affecting almost every character. In addition to Ella and Amy's stories, Sethe remembers the story that an enslaved woman named Nan told her about how Sethe got her name. Sethe's mother named her after her father because he was the only man "she put her arms around" (74). All of her other children were the product of rape, first by the crew on the slave ship, then by "more whites" (74). Stamp Paid also changes his name because of sexual violence. He tells Paul D the story of his wife, Vashti, who was taken from him by a white owner, who wanted her for his own sexual use. Stamp Paid then chooses his new name to indicate that he had paid the world all he could stand. His equating of the abuse of his wife with a monetary metaphor indicates the theft his wife endured, as her body was someone else's property.[20] This abuse is not limited to women. Paul D is haunted by the memory of prisoners in the work camp in Alfred, Georgia, being forced to perform oral sex on the guards every morning, a daily reminder that they do not own their bodies. Because the trauma of this oppression lasts beyond slavery, Baby Suggs's "sermon" is not an admonition to "clean up their lives or to go and sin nor more" (103). She tells them that they are "flesh" and that they must "Love it hard. Yonder they do not love your flesh. They despise it" (103).[21] The formerly enslaved people have to learn to own their own bodies.

The reduction of bodies to property is what Sethe wants to shield her children from by putting them in a world away from slavery. Although Sethe has had the "amazing luck" for someone enslaved of choosing her own husband, her experience with schoolteacher's nephews when they took her milk teaches her all she needs to know about the equation of a female body and property (28). It is an equation she confronts again when the engraver offers to put "Beloved" on a tombstone for ten minutes of sex. She exchanges her body for the one word that would name the child whom she refused to allow to be someone else's property. When Sethe thinks about how to tell all of this to Beloved to explain why she did what she did, she thinks of the "Saturday girls," the prostitutes who waited outside the slaughterhouse on payday. It is the exchange of body for money, or, even worse, the taking of body by a legal owner, from which Sethe tries to save her daughter through claiming her.

While Beloved the daughter is saved from this particular trauma (though murdered in the process), Beloved in this third iteration most likely suffered this very fate. Though their experiences differ, Beloved's multiple identities are linked in the root horror of being treated as simply property. By having this one human/ghost/specter character embody the traumas of being murdered as a property claim, transported as cargo on a ship, and imprisoned as a sexual slave, *Beloved* underscores the various ways people become property and how this conflation, out of all the horrors of slavery, is the catalyst for haunting. As Amy Denver massages Sethe's swollen feet, she warns her, "Anything dead coming back to life hurts" (42). Beloved, haunting in her three guises, is indeed painful because she speaks the language of the dead to demand spectral possession. Coming back to life, her spectral identity questions that "certainty of law" that undergirds slavery.

"124 WAS SPITEFUL"

The battle between legal possession and spectral haunting becomes literalized in the battle over 124 Bluestone Road. If Beloved in her various forms represents the horror of being property, she likewise haunts the physical property of the house because of who owns it. While Baby Suggs and Sethe occupy 124, the house is owned by a white man, Edward Bodwin. His continued ownership is easy to miss given that Baby Suggs and Sethe seemingly pretend the house is theirs. Some critics indeed see 124 as a gendered space, which leaves Paul D having "house-fits" because he does not belong (135). Although I would agree that Baby Suggs and Sethe attempt to make 124, in Michael Hogan's words, "an emblem of female strength and freedom," I would argue that, in the end, they fail (169).[22] Baby Suggs does not achieve full personhood through property ownership, so she remains vulnerable to the white men who come into the yard to claim the property of her daughter-in-law and grandchildren. And Sethe's haunting is amplified through her isolation in a house owned by another white man. Both women simply cannot be free in a house they do not own. Lori Askeland compares 124 with Simon Legree's house in Harriet Beecher Stowe's *Uncle Tom's Cabin* and explains that "124 has always been haunted by the ownership of white men—both by Edward Bodwin's literal ownership and the broader political ownership that allowed the men to invade her home in the name of the law" (172). My reading is in concert with Askeland's, but I offer a connection between Bodwin's ownership and Beloved's haunting of 124. Beloved was killed because she was considered by white society and the law to be property. Her haunting of 124 is not due solely to its proximity to the shed where she died nor because Sethe lives there; she troubles 124 because it continues to be white property. Her attempt at spectral possession echoes Baby Suggs's and Sethe's attempts at physical possession, but 124 proves to be a dangerous place to claim.

In crafting the reader's acquaintance with 124, Morrison explains that she wanted the reader to feel captured:

> The reader is snatched, yanked, thrown into an environment completely foreign, and I want it as the first stroke of the shared experience that might be possible between the reader and the novel's population. Snatched just as the slaves were from one place to another, from any place to another, without preparation and without defense. No lobby, no door, no entrance—a gangplank, perhaps (but a very short one). And the house into which this snatching—this kidnapping—propels

one, changes from spiteful to loud to quiet, as the sounds in the body of the ship itself may have changed. ("Unspeakable" 32)

Entering 124 is entering slavery, and Morrison's language points to the Middle Passage experience that will be central to her examination, but significantly it is not Sweet Home, the plantation house where Sethe is enslaved, that mimics the terror of losing personhood. It is instead 124, the place supposedly beyond slavery. The house is haunted by the baby who played the fox in Sethe's bid to own her children: "124 was spiteful. Full of a baby's venom" (3). When the reader enters in 1873, Sethe and Denver are described as the house's "only victims," with Baby Suggs dead and Sethe's two sons having fled. 124 is a place where hand prints appear, mirrors shatter, and red pools of light pulsate. Denver regards the house "as a person rather than a structure" (35). As Esther Peeren explains, "Rather than a ghost occupying a space, the house *is* the ghost, the space *is* the specter" (85).[23] If Beloved is haunting 124 because she was property, she consequently haunts *as* property, as 124, much like the specters who are fused with houses that I examine in chapter 3.[24] This haunting results in such an intensity that Paul D realizes "compared to 124, the rest of the world was bald" (49).

Strangely enough, this potent house initially signals freedom to Baby Suggs. When her son Halle buys her out of slavery and Mr. Garner takes her to Ohio, he introduces her to the siblings Mr. and Miss Bodwin. When Baby Suggs, bewildered by her change in circumstances, asks, "Where I'm going to be?" Mr. Garner announces, "These two angels got a house for you" (171). Baby Suggs is so "excited about a house with steps," she does not comprehend the import of the agreement they strike: "In return for laundry, some seamstress work, a little canning and so on (oh shoes, too), they would permit her to stay there" (171). Baby Suggs is basically renting the house, with labor instead of money as payment, which certainly sounds harmless enough, and Baby Suggs proceeds to attempt to "[claim] ownership of that freed self" (112). Not only does she discard the name "Jenny Whitlow" assigned to her by a former owner, but she also remodels 124 as if it were her property. Baby Suggs "boarded up the back door," the entrance associated with servants and those enslaved, because "she didn't want to make that journey no more," making the front door the only entrance, so that "if you want to get in 124 you have to come by her" (244). Baby Suggs remodels the house to assert her control over this property. She is not enslaved here but the one with power.

Or so she presumes, until that apocalyptic day when the four horsemen ride into town.[25] Baby Suggs discovers that even if 124 has only the front door, and even if she must be passed for anyone to enter, these men armed with their guns and their whiteness feel free to enter anyway. Hogan argues, "124 is dangerous because it promises what it cannot provide: refuge for its inhabitants. As a free-standing American house, it promises protection; as home to African-American slaves, the disenfranchised and dehumanized, it cannot possibly deliver" (174). The house cannot provide refuge because Baby Suggs does not own the "free-standing American house." Therefore, the connection in the grand narrative of the American dream between being able to own property and establishing not just a self but also crucial barriers between that self and harm does not exist for her and for the others formerly enslaved.

Although Baby Suggs originally imagined that the house corresponded with her claiming of her self, after the apocalypse, she identifies the exact locus of her flaw. When Stamp Paid urges her to continue to preach and asks, "You saying the whitefolks won?," she answers three times, "I'm saying they came in my yard" (211). The white men's violation was trespassing, but the yard she identifies as "mine" is not hers. The real owner is signaled by the white children, a "red-haired boy and a yellow-haired girl," who show up at 124 just as the sheriff is taking Sethe away. They are bringing shoes, telling Baby Suggs "[Mama] says you got to have these fixed by Wednesday" (180). The reminder that she is only renting the house and renting from white people who command her labor serves as a coda to the invasion of the space that she thought was hers. When Stamp Paid later has a conversation with her and asks her if she is looking for a miracle, she answers, "I'm looking for what I was put here to look for: the back door" (211). Baby Suggs gives up on claiming her personhood. Just as the narratives of Harriet Jacobs and Hannah Crafts demonstrate, even those formerly enslaved are not entirely free as long as they inhabit white-owned property, and slavery's dynamics of race and property extend beyond the limits of the South.

The very number of the house betrays a clue to Baby Suggs's problem. Although Halle worked Sundays for five years saving up to buy his mother's freedom, when Mr. Garner transports Baby Suggs north, the debt has not been fully paid. Her supposed freedom is therefore linked to her son's continued slavery. Late in the book, the reader learns that the remaining debt is $123.70, a figure just shy of the 124 of the house. The house thus represents the part of Baby Suggs's person that is still owned by someone else. One white man owns her son and some portion of herself, while another white man owns her house.

Even though Sethe witnessed the white men trespassing into the yard and countered their right to do so by making her own property claim, she seems unaware of the problem of the house's ownership. When Paul D sees the effect that living in a haunted house is having on Denver, he asks, "Who owns this house?" and "They won't let you leave?" (17).[26] His questions strike at the heart of the problem: Sethe appears trapped in property owned by someone else. Confined in a haunted house, Sethe appears to be the damsel in distress in a gothic tale. Sethe, however, answers that she refuses to leave: "No more running—from nothing. I will never run from another thing on this earth. I took one journey and I paid the ticket, but let me tell you something, Paul D Garner, it cost too much" (18). Her assertion that she has already paid all she can echoes Stamp Paid's in claiming his new name. However, though her property claim to her children cost her the life of her daughter, it did not come with the deed to the house. Just as Sethe remains haunted by her complicity with the system of property, she remains trapped in a haunted house that she does not own. She scoffs that Paul D wants her to leave: "as though a house was a little thing—a shirtwaist or a sewing basket you could walk off from or give away any old time. She who had never had one but this one" (26–27). At Sweet Home, she would bring flowers to the Garners' house every day to "feel like some part of it was hers," but this tactic did not work in the end (27). Despite her assertion that she "paid the ticket," Sethe does not own this house either.

Sethe pays for another plot of land with her body when she exchanges sex for a gravesite that would bear the title of her feelings for her daughter: "Beloved." That daughter, though, trades that piece of real estate for 124, where she makes a different kind of claim to the house in haunting it, embodying it with her anger, and later in inhabiting the house in human form. Baby Suggs may claim 124 through her housekeeping, and Sethe may contend that in "paying the ticket" by legally claiming her family that she somehow controls the physical property of the house, but Beloved answers with a spectral claim. Ruth Bienstock Anolik explains that in classic English gothic works, "the true owner of the castle is the possessing ghost" ("Horrors" 667). In her attempt to possess the house, Beloved controls who enters it. Paul D experiences the ghost's presence as a "pool of red and undulating light" the first time he walks into the house (10). Later, he challenges the ghost's claim by shouting "Get the hell out!" and "whipping the table around" (22). The house goes quiet, but Beloved then appears in human form to battle Paul D. She "moves" him out of the house by seemingly casting a spell on him so he cannot sleep inside. When he is gone, even Stamp Paid, who because of his role in the community "took the liberty of walking in your door as though it were his own," cannot enter Beloved's territory (203). Killed as property, her gothic claim counters other claims to the house.

The actual legal property rights to the house, however, belong to Edward Bodwin. Although Bodwin plays the role of the white man thwarting the needs of Baby Suggs, Sethe, and even Beloved to own property and thus to establish personhood, he is not cast as a villain in the text. He and his sister are abolitionists who have repeatedly helped the formerly enslaved people. Stamp Paid says of Bodwin, "He's somebody never turned us down. Steady as a rock" (312). Bodwin is also "the main one kept Sethe from the gallows in the first place" (312). He is therefore not on the level of the slavecatcher or schoolteacher. Even as a "good" white man, though, Bodwin still lives in and perhaps unconsciously perpetuates a system of property that benefits him to the detriment of Baby Suggs and Sethe. One hint of his problem is the bank that Denver sees at the Bodwin house. The bank is in the shape of a black boy: "bulging like moons, two eyes were all the face he had above the gaping red mouth. His hair was a cluster of raised, widely spaced dots made of nail heads. And he was on his knees" (300). His mouth is open and full of coins with the words "At Yo Service" painted across the base of the bank (300). This bank indicates that while Bodwin works on behalf of the enslaved people, the stereotypical Sambo image it portrays is, as Trudier Harris notes, so "pervasive" that "even so-called liberals could not resist its 'charm'" (*Fiction* 336).[27] The degrading image of a black man holding the coins in "service" to the white family points to the system whereby black people can hold property, but only white people can claim it. Although Bodwin has clearly been charitable in renting the house to Baby Suggs in exchange for the labor she can provide and in letting Sethe stay in the house even after the tragic events of Beloved's death, his charity is not enough to grant these women agency. What is lacking for these women is property ownership.

Bodwin is actually extending charity again to yet a third generation, as the Bodwins give Denver a job, and Mr. Bodwin drives his carriage over to 124 to pick her up for her first day. As he makes his way there, he dwells on his childhood memories of living in the house. When Morrison depicts his point of view, it is clear that even though he has not visited 124 in thirty years, he still thinks of himself as the owner. He only rents it because "the tenants at least kept it from the disrepair total abandonment would permit" (306). The house seems to have had a dark existence even before Beloved's death. Bodwin thinks, "Women died there: his mother, grandmother, an aunt and an older sister before he was born" (305). Askeland notes that "Morrison leaves this enigmatic fact unexplained and undeveloped," but more troubling is "Bodwin's seeming indifference to their deaths" (166). His fixation on the house is not due to the loss of his mother and the other women but instead on whether the treasures he buried, "precious things he wanted to protect," including tin soldiers and a watch chain, were still there. Wondering about the treasure leads Bodwin to recall his youth when he and his sister were fighting slavery, and these "good years" are likewise seen by Bodwin as treasure. The house is therefore not just still legally owned by Bodwin, with Baby Suggs and Sethe relegated to unnamed "tenants," but in its connections to his family, childhood, and the treasures he wanted to protect, 124 is still spiritually owned by him as well, even while the spirit of Beloved tries to inhabit and claim it for herself. It is central to Bodwin's conception of himself as crusader and thus to his personhood.

When Bodwin arrives at the house, a battle for its possession is already taking place. Sethe is transfixed by the singing of the women from the community who are attempting to exorcise the ghost from 124, and she, Denver, and Beloved watch the group of women from the porch, not entirely sure what they are doing. When Sethe sees Bodwin, she assumes that he is schoolteacher coming again to claim Beloved: "He is coming into her yard and he is coming for her best thing" (308). The scene echoes Beloved's murder as Sethe again thinks, "No. no. Nonono" and reacts, while Beloved sees Sethe run and feels she has been abandoned: "Alone. Again" (308). This second version of the scene, however, has one significant change. Sethe does not kill her child to make a property claim; this time, she goes after the white man. Only Denver's quick intervention saves Mr. Bodwin from the ice pick that Sethe is holding. This revision may seem satisfying in that Sethe has learned that killing her children to claim them traps them all in the system instead of freeing them from it. Attacking the white man at least directs the violence at the source of the problem. Mr. Bodwin, however, is not schoolteacher, and killing him would, in Stamp Paid's words, "be the worst thing in the world for us" (312). For Sethe, there is no right choice and no action that will keep Beloved with her.

Sethe does not have the agency to make a good decision because it is not "her yard" that Bodwin enters any more than it is Baby Suggs's yard that schoolteacher enters. The women cannot create a safe space to claim their personhood because they do not own property, just as Jacobs does not own that much-desired hearthstone. Paul D and Stamp Paid make the dark joke, "Every time a whiteman come to the door [Sethe] got to kill somebody?" (313). Sethe's turn to violence is a second attempt to claim that door. Within the discourse of property rights, Sethe's attempt fails. Whereas her killing of Beloved thwarts schoolteacher's claim on her and her children, Sethe's attempt to kill Bodwin does not ensure her right to 124 and would not even if she had succeeded. Because Sethe loses Beloved the first time and gains nothing the second time, violence ultimately fails in both scenes, and Sethe is left without agency.

Within the discourse of haunting, however, Sethe's action does effect change. Beloved disappears, suggesting that her spectral claim on both 124 and Sethe has been negated. Perhaps Sethe's choice to destroy the white invader rather than the child relieves the burden of guilt she carries for her complicity. The result is that Sethe has at least some possibility of crafting personhood now that the discourse of haunting no longer claims her. Although she feels that in the disappearance of Beloved, she has lost her "best thing," Paul D tells Sethe, "You your best thing" (322). Paul D tells Sethe that she does indeed own something, not the property of 124 but herself. Sethe may now be able to claim that freed self.

DENVER

In the end, Sethe has one family member left, her daughter Denver. Whereas the violence of claiming property overwhelms Sethe's narrative of kinship with Beloved, Denver is never claimed as property. Denver is only claimed as daughter, allowing her character to counter the gothic haunting of Beloved. In giving Sethe two daughters and in showing Beloved and Denver as having two distinct trajectories, Morrison provides a path for hope, a rare commodity in the world of the novel. Denver emerges as a character of hope because in a gothic narrative where the past fights to affect the present and the present counters by intentional forgetting of the past, she stands in the apex between temporalities. She witnesses the haunting of Sethe by Beloved but is free to build personhood in ways that Beloved, Baby Suggs, Paul D, and Sethe and the others formerly enslaved are not.

Denver understands the history of slavery that these other characters have experienced because she listens to their stories. Throughout most of her life, Denver has feared the past, hearing of Beloved's murder from a classmate. Even though Denver does not fully comprehend the evils of slavery, she understands that "the thing that happened that made it all right for my mother to kill my sister could happen again. I don't know what it is, I don't know who it is, but maybe there is something else terrible enough to make her do it again" (242). But Denver later listens to Sethe's stories explaining why she made the choice she did. Although Beloved does not understand, Denver does. Ashraf H. A. Rushdy notes Morrison's use of point of view: "This moment of understanding, the moment when Sethe articulates her recognition of the reasons she killed Beloved, is filtered through Denver's hearing and understanding" ("Signifyin(g)" 583). Denver has also heard the story of her birth; she then retells the story of Amy Denver to Beloved. Denver is now the age Sethe was during the escape, so she can identify with her mother. As Denver tells the tale, "she stepped into the told story" figuratively walking in Sethe's path as she flees slavery (36). The storytelling in the novel allows Denver to be Sethe's claimed daughter, a vessel for the history of their family.

Denver furthermore becomes the family's pathway to the future. Mae G. Henderson explains that Sethe's "future is figuratively embodied in her relationship to Denver" ("Toni" 75). Denver leaves 124 on her own to seek help from the community when Sethe is drowning in guilt and blame, and they are all starving. After hearing her mother's explanations to Beloved, Denver realizes that it is up to her to secure their survival: "The job she started out with, protecting Beloved from Sethe, changed to protecting her mother from Beloved" (286). Having heard her mother's and grandmother's stories, she is scared to venture away from 124 and hesitates "on the porch of 124 ready to be swallowed up in the world beyond the edge of the porch" (286). She is emboldened, though, through a conversation with what seems to be the spirit of Baby Suggs. Denver pleads that "you said there was no defense," but Baby Suggs answers, "There ain't" but follows with, "Know it, and go on out the yard. Go on" (288). Knowing the past will give Denver the tools to propel her into the future. She can turn the ice pick aside when Sethe tries to kill Bodwin. Although she understands what motivates Sethe's action, she effectively ensures that history will not repeat itself. Because of Denver, the future will not be a gothic doubling of the past.

Denver is therefore singularly important in understanding the past and representing the future. She is able to stand in this intersection of time because she was never property. Denver is, as Sethe declares, a "charmed child. From the beginning" (50). Since Sethe is pregnant with Denver when she leaves Sweet Home, Denver is never schoolteacher's physical property. Sethe actually delivers Denver the moment she steps into the Ohio River, the line dividing slave state from free. Although when schoolteacher arrives, Sethe tries to kill all her children, she does not succeed, so Denver is consequently not claimed by Sethe through destruction. Denver has no personal memory of slavery and no experience of feeling that her body was owned by someone else. In contrast, when Baby Suggs arrives in Ohio, she "suddenly" sees her hands "and thought with a clarity as simple as it was dazzling, 'These hands belong to me. These *my* hands'" (166). Baby Suggs feels her heartbeat and wonders if it had always pounded. Although Denver has imbibed the tragedy of being someone else's property from her mother and grandmother, her hands and heart have always been her own.

While those formerly enslaved each struggle to claim their personhood, Denver, as a representative of the next generation, has a better chance. She is working for the Bodwins, getting an education, and seeking a second job at a shirt factory to help her mother. In symbolizing this glimmer of hope in a very dark and gothic tale, Denver becomes, as Lady Jones describes her, "everybody's child" (290). When she tells Lady Jones that they are starving, the entire community begins to help them. When Denver earlier tells Beloved the story of her namesake Amy Denver, she realizes that "it made her feel like a bill was owing somewhere and she, Denver, had to pay it" (91). Denver indeed owes her life to Amy Denver's charity, her mother's courage, her grandmother's tenacity, and her community's intervention. Free from haunting, Denver can bear witness to their stories of being property.

※ ※ ※

In *A Different Drummer*, when Tucker Caliban and his fellow African Americans leave their southern state, the plot does not follow them. The reader does not know if the destruction and denouncement of white society lead to the finding of a new place to claim as home. Morrison, on the other hand, reveals how the dynamics intertwining race, property, and personhood do not end with slavery. The river that spatially divides Kentucky from Ohio, and the Civil War that temporally divides the era of slavery from the era of Reconstruction are not boundaries strong enough to prevent the ongoing effects of a system built on the conflation of people and property. In *Beloved*, Morrison reveals the horror of people becoming property, the stakes involved in making and unmaking property claims, and the deprivation of being unable to create personhood even after escaping slavery, but also the potential hope of being able to remember the past but not be haunted by it. In constructing this gothic tale, Morrison seeks to create a place:

> There is no place you or I can go, to think about or not think about, to summon the presences of, or recollect the absences of slaves; nothing that reminds us of the ones who made the journey and of those who did not make it. There is no suitable memorial, or plaque, or wreath, or wall, or park, or skyscraper lobby. There's no 300-foot tower, there's no small bench by the road. There is not even a tree scored, an initial that I can visit or you can visit in Charleston or Savannah or New

York or Providence or better still on the banks of the Mississippi. And because such a place doesn't exist (that I know of) the book had to. (qtd in McKay 3)

The book itself becomes the place to counter other places: the false beauty of Sweet Home, the horror of Alfred, Georgia, and the haunting of 124. The book is a territory not owned and proscribed by the laws of property rights that worked to benefit white slaveholders and to devastate those they held in slavery. The book is the yard Baby Suggs and Sethe thought they owned, marking off a place to unlock the circle of iron and create personhood. The book is a site to remember the "sixty million and more" whose very names are lost to history. In making *Beloved* a place, Morrison creates a territory for these ghosts to live again and to haunt the system that made them property.

CHAPTER FIVE

Claiming the Property of History in Octavia Butler's *Kindred* and Natasha Trethewey's *Native Guard*

The question Eric Foner asks, "Who Owns History?" has become particularly significant, with passionate public debates about the meaning of Civil War monuments and with academic fields from economics to history rethinking slavery's role in building the modern capitalist world.[1] That we would be so conflicted about a war waged a century and a half ago points to the myriad ways in which the American narrative of freedom cannot contain the vast impact of three and a half centuries of New World slavery. The struggle over who tells this history and how it is told is understandable. Underlying Foner's question, however, is yet a more fundamental one: How can history be owned? In order for something to be owned, it must be property subject to a claim. Though history is grounded in the tangible entities of numbers and bodies, in the end it is a construct built with words and shaped by language. Ownership therefore cannot be established by a bill of sale but must be claimed through that same medium of language. For literary writers, the language of the gothic has proven particularly powerful in approaching history, as specters often haunt to claim title. Avery Gordon explains that "haunting is a constituent element of modern social life" because "the ghost or the apparition is one form by which something lost, or barely visible, or seemingly not there to our supposedly well-trained eyes, makes itself known or apparent to us" (7, 8). Haunting thus suggests that history is not over and settled but available for a new telling and perhaps new ownership.

Natasha Trethewey's 2006 poetry collection, *Native Guard*, depicts hauntings, both personal and national, as she explores memories of her mother intertwined with the forgotten history of black Union soldiers stationed at Ship Island, Mississippi, during the Civil War. Octavia Butler's 1979 novel, *Kindred*, portrays the African American protagonist Dana living in a 1976 California world with her white husband Kevin when she is pulled abruptly back to an 1815 Maryland world where she must not only interact with her white and black ancestors but must also act the part of an enslaved person herself. In exploring how slavery haunts the present, these works align with the traditional gothic focus, according to Allan Lloyd-Smith, of "the *return* of the past, of the repressed and denied, the buried secret that subverts and corrodes the present" (1).² Butler and Trethewey, however, do not just show how slavery haunts us; they also reveal how we haunt slavery. Haunting backwards becomes a thinkable thought in postmodern narratives when the arrow of time can point either way, so that time, as Elizabeth Deeds Ermarth explains, "is not a neutral and absolute but a function of position, literally of reader position" (22). While Butler's use of time travel posits characters from the twentieth century as ghosts in the nineteenth century, Trethewey uses point of view and photography as portals in a kind of poetic time travel. Moving back and forth on the timeline, their works construct a conversation of haunting. While the haunting *by* the past brings pain, the haunting *of* the past restores power. Butler's and Trethewey's depictions of haunting backwards thus provide a new way to see that "something lost, or barely visible."

Critics of both works discuss the authors' rewriting of history. I will argue, however, that this rewriting is actually a claim to the property of the past that crucially rewrites the paradigm of property and power in slavery.³ In Butler's depiction, enslaved people are bought, sold, and raped as items of property subject to a master's whim. Dana's career as a writer, however, indicates that in addition to experiencing the past of slavery, she is composing the history of this past, claiming it as her own. In Trethewey's depiction, people become literal property, as unclaimed soldiers' bodies molder under the ground. *Native Guard* then constructs and claims the history of these soldiers. While slavery cannot be erased, and ancestors cannot be rescued from bondage, the texts attempt to change who owns this history.

Haunting backwards furthermore allows the authors to reclaim ancestors. Dana discovers the stories behind the names in the family Bible and learns that her "kindred" includes enslaved women with little chance for agency and slaveholders whose cruelty is fed by their environment. Trethewey records both the personal loss of a mother and the national loss of soldiers during the Civil War, recovering her literal and figurative ancestors by giving them voices and elegizing their deaths. In both texts, the texts craft a home, providing a place for these ancestors to exist. In chapter 4, I discussed how Sethe in Toni Morrison's *Beloved* claims her daughter through destruction. These texts enact a kind of resurrection in designating as the "beloved" part of the past the ancestors who lived in slavery and whose ghostly voices need to be reconstructed in the space created by these texts. In doing so, these texts attempt to answer the stubborn problem of property this study has traced from the nineteenth century to the twenty-first. Instead of having to build off the system, con the system, opt in or opt out, these texts intervene backwards into history to change what that history means for the present by claiming ownership of it.

TIME TRAVEL AND THE GOTHIC

From its early iterations in eighteenth-century England, the gothic genre has relied on ruptures in chronological time. The setting of gothic narratives in the ruins of medieval castles and churches primes the reader to be wary of the past's influence. The figure of the ghost or specter then confirms the fear that when the past does not remain past and the dead do not remain dead, chaos ensues in the present. Countering the Enlightenment grand narrative of each generation beginning anew with that *tabula rasa* or blank slate on which to craft identity, the ghost announces that identity comes bound with the weight of history. Eric Savoy explains how this weight then affects the individual in the present: "Gothic texts return obsessively to the personal, the familial, and the national pasts to complicate rather than to clarify them, but mainly to implicate the individual in a deep morass of American desires and deeds that allow no final escape from or transcendence of them" ("Rise" 169). The individual faces both collective guilt and the inability to escape the haunting, all because of the bleeding of the past into the present.

While Butler and Trethewey employ this gothic rupture in their explorations of the past, they also reverse the rupture. When Dana becomes the specter disrupting 1815, and Trethewey employs photography to pull the reader back into a particular moment, this willingness to play with time points to their postmodern context. Ermarth explains that postmodern narratives are not constrained by "the time of history, the time of project, the time of Newton and Kant, the time of clocks and capital" (22). The postmodern fluidity of time is evident in other contemporary literary works as well. James McBride's *Song Yet Sung* (2008) depicts visions of the twentieth-century future appearing to a runaway, although she has difficulty comprehending the events, such as Martin Luther King Jr. speaking about dreams. Louise Erdrich's *Round House* (2012) contains a specter from the future who keeps appearing to the main character until he is in a car accident and sees the specter as a real person helping him in the aftermath. This move in postmodern works to flip the gothic haunting on its head has not yet been noticed by critics, but the effects are significant. Butler and Trethewey use the reversal in true gothic form to scare the reader by showing that the past and present are closely connected, thus implicating the reader in that "morass" of history and the battle over property.

Hence these texts borrow from the gothic genre even as they are revising it for a postmodern context. An interesting obstacle, however, impedes the connection between *Native Guard* and the gothic genre: literary critics who write about the gothic focus almost exclusively on prose. That poetry can employ gothic tropes is evident from the earliest American literature, such as Philip Freneau's 1792 poem "To Sir Toby," which explores the horror of slavery. So, the question is: Why do literary critics prefer to study prose? (And given the reliance on prose in this study, I must include myself here.) David J. Rothman finds "the neglect of poetic sources of the Gothic as a whole" nothing short of "surprising" (175). The lack is at least in part the product of inertia; critics engage in conversation with other critics, and the conversations about the gothic have taken place largely in the prose room. Nonetheless, *Native Guard* is ripe for a gothic approach in its depiction of flowers that whisper "Die early," a ghost that pins the speaker to a bed, dead bodies that "molder" beneath battlefields, and even a poem entitled "Southern Gothic."

Although critics have not used the term "gothic" in discussing *Native Guard*, Daniel Cross Turner uses "undeadness" ("Lyric" 103), Elizabeth Bradford Frye and Coleman Hutchison label her poetry "haunted" (37), and William M. Ramsey sees it as "ghost-haunted" (122). These critics examine Trethewey's exploration of southern history, with Ramsey suggesting that her approach is postmodern in that the poet reconfigures history as a "constitutive act" (134).[4] Using a specifically gothic approach for *Native Guard*, however, not only allows the poetry to be in conversation with that whole room of gothic prose works, but it also allows us to see that, just as in *Kindred*, the haunting works forwards and backwards. The poetry is certainly "ghost-haunted" by Trethewey's loss of her mother and by the slave past of the South, but the true power in the poetry collection lies in Trethewey's own version of time travel to bring the present into the past. Examining the moments of uncanniness reveals that Trethewey claims the property of that past.

For *Kindred*, much of the criticism focuses on the question of genre, but the gothic is generally not part of this discussion.[5] Instead, critics weigh the novel's historical matter against its use of time travel to locate an appropriate label. Since Butler is best known for writing science fiction, critics are tempted to read Dana's odd trips as the unreal fodder of a science fiction novel.[6] Butler herself points out one problem with this classification: "[*Kindred*] obviously was not science fiction. There's absolutely no science in it" ("Black" 14). The text, in fact, never bothers to unveil the modus operandi for Dana's time traveling. A. Timothy Spaulding points out another complication: the "realistic representation of nineteenth-century slavery" (44). Spaulding considers *Kindred* a "postmodern slave narrative" and shares with other critics the view that *Kindred* is largely a historical novel.[7] Jason Haslam, however, argues that Butler's depiction of history is actually gothic.[8] Haslam sees this gothic as "generative" and asks, "Could the walking dead be the talking cure?" ("Slavery" 51). Although I share Haslam's gothic lens, I will argue that the "walking dead," that is, the horrors of the past, are not "generative" as much as threatening. Dana's personhood is endangered by a past where she is only property. The "generative" move comes instead as Dana is able to claim the past as her own property.

HAUNTED BY THE PAST IN *KINDRED*

When *Kindred* opens, Dana and Kevin are inhabiting their contemporary California world, blithely assuming a safe barrier between their present and the past that contains slavery. Although Dana will be haunted by a past that becomes an uncanny home and by being treated as property, Dana and Kevin begin as unwitting victims who are largely ignorant of the experience of slavery because the books and films that have crafted that history are woefully inadequate. Dana tells Kevin that although "I've been watching the violence of this time go by on the screen long enough to have picked up a few things," the enslaved people in the nineteenth century "know more about real violence than the screenwriters of today will ever know" (48). After Dana's second trip to the past, she and Kevin strategize about how she can survive. They land on the idea of forging free papers but realize they have no idea what these papers would look like. They then scour the ten books they own on African American history and find nothing helpful. Later, when Dana returns to the present alone, she again tries to read anything she can find about slavery, even *Gone with the Wind*, but finds "its version of happy darkies in tender loving bondage was more than I could stand" (116). If, as Lloyd-Smith argues, the gothic appears when a "buried secret" is ignored by a culture that "does not want to know," then Dana and Kevin as representations of the modern world are ripe for being haunted (1).

Even their marriage signals their naivety. Kevin assumes his sister, who is his only relative, will "love" Dana, and he is shocked when the sister announces that Dana and Kevin are barred from her home. Dana's uncle, who has been like a father to her, denounces her choice of a white man, while her aunt is happy only because their children will be "lighter" (111). Dana and Kevin take the leap anyway with a clichéd quick trip to Vegas. They decide to pretend they "haven't got relatives," thinking that they can ignore history (112). Spaulding argues that the science part of science fiction is left out of the novel so that Butler can "[replace] the question of *how* Dana travels through time with the more crucial question of *why* such a physical intersection between past and present exists for her" (47). The answer I pose here to that question of why is that Dana and Kevin, as stand-ins for the reader, have repressed or ignored a past that answers with haunting.

Perhaps Dana and Kevin could perceive the haunting approaching, much as Baby Suggs in *Beloved* smells the apocalyptic horsemen, if they knew they were characters in a gothic novel and understood that ghosts usually linger to inhabit property, but they seem not to know even the basic premise of a haunted house. Although critics have not yet noticed the gothic role played by the house, every student of mine who has read the book in a course on gothic literature (and is thus using a gothic lens) immediately worries about the agency of the house. It is in fact the vexed meaning of home as both place and property that reveals most clearly how Dana and Kevin are haunted by the past.[9] The "trouble" begins when Dana and Kevin move into what Dana calls "a house of our own" (12). In emphasizing their joint ownership of the house, Dana is unwittingly traipsing upon a couple of dangerous spots in gothic territory. One is the question of property ownership. Dana claims the house, but it is this place that she always loses when she is pulled back in time. Although Butler does not reveal the mechanics of Dana's time travel, the house itself seems to act as the conduit, tesseract, or wormhole. Dana's claim of ownership is also the concrete effect of her cross-racial relationship with Kevin. The novel highlights the precarious interaction of race and property when Dana's uncle announces that he will not leave her his apartment building for fear that it will "fall into white hands" (112). Dana and Kevin's house represents their brave union in defiance of society and their families, but it also signals how oblivious they are to the historical ramifications of that union. Fraught with questions of people and property, this house is indeed where the "trouble" begins.

Dana and Kevin, however, never suspect that the house may be the source of the haunting. In fact, instead of fleeing from the place where she is yanked back into slavery, Dana refuses to leave the house. After her first trip to the past, Dana admits, "I don't feel secure here," but she continues to think of the house as her safe place, which, given its contrast with the Maryland world of slavery, is certainly understandable. Though she and Kevin have not even unpacked their belongings, she continually refers to the house as "home," a word that is used repeatedly in the narrative. This home encompasses her bond with Kevin as well. When he is concerned that Dana mistook him for a patroller briefly during a shift to the present, he asks, "Do I look like someone you can come home to from where you may be going?" (51). When she answers that she needs him, he replies, "Just keep coming home" (51).

That is easier said than done. Though the modern, familiar 1976 world should be the foil for the brute reality of slave life, the notion of home becomes gothic in the conflation of these two places and the intertwining of race and property. When Dana first realizes that her trips are through space and time, taking her across the country and back a century and a half, she thinks, "I was farther from home than I had thought" (27). She might, however, be much closer. In his essay on the uncanny, Sigmund Freud studies instances that spark an uncanny feeling and the linguistic history of the German word for uncanny, "unheimlich," which has as its root the idea of "homely." He finds that both investigations lead to the conclusion that the uncanny is sparked by things that are "known of old and long familiar" (220). Dolls, doppelgangers, and eerie repetition are among the particular triggers, but all originate from the same place: home. As I examined in chapter 3, this idea of home leads to the tangible symbol of the haunted house in many narratives. In *Kindred*, the uncanniness of home is found in Dana's connection to the past. Dana figures out that Rufus, the white boy whom she repeatedly saves, is her ancestor as is the young enslaved girl she meets named Alice. Dana is thus returning to a place "known of old." For a homely thing to become uncanny, however, it must appear in a different way, such as a doll becoming animate. Dana has previously only had a vague idea of her family line from seeing names in a Bible, and she was not aware that the "Rufus Weylin" listed alongside "Alice Greenwood Weylin" was Alice's white master. This forced cross-racial relationship has been buried in history along with Alice's oppression. The knowledge of her ancestors proves uncanny to Dana as the familiar becomes different and dangerous.

The danger escalates as Dana begins to feel at home in the past, a comfort level that is both helpful and risky. Time is distorted in her time traveling so that a few months' time in the past is equal to only a few minutes when she returns to the present. This distortion makes Dana feel more connected to the world of the past because she is spending more time there, according to her body clock. When Dana realizes that the girl she meets is Alice, she thinks, "These people were my relatives, my ancestors. And this place could be my refuge" (37). But shortly after this thought, Dana is attacked by a white patroller who intends to rape her. In the past, she has no rights and no identity as a person, leaving her as vulnerable as Alice. Later, when Dana travels to Maryland and approaches the Weylin house, she catches herself saying, "Home at last," although she immediately reminds herself that here she is considered property, and this is a "hostile place" (126).

As Dana begins to feels less at home in the present, uncanny doublings between her California home and the "hostile place" of slavery scare her. Even though Dana thinks of Kevin as "my anchor, my tie to my own world," she also sees odd correlations between him and the slaveholders from the past (47).[10] The one disagreement Dana and Kevin have before they marry is when Kevin asks Dana to type his manuscript, and she refuses because she finds the secretarial role demeaning. She finds herself, however, in a parallel circumstance when Rufus asks her to write his letters for him. Spaulding finds that "Kevin's attitude toward Dana in this regard represents a disturbing corollary to Rufus's treatment of her in the past" (54). Dana even admits to being worried that "some part of this place would rub off on [Kevin]" (77). Despite the uncanny doubling, there is no indication that Kevin changes, and towards the end, Dana again calls him "my anchor here in my own time" (246).[11] These moments of mirroring, though, give Dana a new perspective on how her cross-racial relationship in another time period could be shaped by power instead of love, and how powerless her female ancestors were as someone else's property.

Dana's haunting by the past is indeed solidified by the link between home and property and the conflation of property and people. At one point, Rufus wants Dana to destroy the map of Maryland she has brought with her. The map obviously signals Dana's desire to leave, and Rufus assures her, "You're home" (143). As warm and familial as this may sound, Rufus is actually laying claim to her. His home is her home because he thinks that in addition to being his guardian angel, she is his property. Rufus's father, Tom, likewise assures Dana, "You know there's always a home for you here," but this promise is immediately preceded by a threatened "good whipping" and is contingent on Dana's helping Rufus (201). Despite Tom Weylin's acknowledgement of Dana's odd powers, her skin color makes him unable to see Dana as anything but property. Even Rufus eventually treats Dana as property when he sends her to the fields. When Dana regains consciousness after being beaten by the overseer, she realizes, "I was still in hell," the place where she is only property (213). In her early trips, Dana is able to remain separate enough from the past world to maintain a semblance of a safe barrier; she and Kevin are just "observers watching a show. We were watching history happen around us. And we were actors" (98). Yet the longer Dana stays in the past, the more it becomes, though a hell, also a home, and she stops pretending.[12] During her last return to the present, Dana loses her arm in the wall of that troublesome house. Ashraf H. A. Rushdy claims this happens "apparently between 'homes'—between a past that has claim on her and a present on which she has a claim" ("Families" 140). In the end, however, these places are conflated as she is stuck between homes and literally conflated with property.

HAUNTING BACKWARDS IN *KINDRED*

While Dana is haunted by a past that claims her as property, she and Kevin in turn haunt this past as strangers from the future. At first, Dana is not aware of her own ghostly qualities. Rufus asks her if she is "like a ghost," but Dana as a twentieth-century rationalist is quick to respond, "There are no ghosts" (24). When Rufus explains that his mother once saw a ghost, Dana realizes that Margaret Weylin was referring to Dana's first appearance and guesses that "I was probably her ghost" (24). In repeatedly appearing out of thin air just in time to save Rufus, Dana surely has the supernatural oddness of a ghost. Kevin has this oddness as well. Dana describes him as "an unusual-looking white man, his face young, almost unlined, but his hair completely gray and his eyes so pale as to be almost colorless" (54). When this description is read through a gothic lens, Kevin's whiteness becomes creepy. He is the whiter-than-white color of the nameless terror at the end of Edgar Allan Poe's *The Narrative of Arthur Gordon Pym* or the blind Mrs. Dalton in Richard Wright's *Native Son*. His stark whiteness highlights the barrier Dana crosses in marrying him. Dana, however, thinks of him as a "kindred spirit" (57), which points both to their decision to defy family to become "kindred" and the resulting experience when they move into a "house of our own" of becoming "spirits" to the people in the past. When Kevin tries to explain to Rufus that they are real people and "we come from a future time and place," he only confirms Rufus's suspicions about their ghostly quality (62). Tom Weylin later asks Dana, "What are you?" (130). Dana and Kevin may be as human as the Weylins, but in the nineteenth century, they play the role of specters.

One crucial question about these specters from the future is whether they can have any power or effect on the people they haunt. Although most critics assume that Dana and Kevin can change the past, the text is actually ambiguous on this question. Of particular significance is the question of whether Rufus dying before adulthood or Alice refusing him so that they do not produce Hagar would result in Dana no longer existing. Dana herself wonders, "What would have happened to me, to my mother's family, if I hadn't saved [Rufus]," but then she figures that "his life could not depend on the actions of his unconceived descendant. No matter what I did, he would have to survive to father Hagar, or I could not exist. That made sense" (29). Kevin is skeptical that they can have any effect, telling Dana that history "already has happened. We're in the middle of history. We surely can't change it" (100). Without a clear answer, though, Dana decides not to "test the paradox" and continues to save Rufus (29).

In the meantime, she launches into the project of changing Rufus's view of enslaved people as property by using her influence over him. This influence is indeed spectral. Rufus admits that since childhood, he has had nightmares about her (254). She thinks that with this power she can temper his racism. Her very presence proves that the way of life practiced by Rufus's family is not natural and eternal but doomed, as the strict division between the races will disappear in the future. In this time, however, Rufus's views are nurtured by his parents and supported by law. When Dana tells Kevin that she is trying to give Rufus "good memories" of her, to buy some "insurance" for her next visit, Kevin responds that "his environment will be influencing him every day you're gone" and that Dana is "gambling against history" (83). Her gamble does not seem to pay off, as Rufus indeed becomes an authoritarian slaveholder just like his father. Dana's haunting of Rufus might actually have the opposite effect of what she intends. She has insisted throughout their interactions that she is married to Kevin as a way to teach Rufus that people are equal. Rufus uses this information, however, to pressure Alice into submitting to a sexual relationship: "I told her about everything. Even about you and Kevin being married. Especially about that" (124).

Dana's role in Rufus's sustained sexual exploitation of Alice is the point where the questions of whether Dana can effect change in her haunting backwards become particularly complex. Many critics, assuming that Dana needs Hagar to be born to ensure her survival in her own time, blame Dana for not intervening to rescue Alice. Trudier Harris, for example, argues, "We can view Dana's toleration of Rufus's repeated rapes of Alice as Dana's essentially raping Alice herself, which Dana recognizes" (*Scary* 73). Another way to frame this reading would be to say that the past ends up affecting Dana more than she affects the past, and the haunting *by* the past has more power than the haunting *of* the past.[13] Rushdy argues that Dana is not acting out of concern about the survival of her family line, pointing to the scene where Dana urges Alice and Isaac to flee. Rushdy suggests that Dana may be "trying to reconstruct her family tree" ("Families" 145). Dana further shows her willingness to support Alice in whatever decision she makes in regards to Rufus. Although Dana delivers Rufus's ultimatum, she twice declines to give Alice advice on her answer and admits that she herself would refuse. When Alice initially indicates that she will run away, Dana leaves, "to stall Rufus. If I really work at it, I think I can get him to let you off tonight. That will give you a start" (168). Alice, however, resigns herself to accepting Rufus, a decision she depicts as her fate: "He knew I would sooner or later" (168). If it is indeed a fate that cannot be changed, then perhaps Kevin is right, and Dana simply cannot affect the past.

Her possible lack of agency does not assuage her guilt. Dana wonders several times throughout her experience if she should be saving Rufus at all, given his treatment of enslaved people as property. After he sells three people, she wishes she "had left Rufus lying in the mud" because "he's no good. He's all grown up now, and part of the system" (223). Carrie, however, communicates to Dana in her unique sign language what Dana suspects: that if Rufus dies, "the people would be sold without regard for family ties" (223). When Dana murders Rufus to prevent him from raping her, she puts other people in jeopardy to save herself. Harris certainly takes this view, arguing that "it is only when her own vagina is threatened that Dana kills Rufus" (*Scary* 77). By killing Rufus, she is, according to Harris, "executing" him, and she puts every other enslaved person in danger (*Scary* 78). When she and Kevin visit Maryland in the present to trace what happened after Dana left, they find a bill of sale. Carrie's three sons are indeed listed, though Carrie is not, suggesting that her family was split. Even as a specter haunting backwards, Dana is simultaneously haunted herself by the effects of her actions. She seems either to have little power to affect the past or only the power to do ill.

One possibility that counters this reading is Dana's effect on the next generation through her relationship with Margaret Weylin. After Margaret loses three children in childbirth, separates from her husband, and then returns after his death, her personality changes drastically, probably due to her opium addiction. She now likes Dana and spends hours listening to her read. Dana's relationship with Margaret proves as important to the continuation of Dana's family line as the one she has with Rufus. Since Hagar ended up in Baltimore, where Margaret's family lives, Dana guesses that Margaret took Rufus and Alice's children with her there after Rufus's death, perhaps even accepting them as her grandchildren. Although this bond remains conjecture on Dana's part, even Rufus seems to accept the children as his own before he dies by letting them learn to read, signing their free papers, and having them call him "Daddy" (251). That Hagar writes her name in the family Bible as "Hagar Weylin" and her parents as "Rufus Weylin" and "Alice Greenwood Weylin" suggests that she accepted Rufus as her father.

Despite this one small glimmer of hope, the overall effect of Dana's haunting of the past seems to be paltry when we consider Rufus's continuing cruel behavior and Alice's resulting suicide. If slavery's conflation of people with property is the most significant element of the past's haunting, the crucial question is whether this problem of property is overcome in the haunting backwards. Can Dana's modern status as person affect or even erase the past's presumption that she is property? That the presumption is strong is indicated in Rufus's first question to Kevin: "Does Dana belong to you now?" (60). Although Dana repeatedly tells Rufus that Kevin is her husband, pretending that she is his property makes living in this time easier. Her acting job may be too good at times, as Tom Weylin feels free to beat her like any other enslaved person when he catches her reading. When Rufus asks her not to teach anyone else to read, he suggests that his father might sell her. Even though Dana protests that "he doesn't own me," Rufus assures her his father could sell her anyway (139).

Dana may look like property to both Tom and Rufus, but she counters this view in a singularly telling way: she does not die. As I discussed in chapter 4, the ultimate way of claiming the right to property is to destroy it, manifesting ownership by complete mastery. Whenever Tom or Rufus threaten to kill Dana, she disappears back to the present. Tom whips her until she thinks she is going to die, and both Tom and Rufus aim guns at her. When trying to assert their ultimate power, they are confronted with a ghost that disappears from their grasp. If destruction is the sign of ownership, the Weylins do not own Dana because they fail to kill her. Dana exclaims to Kevin late in the book when he asks her if Rufus has raped her, "I am not property" (246). Dana's returning to the present signals that her identity in the end is as a person, even in the nineteenth century. Dana is haunted by her inability to save the enslaved people in the past, but she equally haunts that past by escaping from it. Given Alice's inability to escape alive, the battle over property may appear to be a draw, but, as we will see, Dana's ability to claim the past as property will prove to be the difference.

TRAVELING THROUGH TIME IN *NATIVE GUARD*

In crafting a narrative with a wormhole between 1976 and 1815, Butler uses time travel to show how the past and the present haunt each other. Natasha Trethewey achieves time travel through the use of point of view along with shifting verb tenses to posit who is speaking and when. Although critics have aptly explored Trethewey's attention to history in the volume, focusing on time travel will reveal how the past exerts power on the present in its lingering reminders of loss and death and how the present speaks back to the past, shaping and changing its meaning. In this doubled haunting, the different points in time engage in a kind of conversation, an exchange that opens the door for Trethewey to construct the past as property that she can claim.[14]

This past figures simultaneously as a time and a place, a duality Trethewey establishes with the opening poem, "Theories of Time and Space." The use of second person in the first few lines thrusts the reader into a particular moment and location: "You can get there from here, though/ there's no going home" (1). Throughout the collection, "here" orients the reader to a space/time reference, thus acting as a kind of signal for time travel, while "home" represents the time and space Trethewey will craft and claim.[15] The poem then instructs "you" to travel to a specific place: down interstate 49 in Mississippi and then across the Gulf in a boat to Ship Island. Mile markers indicate that the trip happens concurrently through space and time: "ticking off// another minute of your life." In instructing the reader to take this road trip, Trethewey's poem rewrites Robert Frost's "Directive," which similarly instructs the reader to take a trip into the past in order to get "lost enough to find yourself," with the final "destination" being the time and space of a "children's playhouse" (252, 253). Unlike in "Directive," however, the trip in Trethewey's poem does not end in a "watering place" that allows the reader to be "whole again beyond confusion" (253). For "Theories of Time and Space," the revelation is not housed back in a former time but in the conversation between that time and the present.

This conversation transpires within the very form of the poem, as the use of enjambment allows words to pertain to their current line and the succeeding line at the same time. When, for example, the mile markers are passing, the poet instructs the reader to "Follow this/ to its natural conclusion—dead end// at the coast." The "natural conclusion" of time passing is the "dead end" of death, but when the enjambment carries over into "at the coast," the speaker moves into the future. While the point of view in the poem remains in present tense with the "you" boarding the boat, the poem then switches to the future tense with the prediction that at the dock: "someone will take your picture." Though the poem does not depict the actual experience of visiting the island, something happens to the "you" there because "the photograph—who you were—/ will be waiting when you return." The switch to a past tense ("who you were") is an eerie suggestion that the photograph will show "you" to be a different person in the future after having visited Ship Island. The addition of the future tense ("will be waiting") suggests something ominously lurking.[16] The doubling made possible by the photograph renders the experience uncanny, as the second person "you" will be haunted in the future by a past version of a self.[17]

The trip described in the poem to Ship Island actually parallels the larger journey Trethewey takes readers on in the collection, starting from their lives in the present and moving to the past buried on Ship Island. The notion that "you" will be different after the trip betrays a desire that the reader will share the point of view depicted in the poems and will in essence let himself or herself be haunted. Being haunted by both the past and the future, however, the reader witnesses competing claims to history, as exemplified by "Pilgrimage," where the speaker journeys to the Civil War site of Vicksburg, Mississippi, along with pilgrims who visit during the spring to reenact the battle. The stakes in claiming place and time in this poem are high. The pilgrims travel back into the past explicitly to haunt and to be haunted because they wish to construct or even to own this history. David W. Blight, in writing about the contested meaning of the Civil War for the present, asks, "Who owns the memory of the Civil War?" (279). One of the many possible answers is "those who wish to preserve the sacred group of battlefield parks for the telling of a heroic narrative of shared military glory on all sides" (279). The poem, however, troubles this ownership. The first word, "here," which is repeated twice more in the first ten lines, brings the reader to the space of Vicksburg to witness the passing of time: "the Mississippi carved/ its mud-dark path," and "the river changed its course,// turning away from the city" while the city resides on "abandoned bluffs" (19). The speaker then moves back into the past to share the point of view of a woman in 1863: "I can see her/ listening to shells explode." The speaker looks to the future from a vantage point in the past: the woman writes "herself// into history, asking *what is to become/ of all the living things in this place?*" In depicting her point of view in present tense, the poem causes the reader to share in her haunting by the future, a haunting whose end result the poem reveals in the next line: "This whole city is a grave."

In describing the pilgrimage, the devotees make every spring in the next several couplets, the poem depicts people in the present intentionally haunting the past: "*Pilgrimage*—the living come to mingle// with the dead, brush against their cold shoulders/ in the long hallways" (20). It is as if the visitors are summoning the ghosts of the past; as Frye and Hutchison explain, "These pilgrims (such as they are) seek sanctification via an encounter with holy ghosts" (38). The ghosts, though, respond with "silence and indifference," perhaps because they are not thrilled that future generations "relive/ their dying on the green battlefield." The bloody battle is now entertainment, as if the tourists are watching one of the modern movies Dana refers to in *Kindred* with the "too-red blood substitute" (36). This present generation thus constructs a particular version of history by their willed haunting of the past. The speaker shares the tourists' point of view while visiting a museum where "we marvel at their clothes—/ preserved under glass—so much smaller// than our own." The glass between the objects and the tourists speaks to the safe barrier between the present and the past that Dana and Kevin at first assume. The past appears so distant that the people are a different size. Yet the brochure in the speaker's room calls the experience "living history," a clear signal of the hubris of people from the present who think that sleeping "in their beds" negates the barrier.

This pretense of history evaporates when the poem reveals the name plate on the door: "*Prissy's Room*." As a slave character in *Gone with the Wind*, Prissy famously protests in an exaggerated, hysterical, high-pitched voice that she does not know how to birth babies. In alluding to slavery, the poem indicates that the past has horrors not fully attended to by the tourists. The poem shifts at the end to the first-person point of view as the past haunts the present: "In my dream,/ the ghost of history lies down beside me,// rolls over, pins me beneath a heavy arm."[18] After the series of couplets, the last line stands startlingly alone. The past is not on a "green battlefield" or safely under glass at a museum but is a ghost whose weight is constricting. Daniel Cross Turner explains, "We are not hermetically sealed from the ghost of history's unsettled, unsettling presence" ("Natasha" 326). The past, however, is also not safely sealed from its future, as haunting in both directions evokes fear: the looming future truly terrifies the woman in 1863 about to die, while the "heavy" past equally horrifies the speaker in the present contemplating slavery. The poem thus constructs a conversation of haunting in which the past created and claimed by modern-day pilgrims as they rent rooms in its houses clashes with the past claimed by Prissy as the ghost of slavery.

While "Pilgrimage" explores the public stakes of claiming history, Trethewey's collection further explores how personal histories intertwine haunting and claiming. "Southern Gothic" reveals how the haunting Trethewey describes in a childhood memory mirrors the larger haunting of the South by its history. Katherine R. Henninger explains that although Trethewey's personal poems "seem to present a voice of autobiographical transparency," the voice of the adult child is "carefully crafted" (56). Henninger argues that "as the adult child of her (black) mother and her (white) father, Trethewey offers her bodily self as symbolic 'offspring' of regional, national, and transnational obsessions with race and identity" (57). The personal reflects the larger historical context, a move I read as revealing the complicated tensions of claiming history. "Southern Gothic" opens in first person: "I have lain down into 1970, into the bed/ my parents will share for only a few more years" (40). The present perfect tense of "have lain" indicates that the speaker has traveled back in time, but the action is ongoing in that past.[19] Already evident, however, is the haunting by the future in the hint at the parents' eventual separation in a "few more years." The parents in this moment, though, are troubled by the girl's "endless *why* and *why* and *why*" about the ugly names that she, as a mixed-race child, is called at her school. More glimpses of the future disturb this scene, as the mother in the future will have "cold lips stitched shut," and the father has lines that "deepen/ toward an expression of grief." At this point in time, though, the family is still together: "We're huddled on the tiny island of bed, quiet/ in the language of blood." This bed of shelter, however, is in an "unsteady" house, which is itself "sinking deeper/ into the muck of ancestry." The point of view in 1970 is not only haunted by the future separation of the family, but also by an even more distant past of ancestry, a haunting made concrete, as it is in *Kindred*, by the conduit of an "unsteady" house. In marrying across racial lines, the parents made the brave decision that Dana and Kevin do in *Kindred* to defy society. They actually break the law in Mississippi, as Trethewey points out in her poem "Miscegenation." But just as in *Kindred*, this choice links them to a history of race relations that leads back to slavery. This family, then, on their "tiny island of bed" is haunted: "Oil lamps flicker/ around us—our shadows, dark glyphs on the wall,/ bigger and stranger than we are." The family has claimed the property of this house, but the house proves haunted by the "shadows" of the past. As the poem moves to present tense ("we are"), the shift suggests that the speaker in the present is not just reliving a past memory but that the past is still present and is still haunting. The "we" suggests that this haunting may also include the reader, who has been invited to take the journey of the collection. Although the past haunts this family, the poet moves back into that past to reclaim this moment for the present. The poem constructed in language becomes a form of property that, unlike the sinking, unsteady house, can be claimed. In "Southern Gothic" as well as in "Pilgrimage," the point of view moves backwards and forwards in time to show that haunting comes from the past and the present simultaneously. The reader hence learns to fear the past in the form of ghosts from history and the very shadows of slavery, and to fear the future's promise of eventual loss and death.

PHOTOGRAPHY AS PORTAL IN *NATIVE GUARD*

In addition to employing point of view to travel through time, Trethewey uses photography as a portal to allow the present to gain access to the past and to allow the past to speak to the present. In this exchange is the possibility of capture, of using a photograph to claim the property of a moment in time by freezing it and later by framing it and owning it.[20] Susan Sontag explains that "to photograph is to appropriate the thing photographed" (4). Trethewey has certainly considered photography's ability to capture. In her collection *Bellocq's Ophelia*, Trethewey writes poems about E. J. Bellocq's photographs of New Orleans prostitutes. By photographing women whose bodies are for sale, Bellocq employs a secondary materializing and capture of their bodies. One of the women buys her own camera, however, desiring to claim a moment: "On the crowded street I want to stop/ time, hold it captive in my dark chamber" (46).[21] This method of capturing time makes photography particularly helpful for claiming history.

Trethewey, however, also troubles the stasis of photographic capture by imagining the larger temporal context of a photograph. She explains that "whenever I look at photographs I'm always thinking about a couple of things; the moment just before it, the moment after it, and what the subjects of the photograph could or could not have known about what was to come" ("Conversations" 18). The speaker of the two poems I will examine moves back in time to inhabit the moment captured by the photograph, but this moment becomes haunted by the moments on both sides of that instant. Thadious M. Davis's reading of Trethewey's use of photographs as "enfoldment" shows how the photograph can reflect multiple time frames and points of view. She explains that the photograph "provides both a way to seeing ahead to changes wrought by experience and of looking back at past formations of self; it is Trethewey's agile double subjectivity enfolded into the text and made plain by means of her vision of the camera and the work of the photographic space" ("Enfoldments" 38). What Davis sees as the layering of time and self, I read as the catalyst for the haunting allowed by time travel. Just as the picture taken of "you" in the opening poem reflects a past self you can see, photography allows a rupture in the strict chronology of time and the entrance of haunting. By allowing the present access to the past, photography permits the present to haunt that past. Sontag explains, "All photos are *memento mori*. To take a photograph is to participate in another's person's (or thing's) mortality, vulnerability, mutability" (15). Witnessing that mortality through a photograph is much like traveling back in time to a Civil War battle that the witness knows will end in the death of the inhabitants. The portal of a photograph can moreover allow the past to haunt the present. In describing a photograph of her parents, Trethewey explains that her mother does not look at the camera but watches a young Natasha, and "in loving gaze toward my childhood self has turned away from a future she will never enter" ("Necessary"). Her father, however, "looks straight ahead meeting the gaze I will bring each time I take out the photograph to look." While photography carries the potential for capture and ownership, any claiming must take into account the haunting that occurs with time travel.

"Photograph: Ice Storm, 1971" exemplifies this tension between claiming and haunting. The poem is a series of questions centering on the contrast between the beauty of an icy scene and the evident suffering of a mother: "Why the rough edge of beauty? Why/ the tired face of a woman, suffering,/ made luminous by the camera's eye?" (10). John Berger explains that "photographs bear witness to a human choice being exercised in a given situation. A photograph is a result of the photographer's decision that it is worth recording that this particular event or this particular object has been seen" (292). Yet this photograph of the suffering woman begs the question of choice. Trethewey explains that in writing the poem she was inspired by Dorothea Lange's 1936 photograph *Migrant Mother*, where a woman is clearly starving "and yet, there's something strangely beautiful about her suffering face" (20). One question, asking, "Why remember anything/ but the wonder of those few days,// the iced trees, each leaf in its glassy case?," points to the contrasting impulses to photograph this beautiful event and to write about the ugly context. Giorgia De Cenzo argues that the photograph is "nothing else than a frozen moment, similar to the landscape of 'iced trees' captured by the camera. It tells nothing about the destructive force of 'the storm.' ... as it tells nothing about the tragic future still to come" (26). Yet there is something else: that frozen moment is layered with the memories provided by the speaker, as the poem reflects both the past and the future. The actual photograph of "that first morning" may depict "the front yard a beautiful, strange place," but this scene is haunted by whatever has happened before this day to make the mother's face look "tired" and "suffering" and furthermore by what will happen in the future. That initial wonder of a frosty world is followed by deprivation: "for days, power lines down, food rotting/ in the refrigerator." The speaker looking at the photograph knows that the written record on the back does not include what happened after, the violence indicated by the last lines: "why on the back has someone made a list/ of our names, the date, the event: nothing/ of what's inside—mother, stepfather's fist?" The layering of all of the moments—the moment that made the mother tired, the moment of the photograph that reflects beauty, the moment when food was rotting, the moment when someone wrote names on the back, the moment years later when the adult is looking at the photograph—produces a haunting of each moment by the other points in time. The initial claiming of this moment by photographing it becomes troubled by Trethwey's rewriting and reclaiming of it in her time.

While "Photograph: Ice Storm, 1971" encapsulates Trethewey's reclaiming of her personal history, she uses photography to reclaim public history as well. The ekphrastic poem "Scenes from a Documentary History of Mississippi" explores the documenting and claiming of Mississippi's history in a series of four photographs that exemplify the doubled movement of haunting.[22] In the first section, "King Cotton, 1907," the speaker describes a photograph of a parade celebrating the cotton industry by using present tense. The poem depicts a flurry of movement, as "flags wave down" and "great bales of cotton rise up from the ground" (21). In occupying this moment in 1907, the speaker anticipates the future arrival of President Roosevelt when "the band will march" (21). This past scene, available through the photograph, is, however, haunted by the future: "This is two years before the South's countermarch—/ the great bolls of cotton, risen up from the ground,// infested with boll weevils—a plague, biblical, all around." Although African American children ride the bales in the parade, the speaker knows the devastation that they will face and consequently finds this past haunting, as the children "stare out at us." This second person plural "us" includes the reader in this haunting.

As if in answer to the anticipated suffering, in the next section, entitled "Glyph, Aberdeen, 1913," a photograph depicts a starving and disabled child. A man, presumably the father, "cradles the child's thin arm" (22). The child is "haunting the long hours" of labor in the cotton fields, with the present progressive verb tense indicating that the child's suffering is ongoing. The questions the man asks—*"how much cotton?"* and *"how much food?"*—reach into the future, with the devastating answer in the last line: "like dirt heaped on a grave." The previous section in its celebration of "King Cotton" haunts this photograph taken five years later exposing the consequences of that industry, while the boy's certain death haunts backwards to the man's cradling of him. The moments before and after haunt the captured instant of the photograph. The original photographer doing the documenting found the scenes "worth recording," but in crafting the poem, Trethewey makes "us" claimant to the tragedies depicted.

With the third section "Flood," the poem moves to a different tragedy: people trying to find dry land during a flood but National Guard soldiers blocking the "black refugees" from the high ground until they "*sing* their passage onto land" (23). The claiming of property thus turns literal in the question of who can occupy this land. The first half of the poem is in past tense, suggesting that the speaker remains a viewer separate in time from the action in the photograph. But with "here" acting as signal, the speaker moves back into the past, as "the camera finds them still. Posed/ as if for a schoolday portrait." While the people are "still" in space, frozen and captured by a photograph, they also remain "still" in time, ever present in their poses. Unlike the previous two sections where the future clearly forebodes devastation and death, in this poem the people "fix/ on what's before them." What they see is an "aperture, the captured moment's/ chasm in time." While the capture suggests stasis, the aperture acts as an opening or portal through time. The poem brings the reader back to this time by using present tense to locate the reader "here" in 1927, but the poem also locates these refugees in our present as the "refugees from history" now "are waiting to disembark." With the present progressive "are waiting," the photograph becomes a window to see a past that is still active and still haunting the present.

The fourth and final section "You Are Late" moves history even closer to the speaker and to the reader. A photograph shows a girl with a book in her hands approaching a library, but a sign indicates that it is closed. A second sign dates the photograph: "*Greenwood Public Library for Negroes*" (24). The speaker makes explicit her desire to travel through time: "I want to call her, say *wait*/ But this is history: she can't linger./ She'll read the sign that I read: *You Are Late.*" By reactivating the photograph through ekphrasis, however, Trethewey still "arrives" at this time and makes this history present. Although throughout all four sections of the poem, the pretense of traveling back in time carries with it the desire to intervene and prevent the suffering to come, being "late" indicates that the future cannot ultimately save the past; it can only haunt it. "Scenes from a Documentary History of Mississippi" then aligns with *Kindred* in its haunting backwards. Dana wants to change Rufus and save Alice, but her agency is limited at best. The speaker examining the photographs uses them to travel back to a past that cannot be changed, as the starving boy cannot be saved and the girl cannot be given better and equal access to the world of books. Yet these past scenes are still haunting the present in the conflation of moments, so the boy, the girl, and the "refugees from history" are still "here."

CLAIMING THE PROPERTY OF THE PAST IN *KINDRED*

Both *Kindred* and *Native Guard* thus poignantly depict the inability even with time travel to save characters in the past. In reversing the direction of haunting, however, Trethewey and Butler claim the property of the past so that they can combat the power dynamics of slavery. Margaret Jane Radin explains that establishing personhood is based on "some control over resources in the external environment"; the ability to have this control "[takes] the form of property rights" (35). Thus, to counteract the paradigm of the past that leaves Alice the victim of Rufus, Carrie without her sons, and the flood refugees with no safe place to land, Butler and Trethewey must assert ownership.

They do this through writing, both *in* their texts by having characters write their own stories and *through* their texts by using *Kindred* and *Native Guard* to rewrite the past and thereby own it as a form of property. These writers follow in the wake of the formerly enslaved women I examine in chapter 1, Harriet Jacobs and Hannah Crafts, who use their narratives to create their life stories, thus owning the property of their lives. In a postmodern paradigm that eschews boundaries of time, Butler and Trethewey can claim the life stories of earlier generations. Sherley Anne Williams in her 1986 novel *Dessa Rose* (explored more fully in chapter 2) also illustrates how writing can perform this function. Williams takes the 1829 capture and conviction of a pregnant runaway woman and the 1830 story of a white woman giving sanctuary to enslaved people on her farm and imagines a past where the two women meet. While Williams admits in her preface that the novel is "fiction," she still claims it both as "true" and as her property: "Maybe it is only a metaphor, but I now own a summer in the 19th century" (6). The power to reconstruct the past through storytelling becomes a form of ownership. In *Kindred*, Dana goes from knowing little more about her family than a list of names in a Bible to knowing their story firsthand. She writes this story in the narrative arc of the book by reconstructing her memories of traveling through time. Trethewey's poem "Native Guard" imagines the journal of a formerly enslaved person who is now a soldier on Ship Island as he records the story of the black Union soldiers that history omits. Whether the past can actually be changed is ambiguous in both texts, but the way that past is constructed certainly can. Dana and the soldier can tell their stories while Butler and Trethewey can craft new histories. Although the past in both texts shows a certain resistance to being consumed or contained fully by the present, the story of the past that remains to haunt the present can be changed, reimagined, rewritten, and ultimately claimed as property.

In exploring how Butler claims the property of the past in *Kindred*, I want to return to Dana's comment that the "trouble began" when she and Kevin move into "a house of our own" (12). This comment establishes Dana's claim to the property of the house, but it moreover points to the link between the writing Dana and Kevin do and that property. They are able to purchase this house because of Kevin's "most successful novel," *The Water of Meribah* (193). Dana's phrasing of this transaction is telling, as she thinks of Kevin's book as "the novel that bought us this house" (193). This kind of transaction between writing and property reoccurs in the novel as Dana writes letters for Rufus to his creditors so that he will not have to sell any more enslaved people. Writing equals property, which then equals people. Kelley Wagers points to the detrimental effects of this equation when she reads Dana and Kevin as "victims of a system that reduces the social value of writing to meager monetary exchange" (28). But *Kindred* also depicts the power possible in the ability to use writing to claim property. Kevin's book may have gotten them a troublesome house, but Dana's story could get her a couple of decades in the nineteenth century.

Dana must first, however, have enough agency to craft her narrative. In traveling through time, Dana has to negotiate more than her shifting roles as a modern citizen and a supposedly enslaved person. As a writer, she must also contend with the issue of gender. Dana's phrase, a "house of our own" echoes Virginia Woolf's call for women writers to have a "room of one's own." Woolf asserts the need both for the literal space of a room and for the metaphorical space in the busyness of life to be a writer, boiling it down to a rather spare formula: "A woman must have money and a room of her own if she is to write fiction" (2). That both Kevin and Rufus ask Dana to play secretary for them suggests that the men see her writing as merely a tool for their use. Dana, however, has chosen the blue-collar agency because she loathes typing.[23] Typing is transcribing someone else's words; Dana wants to create her own story. When Kevin quite understandably does not believe at first that Dana went back in time, Dana protests, "I know what I saw, and what I did—my facts. They're no crazier than yours" (16). Because of gender bias, Dana will have to fight to tell the story of her experience.

One way to read Dana's time traveling is to see the past as a kind of room she finds that can be her own. She is able to haunt this past because it is her place, where her family lives, and where she can craft her story apart from the house that Kevin's novel bought them. *Kindred* uses a frame structure, so the novel opens at the end of the action with the police talking to Dana in the hospital after her arm was severed by the wall. Their questions about what happened prompt Dana to think back through her experience and "tell" her story as flashback. Christine Levecq points out the foregrounding of the "constructedness of the narrative" (541), while Rushdy suggests that the novel is "a return to the past in the form of a narrative" ("Families" 137). The framing device that Butler uses certainly highlights that Dana is remembering, sorting, and constructing the experience into a narrative that is then shared with the reader as an answer to that question posed by the police of what happened. Like the invisible man in Ralph Ellison's novel who tells the narrative in flashback to answer why he is so "black and blue," Dana's time traveling is reproduced in the narrative's structure of moving back through time (14).

As she reconstructs her memories, several clues indicate that she is thinking of the story as a book. When she reads *Robinson Crusoe* to Rufus, she thinks of herself as a fictional character, "as a kind of castaway myself" (87). In the middle of her experience when she is back in California for a few days, she finds herself experiencing writer's block, but she assures herself that "someday when this was over, if it was ever over, maybe I would be able to write about it" (116). One episode in particular demonstrates how Dana conceives of her experiences as fodder for future writing. When she finds Rufus in the woods fighting with Isaac, she has to leave Rufus behind to get help but wants to be sure she can navigate back to him. She leaves a proverbial trail of breadcrumbs except that her markings are made of paper, as she "tore pages from my scratch pad and stuck them on trees now and then to mark my trail" (126). Then, at the road, she uses "bits of white paper" to make a kind of "barricade" to stop her when she returns (126). Dana thus uses paper to mark the path she takes through the narrative; she walks through the woods and through the story seemingly constructing it on the paper she uses. Dana even keeps a journal of her experience and wonders "whether I could weave [the pages] into a story" (244).

The story that she ends up weaving of her ancestors gives life to two bare written records from the past: the list of family names in the Bible and the notice of the sale of people held in slavery by Rufus Weylin after his death. The paucity of information on the lives of these particular people mirrors the inadequacy Dana and Kevin find in the history books about slavery. In traveling back to the past to write a different story of slavery, Dana performs what Linda Hutcheon would label a "postmodern" feat. Hutcheon argues that the return to the past in postmodern works is "a critical revisiting, an ironic dialogue with the past of both art and society" (4). She explains that in postmodern works, history is "being rethought—as a human construct" (16). This rethinking of history is especially vital to the recounting of slavery, since sources are so sparse.[24] Dana's construction of Alice's story of becoming enslaved, being forced into a sexual relationship, having children with her master, and choosing to end her life, radically reforms both Dana's story of origins and the larger historical picture of the peculiar institution. The reformed history is not just Dana's own because it is the story of her bloodline; it is also hers because in the logic of exchange in the book writing is a form of property. As she plays specter from the future, Dana thus performs the ghostly role of existing to claim property: the story of her ancestors.

Her bloodline includes not just Alice and the others held in slavery, but also Rufus and the Weylin family, so she recovers their stories as well, filling in the whole picture behind the thin historical record. By saving Rufus repeatedly, Dana discovers how troubled his life is: how his father abuses him and his mother spoils him, so that he grows up in a stifling environment where his only power is over those enslaved. That power is absolute, and it absolutely corrupts him. Dana not only writes how violence and fear keep people enslaved; she also writes how violence and fear make a young white boy into a slaveholder. When Rufus reads a book about slavery that Dana brings back from the present, he protests, "This is the biggest lot of abolitionist trash I ever saw" (140). Yet he is not able to counter what Dana tells him is "history" because he does not write his story. Rufus in fact leaves little trace of his life, and Dana survives to tell his story as her own. At one point, Rufus complains, "You think you own me because you saved my life" (164). Dana actually "owns" Rufus because he becomes a character in her story. When Dana earlier told Kevin she wanted some "insurance" in the nineteenth-century world by establishing a relationship with Rufus, Dana suggests that a friendship would keep her safe, but she could also be establishing ownership since a person can only acquire "insurance" on property. Ultimately, though, Dana claims ownership of Rufus not by saving him but by killing him.[25] After declaring "I am not property," she kills Rufus, asserting not only her right to her body and her life, but also asserting an owner's right to destroy. If we read the narrative as Dana's story, this killing metaphorically could be the author's right to kill off a character. David LaCroix notes that when Dana kills Rufus, she "asserts to a certain point the past must be absolutely past" (115). She also asserts that the past is her territory to construct; it is a room of her own.

Octavia Butler, as the writer behind the writer, is engaged in the project of rewriting history as well. She explains that that idea for *Kindred* came from hearing a man talking angrily about black ancestors "holding us back" ("Interview" 51). This view of the past "was actually the germ of the idea for *Kindred*" ("Interview" 51).[26] At one point, Dana realizes that Sarah, who has not rebelled or tried to escape, "was the kind of woman who would be held in contempt during the militant nineteen sixties. The house-nigger, the handkerchief-head, the female Uncle Tom" (145). Dana, however, now understands Sarah's behavior because she has experienced the harsh realities of the slave system. In crafting a story to tell this history, Butler and her writer/double in the novel, Dana, assert ownership of it. Octavia Butler inherits from slave narratives the move of claiming the property of a life story to counteract the claiming of a person under slavery. To imagine the past anew and to possess it, Butler employs the gothic.

Butler does this, however, with an eye to the hubris of the present, thinking it can fully understand the past. If one critiques history as a "human construct," the next version, even if it is "better" in revealing the bleak lives of enslaved people, is still just a version, a construction that is separate from the lived lives of those people. Although Dana moves from pretending to be enslaved in the past to being whipped, beaten, and actually treated as property, a crucial part of the experience of those around her who are enslaved remains elusive to her. One of the worst aspects of slavery is undeniably the separation of families. With her white "master" as Kevin, Dana is not in danger of losing her husband, and she does not have children. While Dana can be shocked that three of Sarah's children were sold so that Margaret Weylin could have "new furniture, new china dishes, fancy things you see in that house now" (95), she cannot experience this deprivation for herself. Even her knowledge that slavery will eventually end sets her apart, as LaCroix argues (113). This knowledge gives her a boldness that does not allow her to share fully in the despair that drives Alice to suicide. As much as Dana experiences nineteenth-century slavery and retells it to claim it as her story, her assertion is challenged by what part of the past remains unknown. At the end of the novel, when Dana and Kevin travel to present-day Maryland to try to trace what happened after Dana killed Rufus, they find the bill of sale and can only make guesses about the elusive past. *Kindred* shows both the power and the complexities of claiming the past.

CLAIMING THE PAST AS PROPERTY IN *NATIVE GUARD*

Like Butler, Natasha Trethewey constructs a narrative that haunts backwards into the past to claim it as property. This claim is made by and through writing. By constructing the history of African American Union soldiers, Trethewey creates a space owned by the present, although like Butler she also gives just due to the complexity of that past. While the constructedness of *Kindred* is foregrounded by Butler's use of a framing structure, in *Native Guard,* Trethewey uses metaphors of construction, such as the image of stitching. In the opening poem, "Theories of Time and Space," the image appears at the dock where the "you" boards a boat: "riggings of shrimp boats are loose stitches// in a sky threatening rain" (1). In "The Southern Crescent," the mother's name is "stitched/ inside each" homemade dress that she takes on her ill-fated journey. In "At Dusk," after listening to a neighbor calling her cat, the speaker wonders if she can "lift/ my voice" to "send it over the lines stitching here/ to there, certain the sounds I make/ are enough to call someone home" (15). In each instance, the stitching is an attempt to connect one time and place to another time and place, displaying not only the double movement of haunting but also the actual construction needed to tie the separate moments together.

This construction is what the writing *in* the poetry and the writing *of* the poetry do to lay claim to the past. In "Letter," for example, the speaker is writing a note to a friend but misspells "errand" as "errant," a slip that causes her to reflect on the difference between the possibility inherent in a trip (errand) and the ending of possibility with the death of her mother (errant), noting "how suddenly" something "simple" "can go wrong" (12). The writing, even when it goes wrong, is the speaker's way of shaping the past. This act of construction is featured in the central poem of the collection "Native Guard," which depicts a formerly enslaved soldier writing a journal of his experiences at Ship Island. He reuses a journal that he found in a Confederate home, thereby writing his story over another man's story.[27] He also tells of writing letters for the Confederate soldiers held captive on the island, giving words to their messages home. In layering writing about writing that is written on top of writing, the poem highlights the conjunction of different narratives. The soldier must claim his story in the face of competing ones. Written in a series of ten linked sonnets, "Native Guard" is presented as, in Pearl Amelia McHaney's words, "a palimpsest of words, literal intersections of stories as evidence of history" (162).

In telling this story through the voice of the unnamed solider, however, Trethewey herself is reconstructing history, much as Sherley Anne Williams does in *Dessa Rose* by imagining the meeting between the runaway and the white woman. It was in fact a white man named Colonel Daniels who found a diary in a Confederate house and used it for his own journal. When Trethewey read about the journal with the cross-writing, she considered it a "gift," in that the "intersection" of words echoed the intersections she wanted to pose in her book (53). But Trethewey does not use Daniels as the narrator or even his star soldier, a mixed-race slaveholder named Francis Dumas, who freed those he had held in slavery and encouraged them to join the Union Army. Instead, "Native Guard" is in the voice of one of Dumas's ex-slaves, a construction of history from the bottom. We are hearing the ordinary experience of a foot soldier in his own words. Destiny O. Birdsong argues that the use of first person "transfers the power of the record-keeper back to the previously silenced historical subject" (105).[28] In using present tense, the poem transports the reader back to 1862 to hear from a man haunted both by his past in slavery and by war-time atrocities against black soldiers. In occupying 1862, the reader fears the future in which this story of African American Union soldiers has been forgotten, signaled ironically by the epigraph penned by Frederick Douglass: "*If this war is to be forgotten, I ask in the name of all/ things sacred what shall men remember?*" (25). Within the double movement of haunting, though, appears this man's claim to the property of his own time and place, as his story focuses on what he can keep, take, and claim.

The speaker begins by discussing what he wants to keep in memory from his time in slavery. He physically carries history "inscribed upon my back" but will exchange this "record" for the one he will now "keep" in ink. While someone else "inscribed" his previous life, he now grasps ownership through writing. Yet he chooses to remember the past and to remain haunted by slavery, a choice not that difficult when the work assigned to the regiment of black soldiers mimics that of slavery: "no less/heavy than before" with "Half rations" that "make our work/ familiar still." Throughout the poem, the near-repetition of each sonnet's last line by the first line of the next sonnet reflects the doubled temporal movement of the soldier's "remembrance" of his past in slavery as he moves into a future different status as soldier.

His past is the property he can keep, but he also takes the property of others as well when the soldiers loot Confederate homes and take objects including "this journal, near full/ with someone else's words" (26). This depiction of the soldier's acquiring paper to give him the means to write echoes *Absalom,*

Absalom! when Charles Bon writes to Judith during the war using stove polish found in an abandoned home. Unlike that fragment of a letter that raises more questions than it answers, this journal in "Native Guard" seeks to recount a fuller history, as the black soldier's words are "crosshatched" with the white man's, "his story intersecting with my own." He is taking someone else's words, another man's history, in order to record in ink what he will keep from this experience.

The story the soldier tells is of a war that seems to extend his slavery, even as he tries to claim his agency. In the third sonnet, with the key word "here" to signal the reader now shares his time/space reference, he looks out at ships in the harbor: "I can look out/ upon the Gulf and see the surf breaking,/ tossing the ships," perhaps signifying on a famous passage from Frederick Douglass's narrative depicting his jealousy at the seeming liberty of ships: "You are loosed from your moorings and are free; I am fast in my chains, and am a slave!" (67). The soldier "can look" because, unlike Douglass, he is not technically enslaved. The next sonnet, however, finds him witnessing a man with scars "crosshatched" on his back, indicating that the "inscribed" slave past proves difficult to overcome, particularly in a place where these men are called on to be the jailors to Confederate prisoners of war, "those who still/ would have us slaves" (27). Though the speaker counts these people as his property, as part of what he "keeps," he also realizes, "We're all bondmen here," as the white men are captive and the black men are conscripted. "Bond" underscores not just their captivity but also their status as property.

As the soldier works to claim his story through writing, he engages in a second form of writing by crafting letters for captives who are illiterate. The Confederates are "wary/ of a negro writing," with only their signature to make it theirs: "X binds them to the page." The speaker, however, tries to use his words to capture their thoughts: "what I know/ they labor to say between silences/ too big for words." Writing is about binding, capturing, taking possession of something, which happens in this instance across racial lines. This seeming camaraderie, however, is cut short by yet another taking of property, the eating of the dead's "share of hardtack" (28).

Keeping what he remembers and taking what he needs in the present to survive, the speaker then spends the last five sonnets detailing what he will claim as his story of the Civil War. He focuses on three events "which must be accounted for" (29). The first is the aftermath of a skirmish on April 9, 1863, when white Union forces fired on their own regiment of black soldiers as they were retreating, killing several men. Trethewey has her fictional speaker quote the real Colonel Daniels, calling it *"an unfortunate incident"* and claiming "*their names shall deck the page of history*" (28). But the soldier guesses the future in answering, "Some names shall deck the page of history/ as it is written on stone. Some will not" (28). Even as the reader of the poem learns about the erasure of the names from previous history, the poem becomes a new "page of history" and a claim of ownership. The second event is the decision by General Nathaniel Banks in 1863 not to bury black soldiers killed in the battle at Port Hudson. The speaker records Banks's disclaimer: "*I have/ no dead there*" (28). Though Banks leaves the bodies "unclaimed," the speaker through the poem claims them: "I record names" (29). The third event is the renaming of the regiment "Corps d'Afrique," which the speaker remarks will "take the *native/* from our claim." Although time will supposedly "render/mute" the story of these soldiers, the poem reveals that "Beneath battlefields, green again/ the dead molder," the verb "molder" suggesting action instead of stasis (30). Although "we tread upon" the bones in "forgetting," a "we" that includes the reader, the poem ends with "Truth be told," a claim for a story that designates the soldier as a native, one who both guards the land and has claim to it. In telling that "truth," the soldier reverses the power dynamics of slavery where he was only property.

    In the writing of the collection, Natasha Trethewey doubles the soldier/ writer in constructing her ownership of the past. In the penultimate poem, "Elegy for the Native Guards," she speaks through a modern point of view and reverses the erasure of the black soldiers' history, using the poem to erect the memorial that is absent at Ship Island and claiming her own moment in the nineteenth century. The poem fills in the gap left in "Theories of Time and Space" by detailing the trip to the island, and the reader discovers the experience that alters a person enough to make a past photograph seem to be of a different person. The poem includes the reader from the beginning: "We leave Gulfport at noon; gulls overhead/ trailing the boat—streamers, noisy fanfare—/all the way to Ship Island" (44). Written in first-person plural point of view, the poem keeps the reader involved as "we" see the remains of the fort and witness an incomplete construction of history as "we" read the plaque honoring the Confederate soldiers but not the Native Guard. The speaker then asks, "What is monument to their legacy?" The answer is twofold: nature in that the remains of the fort are "half open to the sky,/ the elements—wind, rain—God's deliberate eye," and the reader who has now heard the soldier's history and has taken the journey through space and time to Ship Island. In elegizing the dead who have no actual "grave markers," the speaker, the reader, and the poet in constructing the journey are claiming their story.

Although the collection pays special attention to this one slice of history, other poems illustrate that Natasha Trethewey targets southern history writ large. Trethewey comments that in the collection "I am very much asking, after Eric Foner's *Who Owns History?*, 'Who owns southern history or southern poetry?' History belongs to all of us and our one charge is to present it well with all the complexity and humanity that peoples' lives deserve and that art requires" (*Conversations* 60). That the complexity has previously been missing is clear in her poem "Southern History," where the speaker remembers a high school history class with a textbook claiming of enslaved people, "*Before the war, they were happy*" and using *Gone with the Wind* as evidence (38). The speaker of the poem admits complicity: "our textbook's grinning proof—a lie/ my teacher guarded. Silent, so did I" (38). Yet the poet Natasha Trethewey writes the history of this moment to reverse it. She even figures as a specter haunting back into history in the poem "Pastoral" as she dreams herself into a photograph with the Fugitive Poets. The poem haunts backwards to highlight the limited construction of history.

As adamant as the poetry is in deconstructing a history that would erase the lives of enslaved people and soldiers, Trethewey also shares Butler's trepidations about completely knowing and thereby claiming the past. The collection sheds light repeatedly on the fact that the past exists only as fragments and scraps that the present must try to stitch together. In "What Is Evidence," the speaker dismisses as "evidence" of her mother's suffering the concrete proofs usually used in law: the "fleeting bruises she'd cover/ with makeup" and the missing teeth (11). She claims instead "only the landscape of her body." These "thin bones" are not static, however, and therefore not easy to fix and analyze; they are instead "settling a bit each day, the way all things do."[29] As the speaker remarks in "Providence," a poem about the devastation caused by Hurricane Camille, "What's left is footage" (42). The remains of history, whether in the form of journals, photographs, or bodies, only tell partial stories. Added to this problem of fragments is the difficulty of interpretation. Trethewey has asserted her claim to history through words, but her poetry repeatedly gives attention to gestures that are not contained in language. In "What the Body Can Say," for example, the speaker first presents gestures that are "unmistakable," such as a man kneeling in prayer or a raised thumb for agreement (9). The speaker then asks, "But what was my mother saying/ that day not long before her death—her face tilted up// at me, her mouth falling open, wordless" (9). The attention to this inability fully to capture or interpret the past continues in her 2012 collection *Thrall*. The poem "Illumination" explores how "the past unwritten/ eludes us" (77). In

Native Guard, Trethewey reveals that writing history is a way of haunting backwards to claim property, while acknowledging that some facets of the past will remain beyond ownership.

RECLAIMING KINDRED

While both Trethewey and Butler use their own writing to stake their title to stories of the past, and they depict characters' writing as a way of declaring ownership of their life stories, these claims to property are augmented by the reclaiming of ancestors. Unlike the gothic nightmare of slavery's reduction of people to property, these assertions are made to restore personhood and agency. Trethewey writes *Native Guard* to memorialize her own mother, but the image of her mother is so connected to the image of "home" that they become fused. In this synthesis, Trethewey crafts her own identity as a daughter of her mother, a daughter of the South, and as a "Native Guard." In *Kindred*, Dana finds in Alice a sister and in Rufus a brother; her "kindred" are both black and white. In the complicated history of her origins, she tells the very story of America.

Trethewey's collection links her ancestry to the South. Thadious M. Davis explains, "It is difficult to resist reading the mother in Trethewey's poems as emblematic of the South, racialized as black and abused yet offering a homespace to shape the daughter's subjectivity" (*Southscapes* 70). In the haunting backwards, I read the daughter moreover shaping a homespace for the mother. The epigraph for the first section, a verse from the folksong "The Wayfaring Stranger," illustrates the connection between mother and home: "I'm going there to meet my mother/ She said she'd meet me when I come/ I'm only going over Jordan/ I'm only going over home" (3). The connection, however, comes with complications. Just as "home" in *Kindred* is imbued with the saga of racial oppression, the connection to home in Trethewey's poetry is fraught with the baggage of history. In "My Mother Dreams Another Country," the speaker takes the reader back to when the mother was pregnant: "This is 1966—she is married to a white man" (37). The poem imagines her worry about how the mixed-race child will be treated, a worry born out in "Southern Gothic" set later in time. But in this time—"here," as we are again signaled—the place where her mother waits for childbirth, "Mississippi," becomes a "dark backdrop bearing down/ on the windows of her room." Although she falls asleep with the national anthem playing, she is dreaming of a home in "another country" where marrying a white man is not illegal, and their child will not be bullied. To reclaim her mother's life, Trethewey has to refashion that home.

The difficulty, though, of home is announced in the first lines of the collection in "Theories of Time and Space": "You can get there from here, though/ there's no going home" (1). In "Genus Narcissus," the young girl bringing flowers to her mother finds them while walking "home from school," but the flowers are "treacherous" and whisper "*Die early*" to the mother (7). In "Graveyard Blues," after burying her mother, the speaker notes that, "The road going home was pocked with holes,/ That home-going road's always full of holes" (8). In trying to find her way home, the speaker is left to "wander now among names of the dead:/ My mother's name, stone pillow for my head" (8).

The stone pillar points to one way Trethewey attempts to reclaim her mother and make her mark on the territory of home: building a monument. In "Monument," the speaker watches ants in the cemetery making a mound at her mother's "untended plot" (43). She tries not to "begrudge them/ their industry" when she has not put a marker on the grave. Ramsey explains that "the ants' disturbance and rearrangement of once stationary sediments is a metaphor for historical retrieval as a creative memory act. History goes beyond archeological retrieval. It disturbs, remixes, and alters once-stationary layers" (132). Through her poetry, Trethewey also asserts title to those layers. Just as her "Elegy for the Native Guards" creates the marker for the soldiers that does not exist at Ship Island, in the writing of "Monument" and in the collection as a whole, Trethewey forms a monument to her mother, reclaiming her from the dead.

This reclaiming can take the form of a written monument, much like the book *Beloved* is a figural gravestone for the "sixty million and more" who suffered under slavery. Yet another form is the person of the poet herself. That Trethewey uses a Walt Whitman quote about the South to introduce the third section points to the precedent of writing the self as a way of writing the larger history of a nation. In "Miscegenation," Trethewey reconstructs both her and her mother's connections to home. Every other line in the fourteen-line poem ends with "Mississippi" (36). Most of the poem is in past tense, detailing her parents' decision to marry despite the law, their move to Canada, where they "followed a route the same/as slaves," and the naming of Natasha sparked by her father's reading of *War and Peace*. The poem changes to present tense in the last two lines: "I know more than Joe Christmas did. Natasha is a Russian name—/ though I'm not; it means *Christmas child*, even in Mississippi." The poet in the present reclaims her home.

The declaration of Mississippi as home points to Trethewey's postmodern rewriting of the story of this particular space. In *Postmodern Cartographies*, Brian Jarvis argues, "Given the structural inseparability of space/place/landscape and social relations there can be no geographical knowledge without historical narrative. In other words, all spaces contain stories and must be recognized as a site of struggle over meaning and value" (7). The struggle that Trethewey has to contend with is the story of Mississippi as solely the property of whites. Thadious Davis reveals the larger regional effects of this story: "whites in the South becomes simply 'southerners' without a racial designation, but blacks in the South became simply 'blacks' without a regional designation" (29). Although Trethewey has a "Russian name," its meaning and by extension her person exist "even in Mississippi" (36).

Trethewey inserts herself into a past time to remake the places she then designates as "home." In the final poem of the collection, that place is the "South," the title of the poem. The speaker uses past tense to describe a journey with the repeating refrain of "I returned" (45). The images of "white flags" and "unburied" bodies echo previous poems while the visiting of a battlefield and the coast parallel the journey made through the collection. These returns illustrate the history that haunts the earlier poems. In a "field of cotton," for example, the speaker sees "each boll/ holding the ghosts of generations." The unclaimed bodies, which were reclaimed in "Native Guard," are now covered by "earth's green sheet," with the image of grass as another nod to Whitman. The speaker notes that she has returned to a South "Where the roads, buildings, and monuments/ are named to honor the Confederacy," a history that the collection expands with its focus on African Americans. The last lines, however, shift to the present tense: "I return to Mississippi." In using present tense, she announces ownership: "native/ in my native land, this place they'll bury me." By taking on the descriptor "native," the poet becomes a living monument to the Native Guard of history. Trethewey has claimed the story of the past, reclaimed her own ancestors as well as black soldiers, and here asserts title to her eventual plot of land in the home of the South.

Octavia Butler suggests a larger reclamation as well in setting her novel in the year of America's bicentennial. In her modern world, Dana embraces a cross-racial marriage by claiming Kevin as her "kindred spirit," and in her nineteenth-century world, Dana claims both enslaved people and slaveholders as kindred. The crossing of racial lines, though, renders both worlds tough to navigate. The nineteenth-century laws of property depend upon clear race lines, but these lines become increasingly difficult to maintain when blood relatives exist on both sides of the crucial divide between personhood and property. With such thin lines, the construction is highly tenuous, as Frederick Douglass points out in his slave narrative. Douglass argues that the justification for slavery based on race is questioned by the "different-looking class of people" now "held in slavery" due to children whose masters are also their fathers (19). When children have parents of both races, the racial basis of slavery becomes illogical. In traveling back to slavery, Dana claims all her kindred: Alice as her sister, Rufus as her brother, Hagar as her ancestor, and Kevin as her husband and her kindred spirit. This reclamation challenges racial lines, so in haunting backwards, Dana disturbs the power dynamics of property.

Reading Dana as reclaiming her ancestors can lead to a different reading of her interactions with Alice. Earlier, I examined how Alice's lack of agency haunts Dana, as Dana learns the true horror of the status of enslaved people as property and the violence hidden in her own family tree. While this haunting is devastating, Butler's use of another gothic trope, the double, shows how Dana does not simply leave Alice to her tragic fate of rape and suicide. Dana as Alice's double instead reenacts and rewrites Alice's trajectory but with the benefit of her firm twentieth-century sense of personhood. Sarah Eden Schiff argues that "Dana—fantastically—rewrites, possible even unwrites, the narrative of her ancestor's primary trauma" (122). Schiff uses trauma theory to read the novel and sees "the fantasy of potentially healing a traumatic narrative" (122). If we read the double as a gothic return, however, we also see the reclaiming of kindred as a bid to disrupt the conceptions of property.

Alice does not begin as property; she is born free, and her move from freedom to slavery echoes Dana's time travels from twentieth-century personhood to at least the assumption of bondage in the nineteenth century. Alice only becomes property when she is caught helping her husband, Isaac, escape and is sold to Rufus as her punishment. Before comprehending her change in circumstances, she ironically asks Dana, "What's it like to be a slave?" (156). On parallel tracks, both Dana and Alice discover the answer to the question. Not only do Dana and Alice "look alike," but Dana thinks of Alice as a "sister" (228, 180). Sarah remarks after Alice's death that "you sure fought like sisters" (249). When, for example, Alice recovers her memory after being beaten for helping Isaac escape, she shouts at Dana, "Why didn't you know enough to let me die?" (160). In their fights, Dana and Alice are brutally honest with each other, but they also support each other. Dana vows to help in Alice's potential escape from Rufus, and Alice gives Dana the letters Dana wrote to Kevin, which Rufus lied about mailing. Their relationship seems to be mutually beneficial.

The problem is that Rufus perceives the doubling as well, telling them at one point, "You really are only one woman" (228). Once Alice is gone, Rufus then wants Dana to substitute for her, leading to his attempt to rape her while saying, "You are her. One woman, Two halves of a whole" (257). If we read Dana and Alice as completely separate individuals, then we naturally end up blaming Dana for contributing to Alice's sexual captivity at the same time she is willing to kill Rufus to prevent her own. If, however, we read the characters through a gothic lens and see Dana and Alice as doubles, as in Rufus's words "one woman," then Dana's decision to kill Rufus is her way of fixing the problem of Alice's captivity. Hence Dana does not just write Alice's story to reclaim forgotten history, and she does not just rewrite the story from her modern vantage point to claim the past as property. Dana, as Alice's double, relives the story, choosing a different ending by killing Rufus instead of killing herself, thus claiming ownership instead of being claimed as property. When Dana proclaims, "I am not property," she is allowing Alice to say something other than her body is "Not mine, his. He paid for it, didn't he?" (167). Alice claims her body in the end the only way she can in the nineteenth century by choosing to end her life; Dana reverses the power dynamics of property by not dying.[30] In the fusion of Alice and Dana, Dana reclaims her ancestor.

If this were Dana's only claim, the narrative would be a straightforward recovery of the African American past, but kindred is a more complicated puzzle to Dana. She may think of Alice as her sister, but she must also contemplate Rufus as her brother. Although Dana admits that, at times, she has gotten angry enough to kill Rufus, they still "didn't hate each other" (180). Only Dana is aware of their actual family bond, but she continues to play the role of protective sister (180). As horrible as Rufus is in perpetuating violence, raping Alice, and selling people, Dana feels compelled to continue saving him, not only to ensure her family line (not testing the paradox) but also because of what would happen to the rest of the enslaved people if she did not. That she has to save him repeatedly raises the question of why he is always in danger of dying. He almost drowns in a river, almost burns in a fire, almost dies from falling from a tree, almost dies from a beating, and almost drowns in a puddle. As Dana says to him, "You keep trying to get yourself killed. I keep coming back" (121). Other than being the unluckiest man in the world or having a death wish, the only explanation for Rufus's continual scrapes with death is that he needs Dana in his time period, perhaps to influence his eventual attachment to his children. Likewise, Dana may need to save Rufus to ensure the survival of her family line and her own existence. Their relationship is thus a mutual bid for sheer existence, what Rufus labels as "something mighty crazy" (136). The crazy part is that in the gothic nightmare of traveling back in time, Dana must reclaim her ties to the monster as well as the victim, not only because Rufus makes an appearance in the family Bible, but also because his existence helps Dana understand her family's past. She will certainly never claim that her black ancestors were "holding us back" because she can comprehend the complexity.

Although Kevin and Rufus are not set up as doubles the way Dana and Alice are, the parallels Dana finds between them allow Kevin to be a kind of rewriting of Rufus as well. After Kevin spends five years in the past, Dana notices that he has picked up a "slight accent" that makes him sound "a little like Rufus and Tom Weylin. Just a little" (190). Dana's worry that the past will "rub off on" Kevin is allayed, though. Kevin spends his sojourn in the past helping enslaved people escape; he is still the kindred spirit that she chose. The cross-racial marriage Dana chooses with Kevin revises the relationship Rufus forces on Alice. Dana claims Kevin as the locus of home at the beginning of her experience and reaffirms his value as home at the end. Dana and Kevin are bound by their knowledge of the past. After their experiences, they realize that anyone hearing their story would not think them "sane" (266).

As crazy as their experience is, it has larger implications. Just as Trethewey reclaims her mother as a way of reclaiming her larger native land, Butler has designs on America itself.[31] The 1976 setting, the bicentennial of America's founding, highlights that Dana and Kevin's time traveling speaks to a larger American paradigm. At the beginning, Dana and Kevin realize that the history books do not give them enough information about slavery. Dana's final trip into the past, which ends in Rufus's death and her resulting freedom, happens on July 4th. After Dana finally makes it back into the present, she and Kevin end at a historical society, suggesting that their experience has implications for a re-evaluation of history and its meaning for the present. Butler's use of time travel suggests that the past and the present are so close as to exist simultaneously in an America where "kindred" includes people of both races, all now reclaimed from their status as property.

※ ※ ※

Octavia Butler and Natasha Trethewey mold the gothic into a useful tool for their narratives, taking its supernatural disruption of chronological time and reversing it. This disruption opens up the possibility of traveling through time to witness nineteenth-century slavery, a Civil War encampment, and a 1907 parade celebrating King Cotton. Butler uses the conduit of a troublesome house to propel her character into the past, while Trethewey uses point of view, tense shifts, and photography to erase the passage of time. In both texts, however, the writers are reversing haunting to teach their readers that there is no safe barrier between past and present. When Ermarth explains that postmodern temporality makes time "a function of position, literally of reader position," the net effect is that the reader is thrust into the text: "Readers must continuously recognize that when they read, as when they do other things, their consciousness is active, not passive; that reading time is not a separate arrangement where one brackets or neutralizes life but instead a full exercise of that life" (22–23). At the outset of *Native Guard*, Trethewey asks her reader to "try this" and describes a journey. If the "you," which then shifts to a "we" by the end of the collection, takes the journey, he or she must become haunted by the past, just as the reader of Dana's narrative shares Dana's point of view as a modern person encountering slavery. In both texts, the reader becomes the specter haunting history.

The reader furthermore bears witness to the claiming of history. Trethewey and Butler use the tool of the gothic to change the power dynamics of race and property. From the early narratives of Harriet Jacobs and Hannah Crafts through later depictions of slavery, the key catalyst in southern gothic works of haunting is the conflation of people with property. Butler and Trethewey, as many critics aptly argue, rewrite history in their contemporary narratives, but they do more than this; they claim the property of the past by using writing to craft tales of ownership. If property rights are constructed in language, they can be reconstructed in language. The past can be claimed as property through the vehicle of haunting backwards. In southern gothic texts with the spotlight trained on slavery, the reader learns to fear what happens when people lose personhood. Butler and Trethewey reclaim these people, allowing them to tell their story and transforming them from unclaimed bodies to kindred.

EPILOGUE

What the Gothic Can Do

Harriet Jacobs predicted that future Americans would use her bill of sale to learn the truth of slavery: "I was sold at last! A human being sold in the free city of New York! The bill of sale is on record, and future generations will learn from it that women were articles of traffic in New York, late in the nineteenth century of the Christian religion" (155). My project started by examining Jacobs's call for readers to witness the horror of a person being considered property. In this epilogue, I want to attend to yet a different portion of Jacobs's conclusion: that her freedom came "late in the nineteenth century of the Christian religion" (155). By highlighting that Christianity structures the very marking of time, as year zero is determined by the birth of Christ, Jacobs points out the irony that nineteen centuries into this belief system American culture still upheld the abhorrent practice of slavery. Having just complained that she hears the church bells calling people to church on Sunday morning but did not "[dare] to show my face," the conjoining of Christianity and slavery lands as a weighty critique (154). That the sale happens "late" in the century is not, thus, a comment on how far into the hundred-year span of time it happens, but a sense that Jacobs's freedom should have happened earlier, that the timing is faulty and immoral.

 This problem of wrong timing does not disappear with the passing of more time. From her viewpoint in the twenty-first century, Natasha Trethewey likewise contemplates lateness. In "Scenes from a Documentary History of Mississippi," the speaker describes a photograph of a young girl who is turned away from the library designated "for Negroes" because it is "closed, the door/just out of reach" (24). The speaker wants to help her but confronts the problem that "this is history"; hence "You Are Late" (24). While Jacobs may call on readers in her time to see the lateness of her freedom as a failing of their religion, for her future readers, as for the speaker in Trethewey's poem, the lateness is an indication of being separated in time from the victims of slavery and racism and thus being unable to intervene in the past. Because the arrow of time points one way, readers in the present are simply too late.

Contemporary dialogues on slavery therefore tend to focus instead on acquiring a more accurate record of the past. Stephanie E. Jones-Rogers, for example, counters the typical focus on male slaveholders by examining how white female slaveholders also had "economic investments in slavery" (xiii). She is thus able to "uncover hitherto hidden relationships among gender, slavery, and capitalism" (xiii). In another instance, Kathryn Schulz explains that the outsized attention on the Underground Railroad as a means for escape has "mythologized" the narrative of the South as the sole province of slavery's problems. The Underground Railroad, she argues, "was a Northern institution." Fugitives had to escape from the North because, as Jacobs's narrative proves, the North was not safe. Other scholars are recovering parts of slavery's story that have been conveniently left untold. Rachel L. Swarms writes about how the insurance industry, located in the North, made money from writing policies on enslaved people. Multiple universities have also recently confronted the financial benefits they gained from owning or selling people. Harvard President Drew Gilpin Faust acknowledges that her university had been "directly complicit" in slavery and was "coming to terms with history" (Schuessler).

This coming to terms by trying to tell a more accurate story can often, however, reignite the problems of the past. A flashpoint of the struggle about how to tell the history of slavery has been the question of whether to take down public monuments that commemorate the Confederacy. New Orleans Mayor Mitch Landrieu discovered that for many contemporary citizens, "defending history" means keeping monuments to Confederate generals in place. Landrieu may argue that "the historic record is clear, [that] the Robert E. Lee, Jefferson Davis, and P. G. T. Beauregard statues were not erected just to honor these men, but as part of the movement that became known as the Cult of the Lost Cause," but he still had to use SWAT teams to protect construction workers clad in bullet-proof vests because of the threat of domestic terrorism (219). Over one hundred and fifty years after the Civil War, the nation is still debating its meaning and connection to slavery. The fierce tenor of these debates makes the need to see the past accurately that much more crucial.

While this need cannot be overstated, revising history still does not answer the problem of lateness. With adequate resources, the present moment can understand the past better, but only as a record of what happened. Hence, to answer Jacobs's call to bear witness, we need the power to manipulate time; in other words, we need fiction. In her essay, "Some Notes on Time in Fiction," Eudora Welty explains how fiction can play with temporality. While "clock time has an arbitrary, bullying power over daily affairs that of course can't be got around," Welty argues that "it has not the same power in fiction as it has in life" ("Some" 97). Instead, fiction, as the tangible product of the imagination, has the force to alter time: "Fiction does not hesitate to accelerate time, slow it down, project it forward or run it backward, cause it to skip over itself or repeat itself." ("Some" 97). Most significantly, fiction "can set a fragment of the past within a frame of the present and cause them to exist simultaneously" ("Some" 97). Fiction, whether prose or poetry, can render the past in present tense, as Harriet Jacobs and Hannah Crafts demonstrate when they use fiction to reshape and alter the past. They do not just retell their life stories; they create new lives through words, a power that all of the other authors in this study then harness in their attempt to elide the boundaries of time.

The gothic is fiction with its boundary-flaunting capacity at full magnification. Embracing the imaginative power to ignore the arrow of time, the gothic uses haunting to address wrongs across temporal barriers. When Jacobs haunts Dr. Flint from her attic space; when Crafts resurrects Mr. Trappe as a monster; when the figure of Babo haunts Cereno; when the ghosts of Dessa's loved ones keep her company in jail; when Circe becomes a specter overseeing the destruction of white property; when Beloved returns to haunt Sethe; or when Dana and Kevin become ghosts in the nineteenth century, the gothic disruptions in time allow simultaneity. From Jacobs's and Crafts's slave narratives to Trethewey's twenty-first-century poetry, the works in this study illustrate the potency of the gothic to disturb constructions of race and property, a disruption that can work across time. Fighting against the problem of faulty timing is thus what the gothic can do.

With this gothic ability to traverse time, fiction can then imagine and create new monuments to add yet different points of view to the contemporary discourse on how we should think about the past. A model of this construction is Kevin Young's poem "For the Confederate Dead," which describes one monument while constructing a second through words. The poem begins with a speaker seemingly trapped in time and contemplating apocalypse: "These are the last days/ my television says" (97). This coming disaster is evidenced by weather: "Tornadoes, more/ rain, overcast" (97). Although the speaker then notes that "I do not/ trust weathermen," traces of weather appear throughout the poem, representing the human attempt to predict the future. Michael LeMahieu comments that the poem reveals a "temporality that is out of joint," (114) and, indeed, the references to weather as unpredictable but somehow still "inevitable" provide an apt backdrop for the speaker's musings on the problems of time. The speaker describes a mural commemorating the Confederacy, which has a plaque that "declares war" (97). Its temporal dislocation, however, becomes evident as that war is "not Civil" but for "Southern Independence" (97). As a relic from an earlier time, this mural is like milk that "expires" (97). This past is now "flaking" and losing "More leaves each day" (98). Although the poem uses the present tense to describe the mural's scene, "Negroes bend/ to pick the endless white" (98), the mural existed in a hotel that "no longer/ welcomes guests," pointing to the stasis and death of this image of the past (98). The gothic disruption of time happens instead when the speaker creates a different version of the past from that of the mural: "In my movie there are no/ horses, no heroes/ only draftees fleeing" (98). Unlike the "Confederate Dead" of the title, who are lauded by the mural and by monuments such as those Landrieu fought to remove, these "draftees" do not die. The poem imagines them surviving but hiding: "lying/ burrowed beneath the dead—" (98). They remain silent while the enemy kills off "what is believed//to be the last/ of the breathing" (98). The story of these nonheroes is thus buried but perhaps still breathing and still viable. Although the speaker comprehends the problem of timing, in noting "It is getting later" and "How late/ it has gotten," he then declares, "Forget the weatherman" (99). Lateness is not a problem, and time is not a boundary when we can dig "beside the monument" until "we strike/ water" (99). The gothic transgression of the dead becoming undead allows for the poem itself to be a different monument, a possibility created through fiction.

The gothic refusal of time's boundaries means that we can also reconstruct our textual monuments. In her poem "Declaration," Tracy K. Smith erases portions of the Declaration of Independence to rethink the possibility of freedom and agency imagined in the American dream. In borrowing specific lines from the Declaration while leaving blank spaces between them to indicate the portions left out, Smith locates a different thread entirely. She constructs the voice of a people whose freedom was not declared in 1776: "We have reminded them of the circumstances of our emigration/ and settlement here//—taken Captive// on the high Seas" (19). The generic nature of pronouns allows the speaker to posit "our people" and "we" as enslaved people, signifying on the original document by repeating its words but imbuing them with new meaning. By using the words of revolution against the revolutionaries, Smith uncovers yet a different history that, like the alternative monument in Young's poem, may be buried but is not dead. Smith's poem shows that it is not too late to construct even the story of America's founding anew.

With the recent energy to recover historical records, the contemporary world has powerful tools at its disposal to reassess slavery. While the discipline of history has significant potency, literature and literary criticism have important parts to play in this reassessment as well. What the gothic offers to the conversation is a heightened version of the fictional feat of simultaneity, allowing writers to put a "fragment of the past within the frame of the present." While gothic tropes such as ghosts and haunted houses may seem too silly and ephemeral for a subject as weighty as the dispossession of millions of people over hundreds of years, the eleven texts in this study reveal the gothic's important power to teach readers what to fear. Fiction can make that "fear" happen in the present, clarifying that the impact of slavery's conflation of people with property survives into the twenty-first century. Although contemporary readers of Harriet Jacobs's narrative are "late," in that the present cannot intervene into the past, haunting ignores temporal boundaries so that contemporary readers are able both to see the ghosts of the past and to attend to their stories' persistence in the present. Jacobs asks her readers to bear witness to the devastation that occurs when people become property: "a human being sold." What her narrative teaches is that witnessing is best done in present tense, aided by the time-defying power of the gothic.

NOTES

INTRODUCTION: THE BILL OF SALE:
GOTHIC, PROPERTY, SLAVERY, AND THE SOUTH

1. I will be using the terms "America" and "New World" in this introduction to capture the larger connotations that have been tied to these terms, although I certainly acknowledge that "United States" is a more accurate way of describing the history and literature of the nation.

2. I am using gender-neutral language here to indicate the entire life of this idea into the present when it is applied to men and women. Although the phrase itself, the "American dream" was coined in 1931 when James Truslow Adams used it in his novel *The American Epic*, certainly the idea of being able to move up in class with hard work in America is evident much earlier, from Benjamin Franklin's autobiography to the Horatio Alger stories.

3. Other critics who examine American gothic and race include Brogan, Edwards, Wester, and Winter.

4. In 1853, the abolitionist William Goodall in *The American Slave Code* argued that the status of enslaved people as property was "the theory of American slavery" (27). Goodall outlines various state laws declaring enslaved people as either chattel or real estate and then details how all of the other restrictions on the behavior of enslaved people follow from these declarations.

5. See Rothstein for a discussion of how race impacts property law.

6. I will be referencing the contribution of these critics in individual chapters as I discuss individual works, but for the latest scholarship, see *Critical Insights: Southern Gothic Literature*, *Undead Souths: The Gothic and Beyond in Southern Literature and Culture*, and *The Palgrave Handbook of the Southern Gothic*.

7. For more information on the sentimental novel, its popularity, and demise, see Baym.

8. See Faflak and Haslam for a reading of Disneyland as "the most gothic site in the whole of America" (1).

9. Kafer's book details the history of Brown's Quaker family, including his father's detainment during the revolutionary war because of his pacifism, and argues that this history led Brown to be wary of the new republic and thus open to writing gothic tales of anxiety about what could go wrong.

10. See Warwick for a discussion of the definitions of gothic being "so large as to be meaningless" (8).

11. This approach to the gothic is close to the approaches held by Botting and Garrett in their readings of the gothic as depicting transgression to caution the reader to uphold society's values. I agree with their readings of the gothic's relationship to the reader as one of instruction, but I do not read this instruction as necessarily conservative. Most of the narratives that I am exploring in this study are using the gothic to show the reader that society's view on slavery is wrong or that society has not fully comprehended the awful history and legacy of slavery.

12. See Morgan for a reading of how the distinctions of race intensified as Virginia turned from a labor source made up of indentured servants to chattel slavery (316–37).

13. See Johnson for a history of the expansion of slavery in the early 1800s.

14. Even texts not explicitly focused on slavery can carry the residue of the gothic narrative of dispossession. Robert K. Martin finds that the ur-text of American gothic, *The House of the Seven Gables*, hides a narrative about slavery under its focus on class distinctions. Levine makes a similar argument about Hawthorne's attention to slavery in *The House of Seven Gables* but focuses his reading on the chapter where Alice Pynchon becomes enslaved to Matthew Maule ("Reading").

15. Although slavery existed only in the South in the nineteenth century, Warren argues that our perception of slavery as a southern practice has been skewed by our focus on the antebellum time period. She explains that "slavery was in England's American colonies, even the New England colonies, from the very beginning" and that "the nineteenth century divide of a slave south and a free north does not hold for the early colonial period. In fact, in the mid-seventeenth century, the northern English colonies had more slaves than those in the Chesapeake" (9, 11).

16. In the Palgrave collection, both Davison and Kreyling write about southern gothic in relation specifically to plantation houses. Three recent books approach southern literature and slavery/plantations from the different through somewhat related paradigm of memory and trauma studies: see Adams, Hinrichsen, and Russ.

17. For information about the reward notice issued by then-president George Washington and his wife Mary for the return of their enslaved woman, Oney Judge, see Dunbar.

CHAPTER ONE: FROM DAMSELS TO SPECTERS IN HARRIET JACOBS'S *INCIDENTS IN THE LIFE OF A SLAVE GIRL* AND HANNAH CRAFTS'S *THE BONDWOMAN'S NARRATIVE*

1. The full title is *Uncle Tom's Cabin; or, Life among the Lowly*, although the original subtitle was "The Man That Was a Thing" (Parfait 21).

2. This discrepancy may be due to Stowe's writing of the novel first in serial form. When she gave the story its name, she had only completed part of it. The novel's readers urged her to continue to write and to write a longer novel, which may have affected how the title became less appropriate for the story as more chapters were written after the initial scene in the cabin. See Parfait for information about serialization and publication.

3. Fisher also notes these two oddities in the novel's title.

4. Gutman explains that the terms "aunt" and "uncle" to refer to nonrelatives were originally used by the young people for people their parents' age, but that "nineteenth-century whites used kin terms of address toward slaves for different reasons. They had two purposes: to show their personal attachment and even respect toward adult slaves (usually house servants) and to use a nonreciprocal term of address that defined an essential status difference between a slave and his or her owners. 'Uncle' and 'Mister' lived in related but very different worlds. The slaves had different reasons for using similar terms of address" (217). Baldwin notes how the appellation was used to designate an enslaved person as tame: "Uncle Tom, trustworthy and sexless, needed only to drop the title 'Uncle' to become violent, crafty, and sullen, a menace to any white woman who passed by" (28).

5. See Gates and Hecimovich, xvii.

6. The influence between Stowe and Jacobs is complicated. Jacobs approached Stowe for assistance in getting a publisher, but Stowe instead wanted Jacobs's story as part of her research for *A Key to Uncle Tom's Cabin*. Stowe may already have had access to Jacobs's story because Jacobs was known in abolitionist circles. Stowe may have used the story as a basis for the Cassie episode in *Uncle Tom's Cabin*. Jacobs in turn had read Stowe's novel before writing her narrative; see Scholl and Yellin (Introduction). For a reading of Stowe and Crafts, see Yellin ("*The Bondwoman's*"). For readings of Crafts and Dickens, see Hack, Robbins, and Teukolsky.

7. Although Crafts did not publish her narrative, I will be referring to her "audience" because her narrative (especially her preface) suggests that she did anticipate having readers and shapes her narrative accordingly.

8. Ballinger, Lustig, and Townshend chide Henry Louis Gates Jr. for "becoming the dupe of one of the oldest of tricks" when he takes Crafts's claim of presenting facts seemingly as face value (212). For more information on prefaces and truth claims, see Martin (79–84).

9. For critics in addition to Goddu who discuss the combination of fiction and truth in Jacobs's narrative, see William L. Andrews ("Hannah") and Fabian; for the discussion in Crafts's narrative, see Ballinger, Lustig, and Townshend.

10. Winter, on the other hand, analyzes the similarities between gothic fiction and slave narratives.

11. See also Goddu's argument on Crafts's narrative ("American").

12. Castronovo's argument aligns with Goddu's: "Crafts's ghost-writing is not that gothic after all but is rather a critical aesthetic response to the everyday horrors of slavery" (195).

13. See Gates and Hecimovich, xix.

14. For Jacobs's use of the gothic, see Goddu (*Gothic*), Greeson, and Wardrop. For Crafts's use of the gothic, see Ballinger, Lustig, and Townshend, Castronovo, Cucarella-Ramon, Haslam ("The strange"), Marshall, Sanchez-Eppler, Wald, and Wester.

15. For how the death of the mother functions in fiction, see Nancy Armstrong.

16. Since Crafts's narrative was not published (and therefore not edited) in her lifetime, the contemporary editor decided to leave the grammatical and spelling errors in the text. I will follow their lead and quote directly without indicating throughout this chapter with "*sic*" that the primary text has a spelling or an editing error.

17. Though the damsel-in-distress character is key to the gothic genre, the character predates it and was important to Middle English literature that focused on chivalry.

18. Chaplin explains that during the rise of the gothic novel in the eighteenth century, coverture laws were being challenged and debated, so that "the 1790s was the decade in which Female Gothic fiction emerged as a distinct mode of literary Gothicism and its subject was often the precarious juridical position of women" (139). See also Wallace.

19. The use of second person to address the reader was also popular in American sentimental novels of the nineteenth century. Susanna Rowson, for example, interrupts the storyline multiple times in *Charlotte Temple* to speak directly to the young girls whom she imagines reading her novel.

20. Ballinger, Lustig, and Townshend explain the connection between Trappe and the lawyer Tulkinghorn in Charles Dicken's *Bleak House*. Levine argues that "Trappe is perhaps even more compellingly an amalgam of Chillingworth and Judge Jaffrey Pynchon" ("Trappe(d)" 163).

21. Accomando even posits Jacobs's book as a "symbolic courtroom" where Jacobs is "testifying against all slaveholders and the institution of slavery" (234). For Jacobs's narrative as testimony, see also DeLombard (116) and Stone (73).

22. For example, see Buell ("Bondwoman" 24).

23. Wester explains that "the discussion of women's sexualized bodies in slave narratives frequently appears alongside signs of hybridity. Writers almost always note the woman's 'fair' complexion as the cause of the lascivious master's offending advance" (43).

24. Kreiger traces the Linda's racial heritage by discussing her grandmother (611).

25. Marshall even suggests that Trappe could have fabricated the story of Hannah's mistress (127).

26. Haslam argues that the possibility of characters becoming black opens "a fissure in the domestic purity of the white home" ("The strange" 30). Buell labels this shifting racial identity the narrative's "most distinctive and ingenious plot motif" ("Bondwoman" 26).

27. Levine adds that Mrs. Cosgrove's exploration of the house raises "the question of whether there are any 'whites' to be found in the South" ("Trappe(d)" 287).

28. Humphreys finds that for Linda, "survival depends on a lack of divisions between public and private spaces," hence "the distant cottage is the worst possible place Jacobs can envision not only because she fears being sexually abused there, but because it is outside her protective community" (146, 147).

29. Sanchez-Eppler asks whether, considering Hannah's light skin, the portraits might also be Hannah's ancestors (266).

30. For a gothic reading of this "ghost," see Castronovo and Haslam ("The strange" 36).

31. See chapter 2 for a full explication of this phenomenon.

32. Fabian calls Crafts's text "imagined fiction" and argues "she broke many of the rules that governed literary works by people who had been slaves" ("Hannah" 44).

33. Keyser explains that these shifts to present tense also "engage readers" by making them "waiting witnesses" (92).

34. See Baym for the connection to *Uncle Tom's Cabin*, and see Kesyer for the connection to *Jane Eyre*. For the connection to *Bleak House*, see Hack, Robbins, and Teukolsky.

35. Gates suggests that another reason that Hannah Bond selected the name "Crafts" was to honor Horace Craft, a local farmer who hid her during her escape (xiv).

CHAPTER TWO: PLAYING CON GAMES IN HERMAN MELVILLE'S *BENITO CERENO*, MARK TWAIN'S *PUDD'NHEAD WILSON*, AND SHERLEY ANNE WILLIAMS'S *DESSA ROSE*

1. See Kaplan for a general overview of the critics' divide.

2. Critics who analyze the lack of resolution in the endings are Cox and Porter for *Pudd'inhead Wilson* and Goldner for *Benito Cereno*.

3. Although the term for these characters historically is "confidence man," I will be using the later gender-neutral term "con artist" since some of my examples will be women.

4. See Young, who posits the Americanness of the con artist on the influence of particular people, such as Barnum.

5. See Lenz for a discussion of P. T. Barnum and Davy Crockett as con men.

6. See Thadious Davis for a reading of how games subvert the power structures of property in William Faulkner's *Go Down, Moses* (*Games*).

7. The timing of the novel suggests that Herman Melville was indeed thinking about con artists. *Benito Cereno* was published in three installments in *Putnam's Monthly* in 1855. Matterson explains that Melville proposed his novel *The Confidence-Man* this same year to the publisher Dix and Edwards (viii).

8. Wyn Kelley notes the influence of popular melodrama on Melville's depiction, explaining that Melville "attended performances of Douglas Jerrold's nautical melodramas in London" (25).

9. Edwards calls Babo's performance "minstrelsy" (28).

10. See Morris for a close reading of clothing in *Pudd'nhead Wilson*.

11. Gillman's reading is in concert with mine, as she notes that Tom "harkens back to those pretenders, confidence men, and false claimants whose imposture is exposed" (71).

12. See Sundquist for a reading of Melville's use and revision of the 1805 slave revolt on the *Tryal* (135–221).

13. Tawil adds interesting context: "Lest we think this language of animality would somehow have seemed natural or unremarkable to Melville's original readership, it is worth pointing out that in the same issue of *Putnam's Monthly* in which the third installment of 'BC' was originally published, an article ironically entitled 'About Niggers' satirized the disavowal of black humanity" (40).

14. Cartwright argues that Babo parallels Melville: "It is my contention that Babo, the dictator of the fiction within Melville's tale, is the text's authorial figure. Babo's insurrectional pleasure authorizes the tale and mirrors the bitter pleasures of the novella's plotting artist. Both Babo and Melville rely upon predictable ideological responses to trap the witless reader, and both finally refuse commentary, choosing, through recognition of the inadequacies of language, silence" (184).

15. From this point forward, in discussing *Pudd'nhead Wilson*, I will put "white" and "black" in quotation marks when I am highlighting how these categories are used as societal constructions.

16. See King for an analysis of the stereotype of the black thief.

17. See Esteve, Rowe, and Spangler for readings about the depiction of economics in the novel.

18. Rowe points out the personal context of Twain's depiction of property: "*Pudd'nhead Wilson* was written on the verge of the Panic of 1893 (and rewritten and proofread during the Panic), which was the final blow to Twain's publishing company, Wester and Company, and his dreams for the commercial success of the Paige Typesetter" (147).

19. Kekeh explains that Adam Nehemiah's name "may be a reference to a nineteenth-century preacher called Adam Nehemiah. He was a proslavery clergyman belonging to the Essex Street Church of Boston and published a book in favor of slavery" (221).

20. For readings of the gothic as conservative, see Bernstein, Botting, and Clemens. For readings of the gothic as transgressive, see Bailey, Crow, Garrett, and Goddu (*Gothic*). Anolik traces both possibilities in the English tradition ("Horrors").

21. I have referred to the African crew on the *San Dominick* as "slaves" when discussing them through Delano's view, but in deciphering their own view (through Cereno's deposition), I will refer to them as "blacks" since they are rejecting their slave status.

22. Goldner (66) and Morrell (73) also discuss the continued haunting in different contexts.

23. Cox points out the violence underlying this parentage: "[Tom] is, after all, the son of white men's casual lust gratified by a series of aggressive sexual acts at the expense of their slaves" (229).

24. Rowe broadens this argument by arguing that the blaming of "erroneous inventory" demonstrates Twain's larger satire of a speculative economy: "Twain understands slavery itself as not just a provincial agrarian institution, but the basis for the speculative economy that would fuel industrial expansion, Manifest Destiny, and laissez-faire capitalism. The slave is, after all, the ultimate 'speculation,' insofar as the buyer invests a relatively small amount of money—for purchase and maintenance—in hopes of watching that capital grow into the accumulated labor power of a healthy, long-lived slave" (139).

25. See Douglass for a passage about the misconception of the singing of enslaved people as evidence of their happiness (27–28).

26. See Davison and Kreyling.

27. See Goddu for a close reading of the gothic whiteness in Poe's novel (*Gothic* 76–93).

28. Dawson points out that Nehemiah's "insistence to the Sheriff to have Dessa reveal her scars to the men present recalls the nineteenth-century experience of Sojourner Truth. The men in the audience in Silver Lake, Indiana, in 1850 challenged the famous abolitionist to prove she was a woman by demanding that she bare her breasts. They questioned her womanhood, since her physical strength and oral ability as an abolitionist had led to rumors that she was a man" (28).

CHAPTER THREE: SPECTERS ON STAIRCASES IN WILLIAM FAULKNER'S *ABSALOM, ABSALOM!*, EUDORA WELTY'S *DELTA WEDDING*, AND TONI MORRISON'S *SONG OF SOLOMON*

1. For readings of how Morrison alludes to or rewrites Faulkner in *Song of Solomon*, see Batty, Bauer, Fulton, and Weinstein. For Morrison's comments about Welty, see Morrison *Conversations* (47, 91). Welty has a story entitled "Circe."

2. See Kreyling ("Uncanny") for how the plantation's repetition in southern literature becomes gothic.

3. For a discussion of the connections between Circe and Clytie, see Batty. For a discussion of the connections between Circe and Aunt Studney, see McMahand.

4. See Pan and Byerman for readings of Clytic; see McWhirter for a reading of Aunt Studney; see Fletcher for a reading of Circe.

5. For readings of *Absalom, Absalom!* and the gothic, see especially Brooks, Duck ("Haunting"), Hinrichsen, Kerr, Millgate, and Ramos. Ramos discusses Clytie as well as other characters as ghosts. Hurley argues that "ghost" becomes a verb in the narrative, as the story creates ghosts out of the characters.

6. See Simon for a connection between this narrative of Sutpen's early life and Jean-Jacques Rousseau's *Discourse of the Origin of Inequality*.

7. In examining the ledgers that the lawyer keeps in plotting how to make money from Charles's existence, Benson finds that even Faulkner's discourse is imbued with the "language of calculation," so that in the end, Charles Bon is "quite literally, a product of Sutpen's botched books" (47). Sayers also reads how "the economic logic of the ledger penetrates the novel and its logic of storytelling (224).

8. For a reading of Faulkner's attention to property in *Go Down, Moses*, see Davis (*Games*).

9. Macon's obsession with property affects everyone in the family. As Willis argues, "For Macon Dead, Milkman's father, all human relationships have become fetishized by their being made equivalent to money. His wife is an acquisition; his son, an investment in the future; and his renters, dollar signs in the bank" (38).

10. This description of his entrance into the town and his amazing feat cause both Weinstein and Fulton to find an echo to the story of Thomas Sutpen (62, 19).

11. See Robert K. Martin for a reading of how *Absalom, Absalom!* rewrites *The House of Seven Gables*.

12. For an alternative reading, see Millgate, who argues that the gothic in *Absalom, Absalom!* is similar to the European tradition (162).

13. Faulkner even plays with time to age the house so it can look appropriately haunted; as Coss notes, "the house is rotting away at a rate which seems unnatural" (110).

14. Godden explains that the timeline for Sutpen's actions in Haiti is inaccurate and argues that the Haiti scenes allow Faulkner to a counterrevolution to the idea of slave revolt.

15. Although not explored in this essay, each of the three novels alludes to the original Native American ownership of the land. The Fairchilds live at "Shellmound" and speak of an Indian ghost, and Milkman discovers that his lineage includes displaced Native Americans.

16. Matthews points out that in 1833 Sutpen's importation of enslaved people from Haiti was illegal, adding to the town's perception of them as "wild" (251).

17. Kerr points out that, although many of Faulkner's works deploy the gothic genre, Faulkner relates the entire history of a haunted house only in *Absalom, Absalom!* (32). See Hinrichsen for a reading of how nature works against the haunted house: "Faulkner envisions nature as a gothic space for staging ecological resistance to plantation order" (224).

18. Marrs explains that Eudora Welty's inspiration for Marmion was Waverly, a "once grand plantation that had become derelict," which Welty visited with friends when she was in college (80). An earlier version of this house appears in a short story Welty wrote entitled "The Delta Cousins," but the gothic setting teeming with overgrowth was an addition to the novel (86).

19. Weston argues that the current Fairchild family home, Shellmound, acts as a gothic space because of its "artificial architectural mazes and human family tangles" (101).

20. Griffin explains that "it is imperative that Marmion, of all the Fairchild houses, be the expected Southern-plantation house design, columned and expansive. Marmion was built on the unreality of the southern past, not on the actuality, when the legend of the Old South was at its height" (531).

21. In Welty's story "Circe," Welty depicts Circe as a housekeeper: "In the end, it takes the phenomenal neatness of housekeeping to put it through the heads of men that they are swine" (639).

22. Levins argues that it is only Rosa's narrative that is in the gothic mode in the novel, but my reading will show that Quentin's story has gothic overtones as well.

23. This distance has caused even the critics who write about the African American women in *Delta Wedding* to focus their readings on other characters. For readings of the other African American women, see Costello, Entzminger, and Ladd ("Coming").

24. See Gygax for a different allusion in this scene (22).

25. See Harker for a reading of the scene as Rosa's "lesbian panic" (42).

26. Judith also takes on the voice of the house in this scene, as Donovan-Condron points out in a reading that focuses on Clytie, Judith, and stasis.

27. See O'Donnell for a reading of the house as having a body.

28. Duck ("Haunting") argues that Quentin's participation in the regional haunting is not fated but a choice he makes in recreating Sutpen's story with Shreve (94).

29. See Ford for a reading of how conjure can be beneficial in *Delta Wedding*.

30. Although my reading is focused on Milkman, it should be noted that other characters in *Song of Solomon* do not make this redemptive turn. Milkman's friend Guitar is so focused on getting the gold to finance his revenge killings that he comes after Milkman, and Milkman's ex-girlfriend Hagar dies after attempting to fix her life by buying new clothes and makeup.

CHAPTER FOUR: CLAIMING, KILLING, AND HAUNTING IN TONI MORRISON'S *BELOVED*

1. For discussions about Sethe's decision, see Decker and Phelan.

2. Critics who do discuss the issue of property are Franco, Christopher Peterson, and Harris ("Escaping"). I will address these specific arguments later in the chapter.

3. For discussions about Beloved's identity, see Harris (*Fiction*), Horvitz, and House.

4. For readings of the haunted house, see Hogan, Kawash ("Haunted"), Peeren, and Schmudde.

5. For other readings of Sethe's claim about her milk, see Henderson ("Toni" 71) and Goldman (324).

6. As King explains, "the label thief" is "produced in discourse and is contingent upon the social and political conditions surrounding and informing that discourse" (71, 73). For a broader discussion of stealing and slavery, see chapter 2. For historical context, see Genovase (599–603).

7. For a discussion of *Pierson v. Post* in American literature, see Luck. For a discussion of the case in Faulkner's *Go Down, Moses*, see Thadious Davis (*Games*).

8. See Morgan for a discussion of enslaved women's reproductive capabilities as part of their property value to owners.

9. For discussion of the Margaret Garner case and its relation to *Beloved*, see Gordon, Reinhardt, and Walters.

10. Reinhardt points out another difference; press reports refer to the Garners' daughter as "nearly white," with the suggestion that her owner may be the father (99–100).

11. Goldman posits an interesting link between the ink Sethe makes for schoolteacher and the milk the nephews steal from her (324).

12. For a discussion about the power of literacy in this image, see Gordon, 148.

13. The last Africans brought to America were on the ship *Clotilda*, which traveled from Ouidah to Alabama in 1860; see Diouf.

14. For a counterreading, see O'Reilly, who argues that Beloved cannot be read as human (85–86).

15. For a discussion of "revolutionary suicide" in the novel, see Ryan.

16. See Daina Ramey Berry for a discussion of "ghost value," the value of dead bodies.

17. The ship is the subject as well of J. M. W. Turner's famous 1940 painting *The Slave Ship* and M. NourbeSe Philip's 2008 *Zong*, a profound poetic meditation on the devastation of people becoming property.

18. In December of 2016, *The New York Times* published an article about New York Life's history of writing policies on enslaved people as property. The article discusses other banks who wrote these policies as well; see Swarns.

19. If the Beloved who survives the Middle Passage is fully human, the Beloved who is imprisoned may indeed be the survivor Beloved in her later life in America. House makes this very argument, asserting that Beloved is the survivor all along and is only imagined as Sethe's daughter by the other characters as they construct her identity. Even if, however, there is nothing supernatural about Beloved, she acts as a gothic reminder for Sethe of her

actions. For the purposes of my analysis here, I will treat the runaway Beloved as a separate, third identity.

20. See Harris ("Escaping") for a reading of Stamp Paid's decision in terms of his manhood (330–32).

21. Duvall connects Baby Suggs's sermon on flesh to Rosa's panic over Clytie's touch in *Absalom, Absalom!* (93).

22. See Peeren for another reading of the house as gendered space.

23. Other modern texts do this as well. Shirley Jackson's *The Haunting of Hill House*, for example, portrays the house itself as the specter.

24. Both Beloved and 124 are using names that were assigned later. We do not know the name of the baby Sethe killed, and "Beloved" is on her tombstone because of the words of the funeral mass. Although the book initially identifies the house as "124," the text also says, "it did not have a number then" (3). Decker also makes an interesting argument about the number. She argues that "124" skips "3" in numeric sequence because Beloved is the third child (246).

25. For a discussion of the allusion to the apocalypse, see James Berger (409–10).

26. These questions echo the ones Milkman asks Circe in *Song of Solomon*.

27. Buell compares the bank to Mary's bank in Ralph Ellison's *Invisible Man* (*Dream* 323) while Harris ("Escaping") compares it to the Sambo doll in the same novel (335).

CHAPTER FIVE: CLAIMING THE PROPERTY OF HISTORY IN OCTAVIA BUTLER'S *KINDRED* AND NATASHA TRETHEWEY'S *NATIVE GUARD*

1. For the debate over slavery's place in capitalism, see Beckert and Rockman.

2. Those "buried secrets" come back to haunt because of a desire for justice, according to Derrida, who explains that haunting fulfills the need for "responsibility" for "victims of wars, political or other kinds of violence, nationalist, racist, colonialist, sexist, or other kinds of exterminations" (xix).

3. That writing can somehow establish ownership of an abstraction, such as history, is an idea that has roots in slavery. Stephen Best traces modern laws concerning intellectual property back to laws created to establish slavery. He examines the expansion of the idea of property into more abstract thinking, from the concept of people being property to a person's ideas being treated as property, concluding that "within the text of the law there is an afterlife of slavery" (14).

4. Still other critics place Trethewey's poetry in contexts outside the South. Pereira reads her in mixed-race studies, and Russell reads her as part of the "global south" in his comparison with Seamus Heaney.

5. For discussions about the difficulty of pinpointing a genre for *Kindred*, see Stephanie S. Turner and Flagel.

6. Steinberg has a different reading of the time travel, arguing that it represents a "non-Western conceptualization of history" in which history is cyclical (467).

7. Brogan shares Spaulding's view of how contemporary narratives work to recoup and rewrite history but offers a more expansive view of ghosts in ethnic literature, focusing on Louis Erdrich's *Tracks,* Toni Morrison's *Beloved,* and Cristina Garcia's *Dreaming in Cuba.* Harris also reads *Kindred* as a historical novel but designates the text a "neo-slave narrative" that is crafted to "rewrite history" (*Scary* 62).

8. See also Schiff, who does not use the term "gothic," but he discusses Freud's uncanny and doubling, two key elements of the gothic.

9. Rushdy is the one critic who discusses the meaning of "home" in the novel, though not in connection to haunting ("Families" 139–40).

10. See Foster for a reading of how the time traveling impacts Dana and Kevin's relationship in the present.

11. See Levecq for a counterreading; she argues that the modern world has not progressed from slavery.

12. Certainly, one reason that her performance becomes real is that she is repeatedly physically assaulted. The pure pain of her body makes the past into a reality. Bast explains that "not only is she unable to prevent her body's abuse, but it crucially robs her of control over her movements, explicating the interconnectedness of agency, subjectivity, and the body" (158). The violence forces her closer to the position of property. Even though she earlier observes of the enslaved people "how easily people can be trained to accept slavery" (110), she later has to ask of herself, "*See how easily slaves are made?*" (177). Vint argues that "Dana realizes that bodily experiences have made her a slave" (251).

13. Weinbaum actually argues that Dana is mistaken in thinking she is called back to the past to save Rufus, asserting that the catalyst was instead Alice.

14. Jones argues that Trethewey's collection *Bellocq's Ophelia* also plays with time, "going backwards and forwards and backwards again in time" (424).

15. "Here" appears fourteen times in the collection while "home" appears twelve times.

16. In some poems, even a possible future is evoked. In "Blond," for example, the poet imagines that given her "parents' genes," blond hair was a possibility that the odds "might have brought" (39).

17. In discussing Otto Rank's writing on the double, Freud connects the double to the uncanny (235).

18. Dreams are also employed as a method of time travel in "Myth" and "Pastoral."

19. Other examples of the present tense in tension with a past moment are the line "In 1959 my mother is boarding a train" in "The Southern Crescent" and "This is 1966—she is married to a white man—" in "My Mother Dreams Another Country."

20. In "Pastoral," for example, the speaker imagines that the "flash freezes us" (35).

21. The ability of a photograph to capture a scene is also the subject of a poem in Trethewey's earlier collection *Domestic Work*. In "Three Photographs," a cabbage vendor critiques a photographer who has apparently told her to act "natural" by complaining he will "make a picture hold/ this moment, forever" (7).

22. In a reading of Trethewey's exploration of "throwaway bodies," Goad offers a reading of these photographs: "the speaker facilitates an intimate link between viewer and subject and keeps the subject from historical obscurity" (277).

23. There is an authorial connection to this loathing. Butler explains that her mother's "big dream for me was that I should get a job as a secretary and be able to sit down when I worked. My big dream was never to be a secretary in my life. I mean, it just seemed such an appallingly servile job" ("Interview" 51).

24. See Spaulding, Brogan, and Byerman (*Remembering*) for a discussion of works that attempt to interrogate and rewrite African American history.

25. For most of the novel, Dana plays the part of black savior to the white character, echoing a motif made infamous by Uncle Tom, but Butler turns this motif on its head by having Dana be the one to kill Rufus.

26. Dubey (348) and Spaulding (45) both explore how the novel was written as a response to the 1970s Black Power movement.

27. See McHaney (164) and Ramsey (132) for how the cover of *Native Guard* with a picture of the cross-hatched journal augments the layering of narratives in the poem.

28. For a discussion of Trethewey's choice not to use dialect, see De Cenzo (33).

29. In her reading of *Native Guard*, McHaney discusses the "bodies and body parts" that "pervade each section" (161).

30. See Angelyn Mitchell for a reading of Alice's suicide as a choice that shows her agency.

31. Kubitschek notes that Kevin's last name, Franklin, points to Benjamin Franklin (42).

WORKS CITED

Accomando, Christina. "'The Law Were Laid Down to Me Anew': Harriet Jacobs and the Reframing of Legal Fictions." *African American Review*, vol. 32, no. 2, 1998, pp. 229–45.

Adams, Jessica. *Wounds of Returning: Race, Memory, and Property on the Postslavery Plantation*. U of North Carolina P, 2007.

Alexandre, Sandy. *The Properties of Violence: Claims to Ownership in Representations of Lynching*. UP of Mississippi, 2012.

Anderson, Eric Gary, Taylor Hagood, and Daniel Cross Turner. Introduction. *Undead Souths: The Gothic and Beyond in Southern Literature and Culture*. Louisiana UP, 2015, pp. 1–9.

Andrews, David. "'Benito Cereno': No Charity on Earth, Not Even at Sea." *Leviathan: A Journal of Melville Studies*, vol. 2, no. 1, 2000, pp. 83–103.

Andrews, William L. "Hannah Crafts' Sense of an Ending." *In Search of Hannah Crafts: Critical Essays on "The Bondwoman's Narrative,"* edited by Henry Louis Gates Jr. and Hollis Robbins, Basic Books, 2004, pp. 30–42.

Andrews, William L. *To Tell a Free Story: The First Century of Afro-American Autobiography, 1760–1865*. U of Illinois P, 1986.

Anolik, Ruth Bienstock. "Horrors of Possession: The Gothic Struggle with the Law." *The Legal Studies Forum*, vol. 24, no. 3–4, 2000, pp. 667–86.

Anolik, Ruth Bienstock. *Property and Power in English Gothic Literature*. McFarland, 2016.

Armstrong, Nancy. *Desire and Domestic Fiction: A Political History of the Novel*. Oxford UP, 1987.

Armstrong, Tim. *The Logic of Slavery: Debt, Technology, and Pain in American Literature*. Cambridge UP, 2012.

Askeland, Lori. "Remodeling the Model Home in *Uncle Tom's Cabin* and *Beloved*." *Toni Morrison's Beloved: A Casebook*, edited by William L. Andrews and Nellie Y. McKay, Oxford UP, 1999, pp. 159–78.

Bailey, Dale. *American Nightmares: The Haunted House Formula in American Popular Fiction*. Bowling Green State UP, 1999.

Baldwin, James. "Many Thousands Gone" *Notes of a Native Son*, Beacon, 1955.

Ballinger, Gill, Tim Lustig, and Dale Townshend. "Missing Intertexts: Hannah Crafts's *The Bondwoman's Narrative* and African American Literary History." *Journal of American Studies*, vol. 39, no. 2, 2005, pp. 207–37.

Banner, Stuart. "21st Century Fox: *Pierson v. Post*, Then and Now." *Law and History Review*, vol. 27, no. 1, 2009, pp. 185–88.

Baptist, Edward E. *The Half Has Never Been Told: Slavery and the Making of American Capitalism*. Basic Books, 2014.

Bast, Florian. "'No.': The Narrative Theorizing of Embodied Agency in Octavia Butler's *Kindred*." *Extrapolation*, vol. 53, no. 2, 2012, pp. 151–81.

Batty, Nancy Ellen. "Riff, Refrain, Reframe: Toni Morrison's Song of Absalom." *Unflinching Gaze: Morrison and Faulkner Re-Envisioned*, edited by Carol A. Kolmerton, Stephen M. Ross, and Judith Bryant Wittenberg, UP of Mississippi, 1997, pp. 77–90.

Baucom, Ian. *Specters of the Atlantic: Finance Capital, Slavery, and the Philosophy of History*. Duke UP, 2005.

Bauer, Margaret Donovan. *William Faulkner's Legacy: "What shadow, what stain, what mark."* UP of Florida, 2005.

Baym, Nina. "The Case for Hannah Vincent." *In Search of Hannah Crafts: Critical Essays on "The Bondwoman's Narrative,"* edited by Henry Louis Gates, Jr. and Hollis Robbins, Basic Books, 2004, pp. 315–31.

Beckert, Sven. *Empire of Cotton: A Global History*. Alfred A. Knopf, 2015.

Beckert, Sven. "Slavery and Capitalism." *The Chronicle of Higher Education*, 12 Dec. 2014.

Beckert, Sven, and Seth Rockman. Introduction. *Slavery's Capitalism: A New History of American Economic Development*, edited by Sven Beckert and Seth Rockman, U of Pennsylvania P, 2016, pp. 1–27.

Benson, Melanie R. "The Fetish of Surplus Value, or, What the Ledgers Say." *Global Faulkner: Faulkner and Yoknapatawpha, 2006*, edited by Annette Trefzer and Ann J. Abadie, UP of Mississippi, 2009, pp. 43–58.

Berger, James. "Ghosts of Liberalism: Morrison's *Beloved* and the Moynihan Report." *PMLA*, vol. 111, no. 3, 1996, pp. 408–20.

Berger, John. "Understanding a Photograph." *Classic Essays on Photography*, edited by Alan Trachtenberg, Leete's Island Books, 1980, pp. 291–94.

Bernstein, Stephen. "Form and Ideology in the Gothic Novel." *Essays in Literature*, vol. 18, no. 2, 1991, pp. 151–65.

Berry, Daina Ramey. *The Price for Their Pound of Flesh: The Value of the Enslaved, from Womb to Grave, in the Building of a Nation*. Beacon, 2017.

Best, Stephen. *The Fugitive's Properties: Law and the Poetics of Possession*. U of Chicago P, 2004.

Birdsong, Destiny O. "'Memories that are(n't) mine': Matrilineal Trauma and Defiant Reinscription in Natasha Trethewey's *Native Guard*." *African American Review*, vol. 48, no. 1–2, 2015, pp. 97–110.

Blackford, Holly. "Haunted Housekeeping: Fatal Attractions of Servant and Mistress in Twentieth-Century Female Gothic Literature." *Lit: Literature Interpretation Theory*, vol. 16, no. 2, 2005, pp. 233–61.

Blackstone, William. from *Commentaries on the Laws of England*. 1765. *Perspectives on Property Law*, edited by Robert C. Ellickson, Carol M. Rose, and Bruce A. Ackerman, Little, Brown, 1995, pp. 37–44.

Blight, David W. *Beyond the Battlefield: Race, Memory, and the American Civil War.* U of Massachusetts P, 2002.

Botting, Fred. *Gothic.* Routledge, 1996.

Botting, Fred. "In Gothic Darkly: Heterotopia, History, Culture." *A Companion to the Gothic,* edited by David Punter, Blackwell, 2000, pp. 13–24.

Bradbury, Malcolm. Introduction. *Pudd'nhead Wilson and Those Extraordinary Twins.* By Mark Twain. Penguin, 1969, pp. 7–44.

Brax, Klaus. "The Age of Scientific Racism: Internal Focalization and Narrative Ethics in Toni Morrison's *Beloved.*" *Narrative Ethics,* edited by Jakob Lothe, Rodopi, 2013, pp. 253–67.

Brigham, John. *Property and the Politics of Entitlement.* Temple UP, 1990.

Brogan, Kathleen. *Cultural Haunting: Ghosts and Ethnicity in Recent American Literature.* UP of Virginia, 1998.

Brooks, Cleanth. *William Faulkner: The Yoknapatawpha Country.* Yale UP, 1963.

Brown, Charles Brockden. *Wieland and Memoirs or Carwin the Biloquist.* 1798. Penguin, 1991.

Buell, Lawrence. "Bondwoman Unbound: Hannah Crafts' Art and Nineteenth-Century Literary Practice." *In Search of Hannah Crafts: Critical Essays on "The Bondwoman's Narrative,"* edited by Henry Louis Gates Jr. and Hollis Robbins, Basic Books, 2004, pp. 16–29.

Buell, Lawrence. *The Dream of the Great American Novel.* Harvard UP, 2014.

Busch, Frederick. *A Dangerous Profession: A Book about the Writing Life.* St. Martin's, 1998.

Butler, Octavia. "Black Scholar Interview with Octavia Butler: Black Women and the Science Fiction Genre." *The Black Scholar,* vol. 17, no. 2, 1986, pp. 14–18.

Butler, Octavia. "An Interview with Octavia Butler." By Charles H. Rowell, *Callaloo,* vol. 20, no. 1, 1997, pp. 47–66.

Butler, Octavia. *Kindred.* Beacon, 1979.

Byerman, Keith. *Remembering the Past in Contemporary African American Fiction.* The U of North Carolina P, 2005.

Byerman, Keith. "Untold Stories: Black Daughters in *Absalom, Absalom!* and *The Bluest Eye.*" *Unflinching Gaze: Morrison and Faulkner Re-Envisioned,* edited by Carol A. Kolmerten, Stephen M. Ross, and Judith Bryant Wittenberg, UP of Mississippi, 1997, pp. 128–38.

Cartwright, Keith. *Reading Africa into American Literature: Epics, Fables, and Gothic Tales.* UP of Kentucky, 2002.

Castronovo, Russ. "The Art of Ghost-Writing: Memory, Materiality, and Slave Aesthetics." In *Search of Hannah Crafts: Critical Essays on "The Bondwoman's Narrative,"* edited by Henry Louis Gates Jr. and Hollis Robbins, Basic Books, 2004, pp. 195–212.

Chandler, Marilyn R. *Dwelling in the Text: Houses in American Fiction.* U of California P, 1991.

Chaplin, Sue. "Female Gothic and the Law." *Women and the Gothic: An Edinburgh Companion,* edited by Avril Horner and Sue Zlosnik, Edinburgh UP, 2016, pp. 135–49.

Christian, Barbara. "Beloved, She's Ours." *Narrative,* vol. 5, no. 1, 1997, pp. 36–49.

Clemens, Valdine. *The Return of the Repressed: Gothic Horror from "The Castle of Otranto" to "Alien."* State U of New York P, 1999.

Coates, Ta-Nehisi. *Between the World and Me*. Spiegel & Grau, 2015.
Cobb, Thomas R.R. *An Inquiry into the Law of Slavery in the United States*. 1858. Negro Universities Press, 1968.
Cohn, Dorrit. "Discordant Narration." *Style*, vol. 34, no. 2, 2000, pp. 307–16.
Columbus, Christopher. "Letter of Discovery." 1493. *Norton Anthology of American Literature*, Volume A, Ninth Edition, edited by Robert S. Levine, W.W. Norton, 2017, pp. 59–64.
Coonradt, Nicole M. "To Be Loved: Amy Denver and Human Need—Bridges to Understanding in Toni Morrison's *Beloved*." *College Literature*, vol. 32, no. 4, 2005, pp. 168–87.
Coss, David L. "Sutpen's Sentient House." *Journal of the Fantastic in the Arts*, vol. 15, no. 2, 2005, pp. 101–18.
Costello, Brannon. "Playing Lady and Imitating Aristocrats: Race, Class, and Money in *Delta Wedding* and *The Ponder Heart*." *Southern Quarterly*, vol. 42, no. 3, 2004, pp. 21–54.
Coviello, Peter. "The American in Charity: 'Benito Cereno' and Gothic Anti-Sentimentality." *Studies in American Fiction*, vol. 30, no. 2, 2002, pp. 155–80.
Cox, James B. *Mark Twain: The Fate of Humor*. Princeton UP, 1966.
Craft, William, and Ellen. "Running a Thousand Miles for Freedom; or the Escape of William and Ellen Craft from Slavery." 1860. *Slave Narratives*, edited by William L. Andrews and Henry Louis Gates Jr., Library of America, 2000, pp. 677–742.
Crafts, Hannah. *The Bondwoman's Narrative*. 1858. Edited by Henry Louis Gates Jr., Grand Central, 2014.
Crane, Gregg. "Black Comedy: Black Citizenship and Jim Crow Positivism." *REAL*, vol. 18, 2002, pp. 289–310.
Crow, Charles. *American Gothic*. U of Wales P, 2009.
Cucarella-Ramon, Vicent. "The Black Female Slave Take Literary Revenge: Female Gothic Motifs against Slavery in Hannah Crafts's *The Bondwoman's Narrative*." *Journal of English Studies*, vol. 13, 2015, pp. 19–46.
Cutter, Martha J. "Skinship: Dialectical Passing Plots in Hannah Crafts' *The Bondwoman's Narrative*." *American Literary Realism*, vol. 46, no. 2, 2014, pp. 116–36.
Davis, David Brion. *The Problem of Slavery in the Age of Emancipation*. Alfred A. Knopf, 2014.
Davis, Mary Kemp. "Everybody Knows Her Name: The Recovery of the Past in Sherley Anne Williams's *Dessa Rose*." *Callaloo*, vol. 40, 1989, pp. 544–58.
Davis, Thadious. "Enfoldments: Natasha Trethewey's Racial-Spatial Phototexting." *Southern Quarterly*, vol. 50, no. 4, 2013, pp. 37–54.
Davis, Thadious. *Faulkner's "Negro": Art and the Southern Context*. Louisiana UP, 1983.
Davis, Thadious. *Games of Property: Law, Race, and Gender, and Faulkner's "Go Down, Moses*." Duke UP, 2003.
Davis, Thadious. *Southscapes: Geographies of Race, Region, & Literature*. U of North Carolina P, 2011.
Davison, Carol Margaret. "Southern Gothic: Haunted Houses." *The Palgrave Handbook of the Southern Gothic*, edited by Susan Castillo Street and Charles L. Crow, Palgrave Macmillan, 2016, pp. 55–67.

Dawson, Emma Waters. "Psychic Rage and Response: The Enslaved and the Enslaver in Sherley Anne Williams's *Dessa Rose*." *Arms Akimbo: Africana Women in Contemporary Literature*, edited by Janie Lee Liddell and Yakini Belinda Kemp. UP of Florida, 1999, pp. 17–31.

Day, William Patrick. *In the Circles of Fear and Desire: A Study of Gothic Fantasy*. U of Chicago P, 1985.

De Cenzo, Giorgia. "Natasha Trethewey: The Native Guard of Southern History." *South Atlantic Review*, vol. 73, no. 1, 2008, pp. 20–49.

Decker, Sharon. "'Anything dead coming back to life hurts': The Double Murder of *Beloved*." *Critical Insights: Southern Gothic Literature*, edited by Jay Ellis, Salem, 2013, pp. 243–62.

DeLamotte, Eugenia. *Perils of the Night: A Feminist Study of Nineteenth-Century Gothic*. Oxford UP, 1990.

DeLombard, Jeannine Marie. "Salvaging Legal Personhood: Melville's 'Benito Cereno.'" *American Literature*, vol. 81, no. 1, 2009, pp. 35–64.

Derrida, Jacques. *Specters of Marx: The State of Debt, the Work of Mourning, and the New International*. Translated by Peggy Kamuf, Routledge, 1994.

Dickinson, Emily. *The Poems of Emily Dickinson*. Edited by R.W. Franklin, Belknap Press of Harvard University Press, 1999.

Diouf, Sylviane A. *Dreams of Africa in Alabama: The Slave Ship "Clotilda" and the Story of the Last Africans Brought to America*. Oxford UP, 2007.

Donaldson, Susan V. "Making a Spectacle: Welty, Faulkner, and Southern Gothic." *Mississippi Quarterly*, vol. 50, no. 4, 1997, pp. 567–84.

Donaldson, Susan V. "Making Darkness Visible: An Afterword and an Appreciation." *Undead Souths: The Gothic and Beyond in Southern Literature and Culture*, edited by Eric Gary Anderson, Taylor Hagood, and Daniel Cross Turner. Louisiana State UP, 2015, pp. 261–65.

Donaldson, Susan V. "Subverting History: Women and Narrative in *Absalom, Absalom!*" *Southern Quarterly*, vol. 26, no. 4, 1988, pp. 19–32.

Donovan-Condron, Kellie. "Twisted Sisters: The Monstrous Women of Southern Gothic." *The Palgrave Handbook of the Southern Gothic*, edited by Susan Castillo Street and Charles L. Crow. Palgrave Macmillan, 2016, pp. 339–50.

Doriani, Beth Maclay. "Black Womanhood in Nineteenth-Century America: Subversion and Self-Construction in Two Women's Autobiographies." *American Quarterly*, vol. 43, no. 2, 1991, pp. 199–222.

Douglass, Frederick. *Narrative of the Life of Frederick Douglass, an American Slave*. 1845. Penguin, 2014.

Dubey, Madhu. "Octavia Butler's Novels of Enslavement." *Novel: A Forum on Fiction*, vol. 46, no. 3, 2013, pp. 345–63.

Duck, Leigh Anne. "Haunting Yoknapatawpha: Faulkner and Traumatic Memory." *Faulkner in the Twenty-First Century: Faulkner and Yoknapatawpha*, edited by Robert W. Hamblin, UP of Mississippi, 2003, pp. 89–106.

Duck, Leigh Anne. *The Nation's Region: Southern Modernism, Segregation, and U.S. Nationalism*. U of Georgia P, 2006.

Dunbar, Erica Armstrong. *Never Caught: The Washingtons' Relentless Pursuit of Their Runaway Slave, Ona Judge*. Atria Books, 2017.
Duvall, John N. "Authentic Ghost Stories: *Uncle Tom's Cabin, Absalom, Absalom!*, and *Beloved*," *The Faulkner Journal*, vol. 4., no. 1, 1988, pp. 83–97.
Edwards, Justin. *Gothic Passages: Racial Ambiguity and the American Gothic*. U of Iowa P, 2003.
Ellis, Jay. "On Southern Gothic Literature." *Critical Insights: Southern Gothic Literature*, edited by Jay Ellis, Salem, 2013, pp. xvi-xxxiv.
Ellison, Ralph. "Change the Joke and Slip the Yoke." *Mother Wit from the Laughing Barrel: Readings in the Interpretation of Afro-American Folklore*, Prentice-Hall, 1973, pp. 56–65.
Ellison, Ralph. *Invisible Man*. Vintage, 1947.
Entzminger, Betina. "Playing in the Dark with Welty: The Symbolic Role of African Americans in *Delta Wedding*," *College Literature*, vol. 30, no. 3, 2002, pp. 52–67.
Ermarth, Elizabeth Deeds. *Sequel to History: Postmodernism and the Crisis of Representation Time*. Princeton UP, 1992.
Esteve, Mary. "Shadow Economies: The Distribution of Wealth in and around *Pudd'nhead Wilson*." *ELH*, vol. 78, no. 2, 2011, pp. 359–85.
Fabian, Ann. "Hannah Crafts, Novelist: or, How a Silent Observer Became a 'Dabster at Invention.'" *In Search of Hannah Crafts: Critical Essays on "The Bondwoman's Narrative,"* edited by Henry Louis Gates Jr. and Hollis Robbins, Basic Books, 2004, pp. 43–52.
Fabian, Ann. *The Unvarnished Truth*. U of California P, 2000.
Faflak, Joel, and Jason Haslam. Introduction. *American Gothic Culture: An Edinburgh Companion*, Edinburgh UP, 2016, pp. 1–22.
Faulkner, William. *Absalom, Absalom!* 1936. Vintage International, 1986.
Faulkner, William. "Evangeline." *Uncollected Stories of William Faulkner*, edited by Joseph Blotner, Random House, 1979, pp. 583–609.
Fede, Andrew. "Legitimized Violent Slave Abuse in the American South, 1619–1865: A Case Study of Law and Social Change in Six Southern States." *Law, the Constitution, and Slavery*, edited by Paul Finkelman, Garland, 1989, pp. 31–88.
Fernandez, Angela. "Fuzzy Rules and Clear Enough Standards: The Uses and Abuses of *Pierson v Post*." *University of Toronto Law Journal*, vol. 63, 2013, pp. 97–125.
Fielder, Leslie A. *Love and Death in the American Novel*. Criterion, 1960.
Fisher, Philip. *Hard Facts: Setting and Form in the American Novel*. Oxford UP, 1985.
Fishkin, Shelley Fisher. "Race and Culture at the Century's End: A Social Context for *Pudd'nhead Wilson*." *Essays in Arts and Sciences*, vol. 19, 1990, pp. 1–27.
Flagel, Nadine. "'It's Almost Like Being There': Speculative Fiction, Slave Narrative, and the Crisis of Representation in Octavia Butler's *Kindred*." *Canadian Review of American Studies*, vol. 42, no. 2, 2012, pp. 216–45.
Fletcher, Judith. "Signifying Circe in Toni Morrison's *Song of Solomon*." *The Classical World*, vol. 99, no. 4, 2006, pp. 405–18.
Foner, Eric. *Who Owns History: Rethinking the Past in a Changing World*. Hill and Wang, 2003.

Ford, Sarah. "Nothing 'So Mundane as Ghosts': Eudora Welty and the Gothic." *The Palgrave Handbook of the Southern Gothic*, edited by Susan Castillo Street and Charles L. Crow, Palgrave Macmillan, 2016, pp. 433–44.

Foster, Guy Mark. "'Do I look like someone you can come home to from where you may be going?': Re-mapping Interracial Anxiety in Octavia Butler's *Kindred*." *African American Review*, vol. 41, no. 1, 2007, pp. 143–64.

Franco, Dean J. "What We Talk about When We Talk about *Beloved*." *Modern Fiction Studies*, vol. 52, no. 2, 2006, pp. 415–39.

Franklin, Benjamin. *The Autobiography and Other Writings*. 1789. Penguin, 1986.

Freud, Sigmund. "The 'Uncanny.'" *The Standard Edition of the Complete Psychological Works of Sigmund Freud*, translated by James Strachey, vol. 17, Hogarth, 1925, pp. 219–52.

Frost, Robert. *Selected Poems of Robert Frost*. Holt, Rinehart, and Winston, 1963.

Frye, Elizabeth Bradford, and Coleman Hutchison. "What Remains Where: Civil War Poetry and Photography across 150 Years." *Undead Souths: The Gothic and Beyond in Southern Literature and Culture*, edited by Eric Gary Anderson, Taylor Hagood, and Daniel Cross Turner, Louisiana UP, 2015, pp. 36–51.

Fulton, Lorie Watkins. "William Faulkner Reprised: Isolation in Toni Morrison's *Song of Solomon*." *Mississippi Quarterly*, vol. 58, no. 1–2, 2004, pp. 7–24.

Garrett, Peter K. *Gothic Reflections: Narrative Force in Nineteenth-Century Fiction*. Cornell UP, 2003.

Gates, Jr., Henry Louis, and Gregg Hecimovich. "Preface." *The Bondwoman's Narrative*. Edited by Henry Louis Gates, Jr., Grand Central, 2002, pp. xi–xl.

Genovese, Eugene D. *Roll, Jordan, Roll: The World the Slaves Made*. Pantheon Books, 1974.

Gillman, Susan. *Dark Twins: Imposture and Identity in Mark Twain's America*. U of Chicago P, 1989.

Glasgow, Ellen. "Heroes and Monsters," *Saturday Review of Literature*, vol. 4. May 1935, pp. 3–4, reprinted in *Defining Southern Literature: Perspectives and Assessments, 1831–1952*, edited by John E. Bassett. Cranbury, Associated University Presses, 1997, pp. 357–60.

Gleason, William. "'I Dwell Now in a Neat Little Cottage': Architecture, Race, and Desire in *The Bondwoman's Narrative*." *In Search of Hannah Crafts: Critical Essays on "The Bondwoman's Narrative*," edited by Henry Louis Gates Jr. and Hollis Robbins, Basic Books, 2004, pp. 145–74

Goad, Jill. "Throwaway Bodies in the Poetry of Natasha Trethewey." *South*, vol. 48, no. 2, 2016, pp. 265–82.

Godden, Richard. "*Absalom, Absalom!*, Haiti, and Labor History: Reading Unreadable Revolutions." *William Faulkner's "Absalom, Absalom!": A Casebook*, edited by Fred Hobson, Oxford UP, 2003, pp. 251–81.

Goddu, Teresa. "American Gothic." *The Routledge Companion to Gothic*, edited by Catherine Spooner and Emma McEvoy, Routledge, 2007, pp. 63–72.

Goddu, Teresa. *Gothic America: Narrative, History, and Nation*. Columbia UP, 1997.

Goldman, Anne E. "'I Made the Ink': (Literary) Production and Reproduction in *Dessa Rose* and *Beloved*," *Feminist Studies*, vol. 16, no. 2, 1990, pp. 313–30.

Goldner, Ellen J. "Gothicism and the Bonds of Reason in Melville, Chesnutt, and Morrison." *MELUS*, vol. 24, no. 1, 1999, pp. 59–83.

Gomaa, Sally. "Writing to 'Virtuous' and 'Gentle' Readers: The Problem of Pain in Harriet Jacobs's *Incidents* and Harriet Wilson's *Sketches*" *African American Review*, vol. 43, no. 2–3, 2009, pp. 371–81.

Goodell, William. *The American Slave Code*. 1853. Arno, 1969.

Gordon, Avery. *Ghostly Matters: Haunting and the Sociological Imagination*. U of Minnesota P, 1997.

Gould, Philip. "Slavery in the Eighteenth-Century Literary Imagination." *The Cambridge Companion to Slavery in American Literature*, edited by Ezra Tawil, Cambridge UP, 2016, pp. 16–31.

Greeson, Jennifer Rae. *Our South: Geographic Fantasy and the Rise of National Literature*. Harvard UP, 2010.

Griffin, Dorothy. "The House as Container: Architecture and Myth in Eudora Welty's *Delta Wedding*." *Mississippi Quarterly*, vol. 39, no. 4, 1986, pp. 521–35.

Gross, Louis S. *Redefining the American Gothic: From "Wieland" to "Day of the Dead."* UMI Research Press, 1989.

Gutman, Herbert G. *The Black Family in Slavery and Freedom, 1750–1925*. Pantheon Books, 1976.

Gygax, Franziska. *Serious Daring from Within: Female Narrative Strategies in Eudora Welty's Novels*. Greenwood, 1990.

Hack, Daniel. "Close Reading at a Distance: The African Americanization of *Bleak House*." *Critical Inquiry*, vol. 34, no. 4, 2008, pp. 729–53.

Hadden, Sally. "Judging Slavery: Thomas Ruffin and *State v. Mann*." *Local Matters: Race, Crime, and Justice in the Nineteenth-Century South*, edited by Christopher Waldrep and Donald G. Nieman, U of Georgia P, 2001, pp. 1–28.

Handley, William R. "The House a Ghost Built: 'Nommo,' Allegory, and the Ethics of Reading in Toni Morrison's *Beloved*." *Contemporary Literature*, vol. 36, no. 4, 1995, pp. 676–701.

Harker, Jaime. "'And You Too, Sister, Sister?': Lesbian Sexuality, *Absalom, Absalom!*, and the Reconstruction of the Southern Family." *Faulkner's Sexualities*, edited by Annette Trefzer and Ann J. Abadie, UP of Mississippi, 2010, pp. 38–53.

Harrington, Paula. "Dawson's Landing: On the Disappearance of Domesticity in a Slaveholding Town." *The Mark Twain Annual*, vol. 3, 2005, pp. 91–97.

Harris, Cheryl I. "Whiteness as Property." *Harvard Law Review*, vol. 106, no. 8, 1993, pp. 1707–91.

Harris, Trudier. "Escaping Slavery but Not Its Images" *Toni Morrison: Critical Perspectives Past and Present*, edited by Henry Louis Gates, Jr., and K. A. Appiah, Amistad, 1993, pp. 330–41.

Harris, Trudier. *Fiction and Folklore: The Novels of Toni Morrison*. U of Tennessee P, 1991.

Harris, Trudier. *The Scary Mason-Dixon Line: African American Writers and the South*. Louisiana State UP, 2009.

Harrison, Suzan. "Mastering Narrative/Subverting Masters: Rhetorics of Race in *The Confessions of Nat Turner*, *Dessa Rose*, and *Celia, A Slave*." *Southern Quarterly*, vol. 35, no. 3, 1997, pp. 13–28.

Haslam, Jason. "Slavery and American Gothic: The Ghost of the Future." *American Gothic Culture: An Edinburgh Companion*, edited by Joel Faflak and Jason Haslam, Edinburgh UP, 2016, pp. 44–59.

Haslam, Jason. "'The strange ideas of right and justice': Prison, Slavery and Other Horrors in *The Bondwoman's Narrative.*" *Gothic Studies*, vol. 7, no. 1, pp. 29–40.

Hawthorne, Nathaniel. *The House of Seven Gables*. 1851. Edited by Milton R. Stern, Penguin, 1965.

Henderson, Mae G. "Speaking in Tongues: Dialogics, Dialectics, and the Black Woman Writer's Literary Tradition." *Reading Black, Reading Feminist*, edited by Henry Louis Gates, Jr., Meridian, 1990, pp. 116–44.

Henderson, Mae G. "Toni Morrison's *Beloved*: Re-Membering the Body as Historical Text." *Comparative American Identities: Race, Sex, and Nationality in the Modern Text*, edited by Hortense J. Spillers, Routledge, 1991, pp. 62–86.

Henninger, Katherine R. "What Remains: Race, Nation, and the Adult Child in the Poetry of Natasha Trethewey." *Southern Quarterly*, vol. 50, no. 4, 2013, pp. 55–74.

Higginbotham, A. Leon and Barbara K. Kopytoff. "Property First, Humanity Second: The Recognition of the Slave's Human Nature in Virginia's Civil Law." *Ohio State Law Journal*, vol. 50, no. 3, 1989, pp. 511–40.

Hinrichsen, Lisa. "Writing Past Trauma: Faulkner and the Gothic." *William Faulkner in Context*, edited by John T. Matthews, Cambridge UP, 2015, pp. 219–27.

Hogan, Michael. "Built on the Ashes: The Fall of the House of Sutpen and the Rise of the House of Sethe." *Unflinching Gaze: Morrison and Faulkner Re-Envisioned*, edited by Carol A. Kolmerten, Stephen M. Ross, and Judith Bryant Wittenberg, UP of Mississippi, 1997, pp. 167–80.

Hogle, Jerrold E. "Introduction: Gothic Studies Past, Present, and Future." *Gothic Studies*, vol. 1, no. 1, 1999, pp. 1–9.

Hooper, Johnson Jones. *Adventures of Captain Simon Suggs*. 1845. U of North Carolina P, 1969.

Horvitz, Deborah. "Nameless Ghosts: Possession and Dispossession in *Beloved*." *Studies in American Fiction*, vol. 17, no. 2, 1989, pp. 157–67.

House, Elizabeth B. "Toni Morrison's Ghost: The Beloved is Not Beloved." *Studies in American Fiction*, vol. 18, no. 1, 1990, pp. 17–26.

Humphreys, Debra. "Power and Resistance in Harriet Jacobs' *Incidents in the Life of a Slave Girl*." *Anxious Power: Reading, Writing, and Ambivalence in Narrative by Women*, edited by Carol J. Singley and Susan Elizabeth Sweeney, State U of New York P, 1993, pp. 143–55.

Hurley, Jessica. "Ghostwritten: Kinship and History in *Absalom, Absalom!*" *The Faulkner Journal*, vol. 26, no. 2, 2012, pp. 61–79.

Hurston, Zora Neale. *Their Eyes Were Watching God*. Harper Perennial, 1937.

Huston, James L. *Calculating the Value of the Union: Slavery, Property Rights, and the Economic Origins of the Civil War*. U of North Carolina P, 2003.

Hutcheon, Linda. *A Poetics of Postmodernism: History, Theory, Fiction*. Routledge, 1988.

Jacobs, Harriet. *Incidents in the Life of a Slave Girl*. 1861. Edited by Nellie Y. McKay and Frances Smith Foster, W. W. Norton, 2001.

Jacobs, Harriet. "Letter from a Fugitive Slave." 1853. *Incidents in the Life of a Slave Girl*. By Harriet Jacobs. Edited by Nellie Y. McKay and Frances Smith Foster, W. W. Norton, 2001.

Jehlen, Myra. "The Ties that Bind: Race and Sex in *Pudd'nhead Wilson*." *American Literary History*, vol. 2, no. 1, 1990, pp. 39–55.

Johnson, Paul David. "American Innocence and Guilt: Black-White Destiny in 'Benito Cereno.'" *Phyon*, vol. 36, no. 4, 1975, pp. 426–34.
Johnson, Walter. *River of Dark Dreams: Slavery and Empire in the Cotton Kingdom*. Harvard UP, 2013.
Jones, Meta Duewa. "Reframing Exposure: Natasha Trethewey's Forms of Enclosure." *ELH*, vol. 82, 2015, pp. 407–29.
Jones-Rogers, Stephanie E. *They Were Her Property: White Women as Slave Owners in the American South*. Yale UP, 2019.
Kafer, Peter. *Charles Brockden Brown and the Birth of the American Gothic*. U of Pennsylvania P, 2004.
Kaplan, Sidney. "Herman Melville and the American National Sin: The Meaning of *Benito Cereno*." *The Journal of Negro History*, vol. 42, no. 1, 1957, pp. 11–37.
Kavanagh, James H. "'That Hive of Subtlety:' 'Benito Cereno' and the Liberal Hero." *Ideology and Classic American Literature*, edited by Sacvan Bercovitch and Myra Jehlen, Cambridge UP, 1986, pp. 352–83.
Kawash, Samira. "Fugitive Properties." *The New Economic Criticism: Studies at the Intersection of Literature and Economics*, edited by Martha Woodmansee and Mark Osteen, Routledge, 1999, pp. 277–89.
Kawash, Samira. "Haunted Houses, Sinking Ships: Race, Architecture, and Identity in *Beloved* and *Middle Passage*." *CR: The New Centennial Review*, vol. 1, no. 3, 2001, pp. 67–86.
Kekeh, Andrée-Anne. "Sherley Anne Williams' *Dessa Rose*: History and the Disruptive Power of Memory." *History and Memory in African-American Culture*, edited by Genevieve Fabre and Robert O'Meally, Oxford UP, 1994, pp. 219–27.
Kelley, William Melvin. *A Different Drummer*. Anchor Books, 1959.
Kelley, Wyn. "Introduction." *Benito Cereno*. By Herman Melville. Edited by Wyn Kelley, Bedford St. Martin, 2008, pp. 5–32.
Kerr, Elizabeth M. *William Faulkner's Gothic Domain*. Kennikat Press, 1979.
Keyser, Catherine. "Jane Eyre, Bondwoman: Hannah Crafts's Rethinking of Charlotte Bronte." *In Search of Hannah Crafts: Critical Essays on "The Bondwoman's Narrative,"* edited by Henry Louis Gates Jr. and Hollis Robbins, Basic Books, 2004, pp. 87–105.
Keyssar, Alexander. *The Right to Vote: The Contested History of Democracy in the United States*. Basic Books, 2000.
Kilgour, Maggie. *The Rise of the Gothic Novel*. Routledge, 1995.
Kim, Hyejin. "Gothic Storytelling and Resistance in Charles W. Chesnutt's *The Conjure Woman*." *Orbis Litterarum*, vol. 69, no. 5, 2014, pp. 411–38.
King, Lovalerie. *Race, Theft, and Ethics: Property Matters in African American Literature*. Louisiana State UP, 2007.
Kreiger, Georgia. "Playing Dead: Harriet Jacobs's Survival Strategy in *Incidents in the Life of a Slave Girl*." *African American Review*, vol. 42, no. 3–4, 2008, pp. 607–21.
Kreiswirth, Martin. "Faulkner's Dark House: The Uncanny Inheritance of Race." *Faulkner's Inheritance*, edited by Joseph R. Urgo and Ann J. Abadie, UP of Mississippi, 2007, pp. 126–40.

Kreyling, Michael. "Uncanny Plantations: The Repeating Gothic." *The Palgrave Handbook of the Southern Gothic*, edited by Susan Castillo Street and Charles L. Crow, Palgrave Macmillan, 2016, pp. 231–43.

Kubitschek, Missy Dehn. *Claiming the Heritage: African-American Women Novelists and History*. UP of Mississippi, 1991.

LaCroix, David. "To Touch Solid Evidence: The Implicity of Past and Present in Octavia E. Butler's *Kindred*." *The Journal of the Midwest Modern Language Association*, vol. 40, no. 1, 2007, pp. 109–19.

Ladd, Barbara. "'Coming Through': The Black Initiate in *Delta Wedding*." *Mississippi Quarterly*, vol. 41, no. 4, 1988, pp. 541–51.

Ladd, Barbara. *Nationalism and the Color Line in George W. Cable, Mark Twain, and William Faulkner*. Louisiana State UP, 1996.

Landrieu, Mitch. *In the Shadow of Statues: A White Southerner Confronts History*. Viking, 2018.

Ledoux, Ellen Malenas. "Defiant Damsels: Gothic Space and Female Agency in *Emmeline*, *The Mysteries of Udolpho*, and *Secresy*." *Women's Writing*, vol. 18, no. 3, 2011, pp. 331–47.

LeMaheiu, Michael. "Robert Lowell, Perpetual War, and the Legacy of Civil War Elegy." *College Literature*, vol. 43, no. 1, 2016, pp. 91–120.

Lenz, William E. *Fast Talk and Flush Times: The Confidence Man as a Literary Convention*. U of Missouri P, 1985.

Lepore, Jill. *The Book of Ages: The Life and Opinions of Jane Franklin*. Alfred A. Knopf, 2013.

Levecq, Christine. "Power and Repetition: Philosophies of (Literary) History in Octavia E. Butler's *Kindred*." *Contemporary Literature*, vol. 41, no. 3, 2000, pp. 525–53.

Levine, Robert S. "Reading Slavery and 'Classic' American Literature." *The Cambridge Companion to Slavery in American Literature*, edited by Ezra Tawil, Cambridge UP, 2016, pp. 137–52.

Levine, Robert S. "Trappe(d): Race and Genealogical Haunting in *The Bondwoman's Narrative*." *In Search of Hannah Crafts: Critical Essays on "The Bondwoman's Narrative,"* edited by Henry Louis Gates, Jr. and Hollis Robbins, Basic Books, 2004, pp. 276–94.

Levins, Lynn Gartrell. "The Four Narrative Perspectives in *Absalom, Absalom!*" *PMLA*, vol. 85, no. 1, 1970, pp. 35–47.

Li, Stephanie. *Something Akin to Freedom: The Choice of Bondage in Narratives by African American Women*. SUNY P, 2010.

Lindberg, Gary. *The Confidence Man in American Literature*. Oxford UP, 1982.

Lloyd-Smith, Allan. *American Gothic Fiction: An Introduction*. Continuum, 2004.

Locke, John. *The Second Treatise of Government*. 1689. *Political Writings*, edited by David Wootton, Hackett, 2003, pp. 261–386.

Luck, Chad. *The Body of Property: Antebellum American Fiction and the Phenomenology of Possession*. Fordham UP, 2014.

Macpherson, C. B., ed. *Property: Mainstream and Critical Positions*. U of Toronto P, 1978.

Mantel, Hilary. "The Shape of Absence." *London Review of Books*, vol. 24, no. 15. 8 Aug. 2002, pp. 3–6.

Marrs, Suzanne. "'The Treasure Most Dearly Regarded': Memory and Imagination in *Delta Wedding*." *Southern Literary Journal*, vol. 25, no. 2, 1993, pp. 79–91.

Marshall, Bridget M. *The Transatlantic Gothic Novel and the Law, 1790–1860*. Ashgate, 2011.
Martin, Robert K. "Haunted by Jim Crow: Gothic Fictions by Hawthorne and Faulkner." *American Gothic: New Interventions in a National Narrative*, edited by Robert K. Martin and Eric Savoy, U of Iowa P, 1998, pp. 129–42.
Martin, Terence. *The Instructed Vision: Scottish Common Sense Philosophy and the Origins of American Fiction*. Indiana UP, 1961.
Martinez, Leonard. "Concentric Failures: Melville, Twain, and Shifting Centers." *The Mark Twain Annual*, vol. 13, 2015, pp. 115–29.
Matterson, Stephen. Introduction. *The Confidence-Man: His Masquerade*, by Herman Melville, Penguin, 1990, pp vii–xxxvi.
Matthews, John T. "Recalling the West Indies: From Yoknapatawpha to Haiti and Back." *American Literary History*, vol. 16, no. 2, 2004, pp. 238–62.
McHaney, Pearl Amelia. "Natasha Trethewey's Triptych: The Bodies of History in *Bellocq's Ophelia*, *Native Guard*, and *Thrall*." *Southern Quarterly*, vol. 50, no. 4, 2013, pp. 153–72.
McKay, Nellie Y. Introduction. *Toni Morrison's "Beloved": A Casebook*, edited by William L. Andrews and Nellie Y. McKay, Oxford UP, 1999, pp. 3–20.
McKay, Nellie Y., and Frances Smith Foster. Introduction. *Incidents in the Life of a Slave Girl*. By Harriet Jacobs, W. W. Norton, 2001, pp. ix–xxiii.
McMahand, Donnie. "Bodies on the Brink: Vision, Violence, and Self-Destruction in *Delta Wedding*." *Eudora Welty, Whiteness, and Race*, edited by Harriet Pollack, U of Georgia P, 2013, pp. 165–84.
McWhirter, David. "Secret Agents: Welty's African Americans." *Eudora Welty, Whiteness, and Race*, edited by Harriet Pollack, U of Georgia P, 2013, pp. 114–30.
Melville, Herman. *Benito Cereno*. 1855. Bedford, 2008.
Michaels, Walter Benn. "Romance and Real Estate." *The American Renaissance Reconsidered*, edited by Walter Benn Michaels and Donald E. Pease, Johns Hopkins UP, 1985, pp. 156–82.
Millgate, Michael. *The Achievement of William Faulkner*. Random House, 1963.
Mitchell, Angelyn. "Not Enough of the Past: Feminist Revisions of Slavery in Octavia E. Butler's *Kindred*." *MELUS*, vol. 26, no. 1, 2001, pp. 51–75.
Morgan, Edmund S. *American Slavery, American Freedom: The Ordeal of Colonial Virginia*. W. W. Norton, 1975.
Morgan, Jennifer L. *Laboring Women: Reproduction and Gender in New World Slavery*. U of Pennsylvania P, 2004.
Morrell, Sascha. "Melville's Zombies, North and South." *Undead Souths: The Gothic and Beyond in Southern Literature and Culture*, edited by Eric Gary Anderson, Taylor Hagood, and Daniel Cross Turner, Louisiana UP, 2015, pp. 64–75.
Morris, Linda A. "Beneath the Veil: Clothing, Race, and Gender in Mark Twain's *Puddn'head Wilson*." *Studies in American Fiction*, vol. 27, no. 1, 1999, pp. 37–52.
Morrison, Toni. *Beloved*. Vintage, 1987.
Morrison, Toni. *Conversations with Toni Morrison*. Edited by Danille Taylor-Guthrie. UP of Mississippi, 1994.
Morrison, Toni. *Playing in the Dark: Whiteness and the Literary Imagination*. Vintage Books, 1993.

Morrison, Toni. *Song of Solomon*. Penguin, 1977.
Morrison, Toni. "Unspeakable Things Unspoken: The Afro-American Presence in American Literature." *Michigan Quarterly Review*, vol. 28, no. 1, 1989, pp. 1–34.
Nunes, Ana. *African American Writers' Historical Fiction*. Palgrave Macmillan, 2011.
O'Donnell, Patrick. "Sub Rosa: Voice, Body, and History in *Absalom, Absalom!*" *College Literature*, vol. 16, no. 1, 1989, pp. 28–47.
O'Reilly, Andrea. *Toni Morrison and Motherhood: A Politics of the Heart*. State University of New York Press, 2004.
Pan, Alia C. Y. "Laboring beneath the Father: Plantation in *Absalom, Absalom!*" *Mississippi Quarterly*, vol. 61, no. 3, 2008, pp. 417–33.
Parfait, Claire. *The Publishing History of "Uncle Tom's Cabin," 1852–2002*. Ashgate, 2007.
Parker, Hershel. *Flawed Texts and Verbal Icons: Literary Authority in American Fiction*. Northwestern UP, 1984.
Parry, Marc. "Shackles and Dollars: History and Economics Clash over Slavery." *The Chronicle of Higher Education*. 8 Dec. 2016.
Patterson, Orlando. *Slavery and Social Death: A Comparative Study*. Harvard UP, 1982.
Pedersen, Vidar. "Of Slaves and Masters: Constructed Identities in Mark Twain's *Pudd'nhead Wilson*." *Excursions in Fiction: Essays in Honour of Professor Lars Hartveit on his 70th Birthday*, edited by Andrew Kennedy and Orm Overland, Novus, 1994, pp. 174–90.
Peeren, Esther. "The Ghost as a Gendered Chronotope." *Ghosts, Stories, Histories: Ghost Stories and Alternative Histories*, edited by Sladja Blazan, Cambridge Scholars, 2007, pp. 81–96.
Pereira, Malin. "Re-reading Trethewey through Mixed Race Studies." *Southern Quarterly*, vol. 50, no. 4, 2013, pp. 123–52.
Peterson, Christopher. "The Haunted House of Kinship: Miscegenation, Homosexuality, and Faulkner's *Absalom, Absalom!*" *CR: The New Centennial Review*, vol. 4, no. 1, 2004, pp. 227–65.
Phelan, James. "Sethe's Choice: *Beloved* and the Ethics of Reading." *Style*, vol. 32, no. 2, 1998, pp. 318–33.
Poe, Edgar Allan. "The Fall of the House of Usher." *The Selected Writings of Edgar Allan Poe*, edited by G. R. Thompson, W. W. Norton, 2004.
Porter, Carolyn. "Roxana's Plot." *Mark Twain's "Pudd'nhead Wilson": Race, Conflict, and Culture*, edited by Susan Gillman and Forrest G. Robinson, Duke UP, 1990, pp. 121–36.
Prenshaw, Peggy Whitman. "Woman's World, Man's Place: The Fiction of Eudora Welty." *Eudora Welty: A Form of Thanks*, edited by Louis Dollarhide and Ann J. Abadie, UP of Mississippi, 1979, pp. 46–77.
Punter, David. *Gothic Pathologies: The Text, the Body, and the Law*. St. Martins, 1998.
Purser, John. *Scotland's Music: A History of the Traditional and Classical Music of Scotland from Earliest Times to the Present Day*. Mainstream, 1992.
Radin, Margaret Jane. *Reinterpreting Property*. U of Chicago P, 1993.
Ramos, Peter. "Beyond Silence and Realism: Trauma and the Function of Ghosts in *Absalom, Absalom!* and *Beloved*." *The Faulkner Journal*, vol. 23, no. 2, 2008, pp. 47–66.

Ramsey, William M. "Terrance Hayes and Natasha Trethewey: Contemporary Black Chroniclers of the Imagined South." *The Southern Literary Journal*, vol. 44, no. 2, 2012, pp. 122–35.

Reames, Kelly Lynch. *Women and Race in Contemporary U.S. Writing*. Palgrave Macmillan, 2007.

Redding, Arthur. *Haints: American Ghosts, Millennial Passions, and Contemporary Gothic Fictions*. U of Alabama P, 2011.

Reinhardt, Mark. "Who Speaks for Margaret Garner? Slavery, Silence, and the Politics of Ventriloquism." *Critical Inquiry*, vol. 29, no. 1, 2002, pp. 81–119.

Richards, Jason. "Melville's (Inter)national Burlesque: Whiteface, Blackface, and 'Benito Cereno.'" *American Transcendental Quarterly*, vol. 21, no. 2, 2007, pp. 73–94.

Robbins, Hollis. "Blackening *Bleak House*: Hannah Crafts's *The Bondwoman's Narrative*." *In Search of Hannah Crafts: Critical Essays on "The Bondwoman's Narrative*," edited by Henry Louis Gates Jr. and Hollis Robbins, Basic Books, 2004, pp. 71–86.

Rogin, Michael. "Mutiny and Slave Revolt." *Melville's Short Novels: Authoritative Texts, Contexts, Criticism*, edited by Dan McCall, W. W. Norton, 2002, pp. 317–29.

Rohrbach, Augusta. "'A Silent Unobtrusive Way': Hannah Crafts and the Literary Marketplace." *In Search of Hannah Crafts: Critical Essays on "The Bondwoman's Narrative*," edited by Henry Louis Gates Jr. and Hollis Robbins, Basic Books, 2004, pp. 3–15.

Rose, Carol M. *Property and Persuasion: Essays on the History, Theory, and Rhetoric of Ownership*. Westview, 1994.

Rothman, David J. "'Fantastic terrors never felt before': Southern Gothic Poetry." *Critical Insights: Southern Gothic Literature*, edited by Jay Ellis, Salem, 2013, pp. 173–200.

Rothstein, Richard. *The Color of Law: A Forgotten History of How Our Government Segregated America*. Liveright, 2017.

Rowe, John Carlos. "Fatal Speculations: Murder, Money, and Manners in *Pudd'nhead Wilson*." *Mark Twain's "Pudd'nhead Wilson": Race, Conflict, and Culture*, edited by Susan Gillman and Forrest G. Robinson, Duke UP, 1990, pp. 137–54.

"Runaway Notice for Harriet Jacobs." "Africans in America" PBS.org. Web. 6 July 2016.

Rushdy, Ashraf H. A. "Families of Orphans: Relation and Disrelation in Octavia Butler's *Kindred*." *College English*, vol. 55, no. 2, 1993, pp. 135–57.

Rushdy, Ashraf H. A. *Neo-slave Narratives: Studies in the Social Logic of a Literary Form*. Oxford UP, 1999.

Rushdy, Ashraf H. A. "Signifyin(g) History: The Example of Toni Morrison's *Beloved*." *American Literature*, vol. 64, no. 3, 1992, pp. 567–97.

Russ, Elizabeth, Christine. *The Plantation in the Postslavery Imagination*. Oxford UP, 2009.

Russell, Richard Rankin. "The Black and Green Atlantic: Violence, History, and Memory in Natasha Trethewey's 'South' and Seamus Heaney's 'North.'" *The Southern Literary Journal*, vol. 46, no. 2, 2014, pp. 155–72.

Ryan, Katy. "Revolutionary Suicide in Toni Morrison's Fiction." *African American Review*, vol. 34, no. 3, 2000, pp. 389–412.

Sanchez-Eppler, Karen. "Gothic Liberties and Fugitive Novels: *The Bondwoman's Narrative* and the Fiction of Race." *In Search of Hannah Crafts: Critical Essays on "The Bondwoman's*

Narrative," edited by Henry Louis Gates Jr. and Hollis Robbins, Basic Books, 2004, pp. 254–25.

Saunders, Rebecca. "On Lamentations and the Redistribution of Possessions: Faulkner's *Absalom, Absalom!* and the New South." *Faulkner and His Critics*, edited by John N. Duvall, Johns Hopkins UP, 2010, pp. 66–96.

Savoy, Eric. "The Face of the Tenant: A Theory of American Gothic." *American Gothic: New Interventions in a National Narrative*, edited by Robert K. Martin and Eric Savoy, U of Iowa P, 1998, pp. 3–19.

Savoy, Eric. "The Rise of the American Gothic." *The Cambridge Companion to Gothic Fiction*, edited by Jerrold E. Hogle. Cambridge UP, 2002, pp. 167–88.

Sayers, Philip. "'Just One Thing More': Absalom, Absalom! and the Creditor-Debtor Relationship." *Canadian Review of American Studies/Revue Canadienne D'Etudes Americaines*, vol. 47, no. 2, 2017, pp. 219–38.

Schiff, Sarah Eden. "Recovering (from) the Double: Fiction as Historical Revision in Octavia E. Butler's *Kindred.*" *Arizona Quarterly*, vol. 65, no. 1, 2009, pp. 107–36.

Schmudde, Carol E. "The Haunting of 124." *African American Review*, vol. 26, no. 3, 1992, pp. 409–16.

Scholl, Diane G. "Jacobs's Uncle Tom, Stowe's Incidents: Hiding in the Attic 'Loophole'" *ANQ: A Quarterly Journal of Short Articles, Notes, and Reviews*, vol. 29, no. 2, 2016, pp. 87–91.

Schuessler, Jennifer. "Confronting Academia's Ties to Slavery." *The New York Times*, 5 March 2017, p. C1.

Schultz, Kathryn. "The Perilous Lure of the Underground Railroad." *The New Yorker*, 15 August 2016.

Sedgwick, Eve Kosofsky. *The Coherence of Gothic Conventions*. Methuen, 1980.

Simon, Julia. "Property in *Absalom, Absalom!*: Rousseau's Legacy in Faulkner." *The Faulkner Journal*, vol. 28, no. 2, 2014, pp. 3–24.

Smith, Allan Lloyd. "Postmodernism/Gothicism." *Modern Gothic: A Reader*, edited by Victor Sage and Allan Lloyd Smith, Manchester UP, 1996, pp. 6–19.

Smith, Tracy K. "Declaration." *Wade in the Water*. Graywolf, 2018, pp. 19.

Sontag, Susan. *On Photography*. Farrar, Straus, and Giroux, 1973.

Spangler, George M. "Pudd'nhead Wilson: A Parable of Property. *American Literature*, vol. 42, no. 1, 1970, pp. 28–37.

Spaulding, A. Timothy. *Re-Forming the Past: History, the Fantastic, and the Postmodern Slave Narrative*. Ohio State UP, 2005.

State v. Mann, 13 N.C. 263 (1829).

Steinberg, Marc. "Inverting History in Octavia Butler's Postmodern Slave Narrative." *African American Review*, vol. 38, no. 3, 2004, pp. 467–76.

Stone, Edward. "Usher, Poquelin, and Miss Emily: The Progress of Southern Gothic." *The Taboo*, edited by Harold Bloom, Infobase, 2010, pp. 165–76.

Stowe, Harriet Beecher. *Uncle Tom's Cabin*. 1852. Edited by Elizabeth Ammons, W. W. Norton, 2018.

Street, Susan Castillo, and Charles L. Crow. "Introduction: Down at the Crossroads." *The Palgrave Handbook of the Southern Gothic*, edited by Susan Castillo Street and Charles L. Crow, Palgrave Macmillan, 2016, pp. 1–6.

Sugimori, Masami. "Racial Mixture, Racial Passing, and White Subjectivity in *Absalom, Absalom!*" *The Faulkner Journal*, vol. 23, no. 2, 2008, pp. 3–21.

Sundquist, Eric J. *To Wake the Nations: Race in the Making of American Literature*. Harvard UP, 1993.

Swarns, Rachel L. "Insurance Policies on Slaves: New York Life's Complicated Past." *The New York Times*, December 18, 2016.

Tawil, Ezra F. "Captain Babo's Cabin: Stowe, Race and Misreading in 'Benito Cereno.'" *Leviathan: A Journal of Melville Studies*, vol. 8, no. 2, 2006, pp. 37–51.

Teukolsky, Rachel. "Pictures in Bleak Houses: Slavery and the Aesthetics of Transatlantic Reform." *ELH*, vol. 76, no. 2, 2009, pp. 491–522.

Thoreau, Henry David. "Resistance to Civil Government." 1849. *The Norton Anthology of American Literature*, volume B, ninth edition, edited by Robert S. Levine, W. W. Norton, 2017, pp. 953–69.

Trethewey, Natasha. *Bellocq's Ophelia*. Graywolf, 2002.

Trethewey, Natasha. *Conversations with Natasha Trethewey*. Edited by Joan Wylie Hall, UP of Mississippi, 2013.

Trethewey, Natasha. *Domestic Work*. Graywolf, 2000.

Trethewey, Natasha. *Native Guard*. Houghton Mifflin, 2006.

Trethewey, Natasha. *Thrall*. Houghton Mifflin Harcourt, 2012.

Truth, Sojourner. "Narrative of Sojourner Truth, a Northern Slave, Emancipated from Bodily Servitude by the State of New York, in 1828." *Slave Narratives*, edited by William L. Andrews and Henry Louis Gates Jr., Library of America, 2000, pp. 567–676.

Turner, Daniel Cross. "Lyric Dissections: Rendering Blood Memory in Natasha Trethewey's and Yusef Komunyakaa's Poetry of the Black Diaspora." *Southern Quarterly*, vol. 50, no. 4, 2013, pp. 99–122.

Turner, Daniel Cross. "Natasha Trethewey's Civil War." *A History of Civil War Literature*, edited by Coleman Hutchison, Cambridge UP, 2016, pp. 316–30.

Turner, Stephanie S. "'What Actually Is': The Insistence of Genre in Octavia Butler's *Kindred*." *FEMSPEC*, vol. 4, no. 2, 2004, pp. 259–80.

Twain, Mark. *Pudd'nhead Wilson*. 1894. Penguin, 2004.

Varnado, S. L. *Haunted Presence: The Numinous in Gothic Fiction*. U of Alabama P, 1987.

Vint, Sherryl. "'Only by Experience': Embodiment and the Limitations of Realism in Neo-Slave Narratives." *Science Fiction Studies*, vol. 34, no. 2, 2007, pp. 241–61.

Wagers, Kelley. "Seeing 'from the far side of the Hill': Narrative, History, and Understanding in *Kindred* and *The Chaneysville Incident*." *MELUS*, vol. 34, no. 1, 2009, pp. 23–45.

Wald, Priscilla. "Hannah Crafts." *In Search of Hannah Crafts: Critical Essays on "The Bondwoman's Narrative,"* edited by Henry Louis Gates Jr. and Hollis Robbins, Basic Books, 2004, pp. 213–30.

Wallace, Diana. "'The Haunting Idea': Female Gothic Metaphors and Feminist Theory." *The Female Gothic: New Directions*, edited by Diana Wallace and Andrew Smith, Palgrave Macmillan, 2009, pp. 26–41.

Walters, Delores M. "Re(dis)covering and Recreating the Cultural Milieu of Margaret Garner." *Gendered Resistance: Women, Slavery, and the Legacy of Margaret Garner*, edited by Mary E. Frederickson and Delores M. Walters, U of Illinois P, 2013, pp. 1–22.

Walvin, James. *The Zong: A Massacre, the Law and the End of Slavery*. Yale UP, 2011.

Wardrop, Daneen. "'What Tangled Skeins Are the Genealogies of Slavery!': Gothic Families in Harriet Jacobs' *Incidents in the Life of a Slave Girl*." *Literary Griot*, vol. 14, no. 1–2, 2002, pp. 23–43.

Warhol, Robyn R. "'Reader, Can You Imagine? No, You Cannot': The Narratee as Other in Harriet Jacobs's Text." *Narrative*, vol. 3, no. 1, 1995, pp. 57–72.

Warren, Wendy. *New England Bound: Slavery and Colonization in Early America*. Liveright, 2016.

Warwick, Alexandra. "Feeling Gothicky?" *Gothic Studies*, vol. 9, no. 1, 2007, pp. 5–15.

Weinauer, Ellen. "Law and the Gothic in the Slaveholding South." *The Palgrave Handbook of the Southern Gothic*, edited by Susan Castillo Street and Charles L. Crow, Palgrave Macmillan, 2016, pp. 271–83.

Weinbaum, Alys Eve. "The Afterlife of Slavery and the Problem of Reproductive Freedom." *Social Text*, vol. 31, no. 2, 2013, pp. 49–69.

Weinstein, Philip M. "David and Solomon: Fathering in Faulkner and Morrison." *Unflinching Gaze: Morrison and Faulkner Re-Envisioned*. edited by Carol A. Kolmerton, Stephen M. Ross, and Judith Bryant Wittenberg, UP of Mississippi, 1997, pp. 48–74.

Welty, Eudora. "Circe." *Eudora Welty: Stories, Essays, and Memoir*. Library of America, 1998, pp. 639-646.

Welty, Eudora. *Delta Wedding*. 1946. *Eudora Welty: Complete Novels*. Library of America, 1998, pp. 89–336.

Welty, Eudora. "Eudora Welty: An Interview." By Alice Walker. *Conversations with Eudora Welty*, edited by Peggy Whitman Prenshaw. UP of Mississippi, 1984, pp. 131–40.

Welty, Eudora. *The Eye of the Story: Selected Essays and Reviews*. Vintage, 1942.

Welty, Eudora. *Losing Battles*. 1970. *Eudora Welty: Complete Novels*. Library of America, 1998, pp. 425–880.

Welty, Eudora. "Some Notes on Time in Fiction." 1973. *On Writing*. Modern Library, 2002, pp. 94–106.

Wester, Maisha L. *African American Gothic: Screams from Shadowed Places*. Palgrave Macmillan, 2012.

Weston, Ruth D. *Gothic Traditions and Narrative Techniques in the Fiction of Eudora Welty*. Louisiana State UP, 1994.

Whitley, John S. "*Pudd'nhead Wilson*: Mark Twain and the Limits of Detection." *Journal of American Studies*, vol. 21, no. 1, 1987, pp. 55–70.

Williams, Adebayo. "Of Human Bondage and Literary Triumphs: Hannah Crafts and the Morphology of the Slave Narrative." *Research in African Literatures*, vol. 34, no. 1, 2003, pp. 137–50.

Williams, Eric. *Capitalism and Slavery*. Russell & Russell, 1944.

Williams, Sherley Anne. *Dessa Rose*. Harper Perennial, 1986.

Willis, Susan. "Eruptions of Funk: Historicizing Toni Morrison." *Black American Literature Forum*, vol. 16, no. 1, 1982, pp. 34–42.

Winter, Kari J. *Subjects of Slavery, Agents of Change: Women and Power in Gothic Novels and Slave Narratives, 1790–1865*. U of Georgia P, 1992.

Woolf, Virginia. *A Room of One's Own*. Barnes & Noble, 1929.

Wright, Gavin. *Slavery and American Economic Development*. Louisiana State UP, 2006.

Yaeger, Patricia. "Ghosts and Shattered Bodies, or What Does It Mean to Still Be Haunted by Southern Literature?" *South Central Review*, vol. 22, no. 1, 2005, pp. 87–108.

Yellin, Jean Fagan. "*The Bondwoman's Narrative* and *Uncle Tom's Cabin*." *In Search of Hannah Crafts: Critical Essays on "The Bondwoman's Narrative,"* edited by Henry Louis Gates, Jr. and Hollis Robbins, Basic Books, 2004, pp. 106–16.

Yellin, Jean Fagan. "Introduction." *Incidents in the Life of a Slave Girl*. Harvard UP, 1987, pp. xiii–xxxiv.

Young, Kevin. *Bunk: The Rise of Hoaxes, Humbug, Plagiarists, Phonies, Post-Facts, and Fake News*. Graywolf, 2017.

Young, Kevin. "For the Confederate Dead." *For the Confederate Dead*, Alfred A. Knopf, 2007, pp. 97–99.

INDEX

Accomando, Christina, 53, 199n21
Adams, James Truslow, 196n2
Adams, Jessica, 197n16
Alcott, Louisa May, 52
Alexandre, Sandy, 6
Alger, Horatio, 196n2
Allewart, Monique, 26
America, 98–99, 189, 196n1
American dream: and freedom, 7, 23, 27–28, 194; history of, 196n2; and the North, 24; and property, 3, 5, 11, 72, 101, 103, 105, 122, 127, 146; and prosperity, 22, 103. *See also* Enlightenment
American nightmare, 4–7, 11, 23–24, 27–28, 127
American Revolution, 18–19
ancestors, 155, 160–61, 176–78, 184–89
Anderson, Eric Gary, 26
Andrews, David, 71
Andrews, William L., 31, 57, 198n9
Anolik, Ruth Bienstock, 18–19, 33, 41, 147, 201n20
Armstrong, Nancy, 198n15
Armstrong, Tim, 21, 138
Askeland, Lori, 144, 148

Bailey, Dale, 19, 101, 201n20
Baldwin, James, 198n4
Ballinger, Gill, 60, 198nn8–9, 198n14, 199n20
Banner, Stuart, 20
Baptist, Edward, 8, 22–23
Barnum, P. T., 62, 65, 200nn4–5

Bast, Florian, 206n12
Batty, Nancy Ellen, 123–24, 202n1, 202n3
Bauer, Margaret Donovan, 202n1
Baucom, Ian, 141
Baym, Nina, 196n7, 200n34
Beckert, Sven, 7–8, 22–23, 205n1
Bennett, Jane, 26
Benson, Melanie R., 202n7
Berger, James, 205n25
Berger, John, 171
Bernstein, Stephen, 201n20
Berry, Daina Ramey, 204n16
Best, Stephen, 205n3
Birdsong, Destiny O., 180
Blackford, Holly, 116
Blackstone, William, 71–72, 135
Blight, David W., 167
Botting, Fred, 13, 16, 25, 78, 197n11, 201n20
Bradbury, Malcolm, 89
Brax, Klaus, 136
Brigham, John, 17
Brogan, Kathleen, 196n3, 206n7, 207n24
Brontë, Charlotte, 56, 200n34
Brooks, Cleanth, 202n5
Brown, Charles Brockden, 5, 11–12, 33, 35, 196n9
Buell, Lawrence, 199n22, 199n26, 205n27
Busch, Frederick, 83–84
Butler, Octavia: "Interview," 178, 207n23; *Kindred*, 10, 15, 27, 154–66, 168, 173–79, 183–84, 186–90
Byerman, Keith, 69, 109, 202n4, 207n24

INDEX

capitalism: history of, 8, 22–23; and slavery, 154, 205n1
captivity narrative, 33, 48–49. *See also* Rowlandson, Mary
Cartwright, Keith, 200n14
Castronovo, Russ, 198n12, 198n14, 199n29
Chandler, Marilyn, 4
Chaplin, Sue, 41, 44, 199n18
Chesnutt, Charles, 120
Christian, Barbara, 131
Christianity, 47, 50, 191
Civil War, 154, 167–68, 171, 179–83, 189, 192. *See also* Confederacy
Clemens, Valdine, 201n20
clothing, 67–68, 85, 200n10
Coates, Ta-Nehisi, 22
Cobb, Thomas, 36
Cohn, Dorrit, 82, 89
Columbus, Christopher, 16–17, 98
con men. *See* confidence games
Confederacy, 179–83, 186, 194. *See also* Civil War
confidence games: in American history, 62–65, 200nn3–4; in *Benito Cereno*, 66–67, 200n11; in *Dessa Rose*, 69, 94–99; in *Pudd'nhead Wilson*, 67–68, 87–92; and slavery, 65–69, 81–85, 134, 200n7
conjure, 102, 119–20, 125–27, 203n29
Cooper, James Fenimore, 135
Coss, David L., 202n13
Costello, Brannon, 103, 203n23
Coviello, Peter, 80, 82
Cox, James B., 200n2, 201n23
Craft, William, 39
Crafts, Hannah: as author, 51–59, 198nn6–8; *The Bondwoman's Narrative*, 9, 23, 27, 29–41, 45–53, 55–61, 131, 133, 137, 146, 174, 190, 193
Crockett, Davy, 200n5
Crow, Charles, 12–13, 26–27, 52, 201n20
Cucarella-Ramon, Vicent, 198n14
Cutter, Martha J., 39

damsel in distress: as gothic device, 31–41, 54, 58, 85, 89, 147; history of, 199n17

Darwin, Charles, 62
Davis, David Brion, 70
Davis, Mary Kemp, 75
Davis, Thadious M., 25, 116, 170, 184, 186, 200n6, 202n8, 204n7
Davison, Carol Margaret, 101, 197n16, 201n26
Dawson, Emma Waters, 201n28
Day, William Patrick, 204n1
De Cenzo, Giorgia, 171, 207n28
Decker, Sharon, 134, 205n24
Defoe, Daniel, 176
DeLamotte, Eugenia, 13, 91, 115
DeLombard, Jeannine Marie, 81, 199n21
Derrida, Jacques, 105n2
detective genre, 89
Dickens, Charles, 30, 56, 198n6, 199n20, 200n34
Dickinson, Emily, 50
Diouf, Sylviane A., 204n13
discordant narration, 82, 89
Disney, 11, 196n8
Donaldson, Susan, 25, 110, 124
Donovan-Condron, Kellie, 203n26
Doriana, Beth Maclay, 53
Douglass, Frederick, 60, 180–81, 187, 201n25
Dred Scott v. Sandford, 6
Dubey, Madhu, 207n26
Duck, Leigh Anne, 24, 202n5, 203n28
Dunbar, Erica Armstrong, 197n17
Duvall, John N., 205n21

Edwards, Justin, 196n3, 200n9
ekphrasis, 172–73
Ellis, Jay, 26–27
Ellison, Ralph, 65–66, 176
Enlightenment, 3–4, 7, 12, 18, 64, 156. *See also* American dream
Entzminger, Betina, 203n23
Erdrich, Louise, 156
Ermarth, Elizabeth Deeds, 155–56, 190
Esteve, Mary, 201n17

Fabian, Ann, 30, 198n9, 199n32
Faflak, Joel, 196n8

INDEX

Fair Housing Act, 6
fairy tales. *See* "Hansel and Gretel"
Faulkner, William: *Absalom, Absalom!*, 5, 9–10, 100–109, 112, 114–24, 126–27, 180–81; "Evangeline," 123–24; *Go Down, Moses*, 135, 200n6, 202n8; as gothic writer, 8, 11, 24–25; and the grotesque, 110
Faust, Drew Gilpin, 192
Fede, Andrew, 132
Female Gothic, 199n18
Fernandez, Angela, 135
Fiedler, Leslie, 5–6, 11
Fisher, Philip, 198n3
Fishkin, Shelley Fisher, 84, 88
Flagel, Nadine, 205n5
Fletcher, Judith, 113, 124–25, 202n4
Foner, Eric, 154, 183
Ford, Sarah, 203n29
Foster, Frances Smith, 59–60, 206n10
Franco, Dean J., 134, 204n2
Franklin, Benjamin, 3–4, 8, 51–52, 57, 64–65, 196n2
Freneau, Philip, 157
Freud, Sigmund, 13, 105, 160, 206n17
Frost, Robert, 166
Frye, Elizabeth Bradford, 157, 168
fugitive poets, 183
Fugitive Slave Act, 28, 44, 58, 128, 133, 136–37
Fulton, Lorie Watkins, 202n1, 202n10

Garner, Margaret, 136–37, 204nn9–10
Garrett, Peter K., 13, 16, 60–61, 197n11, 201n20
Gates, Henry Louis, Jr., 59–60, 198n5, 198n8, 198n13, 200n35
Genovese, Eugene D., 23, 73–74, 204n6
ghost: as a dead person, 93, 138–39, 202n5; as haunting, 63; as a property claim, 16, 147, 159; as a supernatural being, 162, 199n30. *See also* haunting; specter; spectral possession
Gilbert, Olive, 58
Gillman, Susan, 200n11

Glasgow, Ellen, 25, 28
Gleason, William, 45, 47, 51
Goad, Jill, 206n22
Godden, Richard, 202n14
Goddu, Teresa: on Edgar Allan Poe, 201n27; on Hannah Crafts, 34, 38, 198n11; on Harriet Jacobs, 31, 34, 201n20; on historical approach to the gothic, 5–6, 9, 15–16, 24, 27, 31, 98, 201n20
Goldman, Anne E., 204n5, 204n11
Goldner, Ellen J., 200n2, 201n22
Gomaa, Sally, 41
Gone with the Wind, 158, 168
Goodell, William, 36, 196n4
Gordon, Avery, 40, 137, 154, 204n9, 204n12
gothic: and architecture, 11–12, 45–46, 86, 91, 115–19; and the body, 94–95, 117; definitions of, 12–16, 26–27, 197n10, 201n20; devices, 4–5, 14, 64, 77, 79–80, 83, 91, 97, 102; doubling, 85–86, 160, 167, 189; in English literature, 18–19; and fear, 14–16, 63, 77–78, 81–98, 111, 127; the Female Gothic, 199n18; as a genre, 7–8, 11–16, 157–58, 191–95; historical approach to, 15–16; history of, 11–14; and monsters, 34–35, 57, 85; and opposition to the law, 16, 36–37, 52, 129; and the reader, 14–15, 197n11; and slavery, 5, 15–16, 31–35, 40–58, 77–98, 108–26, 133–50, 156–89, 193–95; and the South, 23–28; southern, 8, 23–28, 190; and time, 114–15, 127, 155–56, 189, 193–95. *See also* damsel in distress; ghost; haunted house; haunting; specter; spectral possession
Gould, Philip, 18
Greeson, Jennifer Rae, 23–24, 198n14
Griffin, Dorothy, 203n20
Gross, Louis S., 77
Gutman, Herbert G., 198n4
Gygax, Franziska, 203n24

Hack, Daniel, 198n6, 200n34
Hadden, Sally, 132–33
Hagood, Taylor, 26
Handley, William R., 141

"Hansel and Gretel," 100, 113, 121
Harker, Jaime, 203n25
Harrington, Paula, 72, 86–87
Harris, Cheryl I., 6, 20–21, 38–39, 74
Harris, Trudier, 148, 163–64, 204nn2–3, 205n20, 205n27, 206n7
Harrison, Suzan, 111
Haslam, Jason, 158, 196n8, 198n14, 199n26, 199n29
haunted house: approaches to, 203n17, 204n4; as connected to the past, 100–102, 114–19, 122–25, 159–60; as critiques of America, 19, 147; as questionable acquisition, 5, 105–7; as refuge, 40–51, 86–88; as white-owned space, 40–51, 109–11, 113–14, 128, 144–50. *See also* ghost; gothic; haunting; specter
haunting: as reflection of fear, 63, 93, 101–2; as reflection of the future, 155–90; as reflection of guilt, 129, 138–39, 150; as reflection of the past, 16, 142–45, 169–74; as reflection of reality, 40, 154. *See also* haunted house; ghost; gothic; specter; spectral possession
Hawthorne, Nathaniel: and the gothic genre, 11–12; *The House of Seven Gables*, 5, 13, 18, 56, 101, 105, 125–27, 197n14, 202n11
Hecimovich, Gregg, 59, 198n5, 198n13
Henderson, Mae Gwendolyn, 76, 151, 204n5
Henninger, Katherine R., 169
Higginbotham, A. Leon, 21–22
Hinrichsen, Lisa, 197n16, 202n5, 203n17
history: as construction, 177, 180–83; as property, 154–56, 158, 167–68, 174, 178–79, 190; rewriting of, 154–55, 178, 191–95
Hogan, Michael, 144, 146, 204n4
Hogle, Jerrold E., 11–12, 33
Hooper, Johnson Jones, 64
Horvitz, Deborah, 138, 140, 204n3
House, Elizabeth B., 140, 142, 204n3
housekeeping, 101, 108, 116, 125, 147
houses. *See* property
Humphreys, Debra, 45, 199n28

Hurley, Jessica, 202n5
Huston, James L., 19, 37
Hutcheon, Linda, 177
Hutchison, Coleman, 157, 168

infanticide, 85, 128, 133
Irving, Washington, 4, 12, 74

Jackson, Shirley, 19, 205n23
Jacobs, Harriet: and abolitionist movement, 58; as author, 51–59, 198n6; *Incidents in the Life of a Slave Girl*, 3–5, 7–9, 23, 28, 29–45, 51–55, 57–61, 129–30, 137, 146, 149, 174, 190–91, 193, 195
Jefferson, Thomas, 4
Jehlen, Myra, 68, 84–85
Johnson, Paul David, 71
Johnson, Walter, 197n13
Jones, Anne Goodwyn, 25
Jones, Meta Duewa, 206n14
Jones-Rogers, Stephanie E., 192
Judge, Oney, 197n17

Kafer, Peter, 12, 196n9
Kaplan, Sidney, 82, 200n1
Kavanagh, James H., 82
Kawash, Samira, 43, 204n4
Kekeh, Andrée-Anne, 75, 90, 201n19
Kelley, William Melvin, 128, 130, 131, 137, 152
Kelley, Wyn, 200n8
Kerr, Elizabeth M., 202n5, 203n17
Keyser, Catherine, 199n33, 200n34
Keyssar, Alexander, 19
Kilgour, Maggie, 13–14
kindred. *See* ancestors
King, Lovalerie, 201n16, 204n6
Kopytoff, Barbara K., 21–22
Kreiger, Georgia, 43, 199n24
Kreiswirth, Martin, 106
Kreyling, Michael, 197n16, 201n26, 202n2
Kubitschek, Missy Dehn, 207n31

LaCroix, David, 177–78
Ladd, Barbara, 89, 203n23
Landrieu, Mitch, 192, 194

Lange, Dorothea, 171
law: legal possession, 31–32, 36–40, 129, 131; and opposition to the gothic, 16, 36–37, 52; and property, 10, 17–20, 129, 131–32, 134–35, 196n5; in trials, 88–90, 199n21. *See also* personhood, legal
Ledous, Malenas, 41
legal possession. *See* law
LeMahieu, Michael, 193–94
Lenz, William E., 64, 200n5
Lepore, Jill, 52
Levecq, Christine, 176, 206n11
Levine, Robert S., 56, 82, 197n14, 199n20, 199n27
Levins, Lynne Gartrell, 203n22
Li, Stephanie, 48
Lindberg, Gary, 64–65
Lloyd-Smith, Allan, 155, 158
"Loch Lomond," 126
Locke, John, 4, 18
Luck, Chad, 204n7
Lustig, Tim, 60, 198nn8–9, 198n14, 199n20
lynching, 6

Macpherson, C. B., 17
Mantel, Hilary, 52
Marrs, Suzanne, 203n18
Marshall, Bridget M., 40, 50, 198n14, 199n25
Martin, Robert K., 197n14, 198n8, 202n11
Martinez, Leonard, 84
Matterson, Stephen, 200n7
Matthews, John T., 123, 203n16
McBride, James, 156
McHaney, Pearl Amelia, 179, 207n27, 207n29
McKay, Nellie Y., 59–60
McMahand, Donnie, 112, 120, 125, 202n3
McWhirter, David, 110, 202n4
Melville, Herman, *Benito Cereno*, 9, 15, 27, 62–64, 66–73, 77–84, 88–90, 92–93, 97–99, 130, 193
Michaels, Walter Benn, 126–27
Middle Passage, 129, 138–43, 145
Millgate, Michael, 202n5, 202n12
Mitchell, Angelyn, 107n30

monsters, 34–35, 57, 85
Morgan, Edmund S., 7, 197n12
Morgan, Jennifer L., 204n8
Morrell, Sascha, 201n22
Morris, Linda A., 68, 85–86, 200n10
Morrison, Toni: *Beloved*, 10, 13, 128–53, 155, 159, 185, 193; *Conversations*, 136–37, 139–40, 142, 202n1; and the gothic, 11; *Playing in the Dark*, 7, 9, 12, 15–16, 94; *Song of Solomon*, 9–10, 100–105, 107–8, 112–15, 121–22, 124–25, 127, 193; "Unspeakable," 144–45
mythology, 107, 113, 126

narratology, 82
Native Americans, 202n15
Nunes, Ana, 91, 94

O'Donnell, Patrick, 203n27
O'Reilly, Andrea, 204n14

Pan, Alia C. Y., 109–10, 202n4
Parfait, Claire, 197n2
Parker, Hershel, 84
Patterson, Orlando, 21
Pedersen, Vidar, 68
Peeren, Esther, 145, 204n4, 205n22
Pereira, Malin, 205n4
personhood, legal: and property, 4, 6, 18, 29–30, 36–38, 71, 111–13; and slavery, 29–37, 77, 81, 84, 87, 89, 93, 95–96, 102, 130, 152
Peterson, Christopher, 134, 137, 204n2
Phelan, James, 136, 201n1
Philip, M. NourbeSe, 204n17
photography, 155, 167, 170–74, 182, 190–91, 206nn21–22
Pierson v. Post, 10, 129, 134–36, 204n7
plantation house, 94, 101, 131, 197n16, 202n2. *See also* haunted house
Poe, Edgar Allan: "The Fall of the House of Usher," 19, 79–80, 101, 106, 122, 125; as gothic writer, 12, 49; "The Narrative of Arthur Gordon Pym," 94, 162; "The Raven," 118

point of view: contrasting, 84–85, 90–91, 135–36, 148–51, 167–69; first person, 180–82; multiple, 170–73; second person, 166–67, 182, 190, 199n19
Porter, Carolyn, 88, 200n2
postmodernism, 155–58, 174, 177, 186, 190
Prenshaw, Peggy Whitman, 111
property: and American Revolution, 18–19; and civic identity, 19–20; claims of, 129–30, 133–37, 139, 141, 146–50, 152, 180–82; definition of, 16–18; destruction of, 102, 114, 123–25, 127–30, 132–37, 165, 177; as house, 4, 18, 71, 130, 159; law, 10, 17–20, 129, 131–32, 134–35; and legal personhood, 4, 6, 18, 29–30, 36–38, 71, 111–13; ownership, 41–51, 71, 87, 101, 103–8, 119–21, 144–50, 159; and performance, 66–69; and race, 5, 20–23, 128; rights, 18, 116, 129, 131–32; writing as, 58–61, 174–78, 182
Punter, David, 14, 16, 52, 129
Purser, John, 126

race: body, constructions of, 7, 22, 38–39, 62–63, 65, 69–70, 72–75, 78, 83, 186; cross-racial relationships, 161–62, 169, 186, 189; distinctions of, 36–40, 71–72, 87–89, 199n29; mixing of, 109, 111, 159–60, 199n23–27; passing, 68, 88–89, 199n25–26
Radin, Margaret Jane, 18, 174
Ramos, Peter, 202n5
Ramsey, William M., 157, 207n27
rape, 35–38, 108, 142–43, 163–65, 188
reader: discordant narration, 82, 89; response, 78, 82, 90–91, 169, 190; second person, 33–34, 37, 58, 166–67, 182, 190, 199n19
Reames, Kelly Lynch, 94
Redding, Arthur, 99
Reinhardt, Mark, 204nn9–10
Richards, Jason, 66–67
Robbins, Hollis, 35, 198n6, 200n34
Rockman, Seth, 23, 205n1
Rogin, Michael, 66

Rohrback, Augusta, 59
Rose, Carol M., 135
Rothman, David J., 157
Rothstein, Richard, 196n5
Rousseau, Jean-Jacques, 202n6
Rowe, John Carlos, 201nn17–18, 201n24
Rowlandson, Mary, 31–32. *See also* captivity narrative
Rowson, Susanna, 199n19
Rushdy, Ashraf H. A., 69, 96, 150–51, 163–64, 176, 206n9
Russ, Elizabeth Christine, 107, 197n16
Russell, Richard, 205n4
Ryan, Katy, 204n15

Sanchez-Eppler, Karen, 60, 198n14, 199n29
Saunders, Rebecca, 103
Savoy, Eric, 86, 101, 156
Sayers, Philip, 202n7
Schiff, Sarah Eden, 187, 206n8
Schmudde, Carol E., 204n4
Scholl, Diane G., 198n6
Schuessler, Jennifer, 192
Schultz, Kathryn, 192
science fiction, 157–59
Sedgwick, Eve Kosofsky, 13, 46, 78, 80
sentimental genre, 11, 80, 196n7, 199n19
Simon, Julia, 202n6
slave narratives: and gothic fiction, 198n10; and veracity, 30–31. *See also* Crafts, Hannah; Jacobs, Harriet
slavery: and capitalism, 8, 22–23, 154, 205n1; and conflation with property, 4, 6, 8, 12–22, 29–31, 36–40, 66–77, 100–102, 108–12, 114, 118, 123–24, 127–29, 131–33, 138–45, 153, 161–65, 187, 190, 195, 196n4; and depictions of animals, 55, 62, 71–73, 75–77, 131, 136, 200n13; and the gothic, 5, 15–16, 31–35, 40–58, 77–98, 108–26, 133–50, 156–89, 193–95; and history, 158, 161–62; and infanticide, 85, 128, 133; and personhood, 29–37, 77, 81, 84, 87, 89, 93, 95–96, 102, 130, 152; and property, 20–23; and rape, 35–38, 97, 108, 142–43, 163–65, 188; and separation of families,

67–68, 85, 93, 96, 178; and the South, 7–8, 23–28, 58, 186, 197n15. *See also* race
Smith, Allan Lloyd, 13
Smith, Tracy K., 194
Sontag, Susan, 170–71
South: and architecture, 107, 203n20; definition, 24–25; and the gothic, 23–28; history, 172–73; and slavery, 7–8, 23–28, 58, 186, 197n15
Spangler, George M., 201n17
Spaulding, A. Timothy, 138, 159, 161, 206n7, 207n24, 207n26
specter, 44, 100–127, 154, 162, 164, 177, 190. *See also* ghost; haunting; spectral possession
spectral possession, 40–58, 118–20, 126, 129–30, 137–45, 150. *See also* ghost; haunting; specter
staircases, 109, 113, 115–19
State v Mann, 10, 132–33
Steinberg, Marc, 205n6
Stone, Edward, 199n21
storytelling, 151
Stowe, Harriet Beecher: influence on Jacobs, 198n6; *Uncle Tom's Cabin*, 29–32, 41, 56, 58–59, 144, 197nn1–2, 200n34
Street, Susan Castillo, 26–27
Sugimori, Masami, 117
Sundquist, Eric, 200n12
Swarns, Rachel L., 192, 204n18

Tawil, Ezra F., 82, 200n13
Teukolsky, Rachel, 198n6, 200n34
Thoreau, Henry David, 19, 50
time: disruptions, 114–15, 127, 155–56, 189, 193–95; faulty, 191–93; travel, 155–56, 158–60, 166–78, 189, 205n6, 206n10
Townshend, Dale, 60, 198nn8–9, 198n14, 199n20
Trethewey, Natasha: "At Dusk," 179; *Bellocq's Ophelia*, 170, 206n14; "Blond," 206n16; *Conversations*, 170, 183; *Domestic Work*, 206n21; "Elegy for the Native Guards," 182, 185; "Genus Narcissus," 185; "Graveyard Blues," 185; "Illumination," 183; "Letter," 179; "Miscegenation," 185; "Monument," 185; "My Mother Dreams Another Country," 184–85, 206n19; "Myth," 206n18; *Native Guard*, 10, 154–57, 166–75, 179–86, 189–90; "Native Guard," 179–82, 186; "Necessary," 171; "Pastoral," 183, 206n18, 206n20; "Photograph: Ice Storm, 1971," 171–72; "Pilgrimage," 167–69; "Scenes from a Documentary History of Mississippi," 172–74, 191–92; "South," 186; "The Southern Crescent," 179, 206n19; "Southern Gothic," 168–69; "Southern History," 183; "Theories of Time and Space," 166–67, 179, 182, 185; *Thrall*, 183; "Three Photographs," 206n21; "What Is Evidence," 183; "What the Body Can Say," 183
trickster figure, 64–65
Truth, Sojourner, 45, 58, 201n28
Turner, Daniel Cross, 26, 157, 168
Turner, Stephanie S., 205n5
Twain, Mark, *Pudd'nhead Wilson*, 9, 15, 62–64, 67–70, 72, 74–75, 77–78, 81, 84–90, 97–99, 130, 133

undeadness, 26–27

verb tense, 55–56, 166–69, 180, 186, 190, 199n33, 206n19
Vint, Sherryl, 206n12

Wagers, Kelley, 175
Wald, Priscilla, 46, 198n14
Wallace, Diana, 199n18
Walpole, Horace, 11, 33
Walters, Delores M., 204n9
Walvin, James, 141
Wardrop, Daneen, 39, 198n14
Warhol, Robin R., 34
Warren, Wendy, 197n15
Warwick, Alexandra, 197n10
Washington, George, 197n17
Weinauer, Ellen, 37
Weinbaum, Alys Eve, 206n13

Weinstein, Philip M., 202n1, 202n10
Welty, Eudora: "Circe," 203n21; *Delta Wedding*, 9–10, 15, 100–108, 110–12, 114–15, 119–22, 125–27; and gothic, 8, 25; "Some Notes on Time in Fiction," 192–93
West, 98–99
Wester, Maisha L., 196n3, 198n14, 199n23
Weston, Ruth D., 102, 203n19
Whitehead, Colson, 99
whiteness, 20, 38–39, 67, 69, 73–74, 94–95, 162, 199n27, 201n27
Whitley, John S., 88–89
Whitman, Walt, 185–86
Williams, Adebayo, 55
Williams, Eric, 22
Williams, Sherley Anne, *Dessa Rose*, 9, 62–64, 69–70, 75–78, 90–99, 130, 133, 137, 174, 180, 193
Willis, Susan, 202n9
Winter, Kari J., 35, 196n3, 198n10
witch, 113, 121. *See also* ghost; specter
Woolf, Virginia, 175
Wright, Gavin, 22
Wright, Richard, 5, 13, 162

Yaeger, Patricia, 27
Yellin, Jean Fagan, 44, 58–60, 198n6
Young, Kevin: *Bunk*, 62, 64, 200n4; "For the Confederate Dead," 193–94

Zong, 140–41

ABOUT THE AUTHOR

Sarah Gilbreath Ford is a professor of American literature at Baylor University and the director of the Beall Poetry Festival. She is the author of *Tracing Southern Storytelling in Black and White* (2014). In 2017, she received the Phoenix Award from the Eudora Welty Society, and in 2019, she was named a Baylor Centennial Professor.

www.ingramcontent.com/pod-product-compliance
Lightning Source LLC
Chambersburg PA
CBHW030619230426
43661CB00053B/2068